ON CONCEPTS OF CAPITAL
AND TECHNICAL CHANGE

TO MY WIFE AND PARENTS

ON CONCEPTS OF
CAPITAL AND
TECHNICAL CHANGE

THOMAS K. RYMES

Professor of Economics,
Carleton University, Ottawa

CAMBRIDGE
AT THE UNIVERSITY PRESS
1971

Published by the Syndics of the Cambridge University Press
Bentley House, 200 Euston Road, London N.W.1
American Branch: 32 East 57th Street, New York, N.Y.10022

© Cambridge University Press 1971

Library of Congress Catalogue Card Number: 72-149438

ISBN: 0 521 08103 3

Printed in Great Britain
at the University Printing House, Cambridge
(Brooke Crutchley, University Printer)

CONTENTS

PREFACE

This study represents an introductory probe into the theory of capital as an input in the process of economic production. It is concerned almost entirely with matters of definition and measurement. It is necessary to get these clearly out of the way if one wishes to proceed further. I come down heavily in favour of the concept of capital advanced by Sir Roy Harrod and Joan Robinson. It is a very old concept of capital, traceable back to Ricardo. Support of this concept of capital logically entails support of the Harrod–Robinson concept of technical advance and rejection of the entire neoclassical line of thought based on the distinction between commodity-capital accumulation and technical advance of the Hicksian type. All of this I found necessary to get settled first. This book records that attempt and is a stepping-stone to more important matters. In its unemended form, the essay was my doctoral thesis submitted to McGill University in the fall of 1968.

My greatest debt is to Professor Joan Robinson who, during the winter of 1969–70, subjected various drafts to patient, relentless but kindly criticisms. While at Cambridge, and, in particular, as a result of conversations with Dr L. L. Pasinetti, I came to believe that a new economics, based on Ricardo and Keynes, is being founded there – a new economics which is different from the neoclassical tradition. It was an exciting experience to become aware of new thoughts percolating all around and to see whole new questions emerging. I shall always be grateful to the hospitality of Cambridge University for the chance to share in it.

I cannot give an adequate account of what I owe to Professor Lawrence Read of the Department of Religion at Carleton University. He delivered a paper on productivity measurement at the Dominion Bureau of Statistics in the summer of 1961, while I was working there on the problem of capital measurement. Conversations with Read (and a fortunate coincident reading of Mrs Robinson's *The Accumulation of Capital*) convinced me that not only was Read's concept of 'total factor productivity', 'technological change' or what you will, correct, but, much more importantly, that he was providing a way of coming to grips with 'capital as a factor of production'. My agreement with, and development of, Read's argument is to be found in the May 1968 issue of the *Canadian Journal of Economics*. Chapter 5 of this book constitutes the core of my argument and is a greatly expanded and developed version of the statement in the *Journal*.

My next greatest debt is to Professor J. C. Weldon, my research director, for his brilliant 'firm but loose' guidance. When I told him that I wished to pursue the 'problem of capital' as a thesis, he agreed and let me proceed

vii

freely as I saw fit. He warned that my labours might prove wholly bankrupt. It was (is?) a risk which was fun to take up and I appreciate fully the freedom he provided me.

A large number of people helped me along the way. In particular, I must thank Professor S. F. Kaliski, of Queen's University, and Dr S. A. Goldberg, of the Dominion Bureau of Statistics, for their continued confidence that, in the respective areas of capital theory and measurement, something useful would eventually emerge out of all my flounderings. There are three other people at D.B.S. whom I must mention: Jack Sawyer, now at the University of Toronto, whose approach to social accounting taught me the necessity of 'seeing the whole system'; Paul Pitts, whose brilliant mind served as a constant challenge and stimulation; and Miss Betty Jean Emery, with whom I enjoyed many hours of collaboration and who cured me of the fear of index numbers. Finally, I must record an everlasting debt to the late David McCord Wright who, during his stay at McGill, taught me the limitations of economics. I know he would not have liked the kind of analysis used in this essay. It is too sterile, too unlike the growing changing world we live in. Yet I think it is a start in the right direction.

The Government of Canada, through academic leave and a pre-doctoral fellowship from the Canada Council, helped to make some free time available during my initially sporadic attempts at the writing of my thesis. Earlier, the Earhart Foundation, with the intervention on my behalf of Dr Wright, helped finance a year of residence study in Oxford.

I am also indebted to Carleton University and the Canada Council who, through sabbatical leave and a Council Leave Fellowship, supported my stay in Cambridge during the academic year 1969–70.

The Research Fund of the Dean of the Faculty of Arts at Carleton University provided funds for typing. I should like to thank the typists at Carleton, Barbara McClellan, Sadie Hodgins, Audrey McCallum, Evelyn Aldridge and, in particular, Gill Chater, for their stoic handling of my handwriting and the typing chores. Mrs Sheila Isaac checked the quotations, drew the graphs and did most of the proof reading. Her assistance was invaluable.

To all those who helped me along the way, then, my thanks. As usual, though, all the errors and omissions are mine.

Finally, I would like to thank my wife Betsy – for everything.

THOMAS K. RYMES

Carleton University
Ottawa
Spring 1969

Cambridge
Spring 1970

1

INTRODUCTION

For fifteen years a theoretical controversy has raged between two groups of economists interested in the theory of growth and capital:[1] on the one hand, we have, for the Cambridge, U.K., group, Professors Joan Robinson and Nicholas Kaldor and Dr L. Pasinetti as the leading Keynesians and on the other, leading the Cambridge, Mass., Walrasians, we have Professors Samuelson and Solow. The Cambridge controversy, as it may be called, has a number of foci of disagreement, *viz.* (i) Should full employment be assumed or generated by the analysis? (ii) What are the assumed properties of the investment behaviour of entrepreneurs? (iii) Which savings assumptions – neoclassical or Anglo-Italian – should be employed? (iv) What is the relevance of steady-state equilibrium analysis when economic growth results from a sequence of short-run decisions – the only 'run' in which decisions can be made? (v) What role, if any, does money play in the process of economic growth? The controversy may be summarized by asking: Do we develop a 'better' theory of economic growth by extending Keynes or Walras into the dynamics of the long run? This monumental issue is not my immediate concern. Another focus of disagreement which attracts considerable attention is capital measurement. The questions are: What is meant by capital as a factor of production? How is it to be measured? Which concept of technological change is valid and how is it to be measured? Can we distinguish between shifts of and movements along a production function? What is meant by the marginal product of capital? Can one distinguish between embodied and disembodied technical change? This focus of disagreement has an *ex post* flavour. It is redolent of the investment–savings controversy of the late 1930s. It *is* a dispute about definitions, taxonomy and measurement. Nonetheless, it is important to get the dispute settled so that the larger issue may be debated uncluttered by a never-ending discussion about the difficulties of measuring capital and other related matters. It is in this

---

[1] Some aspects of this controversy have been recently examined in G. C. Harcourt, 'Some Cambridge controversies in the theory of capital', *Journal of Economic Literature*, vii, June 1969, 369–405.

spirit that this study is offered. It may have by-products which are important for the greater questions. If doubts are cast upon the conceptual validity of the marginal product of capital, then the Anglo-Italian savings theory for the determination of the rate of return to capital receives increased support. If the measurement of capital is merely an aggregation problem, Walrasian theory can easily handle a disaggregated system, although, of course, Walrasian empirical work must proceed very cautiously indeed.

Much of the criticism directed by Robinson, Kaldor, Pasinetti and other Keynesians against the Walrasian position *seems* to rely on the 'hard' facts that 'capital', as a factor of production, is in reality a most heterogeneous basket of different things, that no meaning can be attached to such concepts as an aggregate stock of capital and an aggregate production function and that marginal products of 'capital' do not exist in a world where technology is characterized by fixed coefficients. In fact, the Walrasian (or more exactly, neo-Walrasian) analysis is impervious to such criticism. In Walrasian theory, no aggregate stock of capital or production function is needed and smooth substitution amongst inputs is not required for there to exist determinate rates of return to capital formation and 'shadow wage and capital rentals' imputed to the various 'factors' of production. The Walrasians rightly become exasperated by the need to defend their *theories* against such misplaced criticisms.

What is seldom realized, however, is that the question posed by the critics of the Walrasian line of thought runs much more deeply. That question, to which in my view the Walrasians have given the wrong answer, is: In a world of technological progress, in what sense can capital, defined as a flow or stock of commodities, be regarded as a primary input? What concept of capital is appropriate for such a context? What concept of technological change logically follows? In this essay, I show that the Harrod–Robinson concepts of capital and technological change are correct and that Walrasian ones, based on Hicks' distinction between capital accumulation and technological change, are incorrect.

The main implication of such a finding is that virtually all current measures of technological progress, whether they be calculations of 'Residuals' or more sophisticated econometric estimates (based as they are on neoclassical concepts), are invalid. The numbers generated by Denison, Kendrick, Salter, Solow, Griliches and Jorgenson are meaningless. Many corollaries follow. There is no meaningful distinction to be drawn between embodied and disembodied technical change. Statistical agencies round the world are today, under the instigation of the U.N., busily turning out measures of output at the sectoral level which are erroneous. *Much of the theoretical and empirical work on production which*

2

has been done in the last fifteen years must therefore be written off as theoretically incorrect.

This essay then is concerned with certain aspects of the theory and measurement of capital. I seek to achieve two things. First, I argue that for economic systems which are dynamic in the non-trivial sense of incorporating progress in technology, the most meaningful way of assessing capital as an *input* in the processes of economic production would appear to be the Harrod–Robinson concept of capital. The concept has, of course, a long historical lineage back through Wicksell, Böhm-Bawerk, Marx and Ricardo. It was David Ricardo who said

capital may increase without its value increasing, and even while its value is actually diminishing; not only may an addition be made to the food and clothing of a country, but the addition may be made by the aid of machinery, without any increase, and even with an absolute diminution in the proportional quantity of labour required to produce them. The quantity of capital may increase, while neither the whole together, nor any part of it singly, will have a greater value than before, but may actually have a less.[1]

Second, I extend and elaborate Professor Read's seminal procedure for making operational the Harrod–Robinson concepts of technological change.[2] I extend this idea to cover such related aspects as the debate on disembodied versus embodied technological progress and the validity of different concepts for the measurement of output.

As indicated, I argue that Walrasian or neoclassical concepts of technological change and commodity capital as a primary input in the process of economic production are essentially empty. The analysis is, I find when I have worked it all out, pretty obvious. Yet innumerable books and journal articles are pouring out written in the neoclassical manner. An understanding of the writings of Harrod and Robinson makes one doubt the validity of this literature. In this essay I show why I think the neoclassical formulation is wrong and indicate the reasons for my sympathies with the theories advanced by Harrod and Mrs Robinson.

I claim no great theoretical insights. There are no behavioural postulates which constitute new dynamic axioms. Perhaps they will come later. In short, the essay is essentially definitional. Nevertheless, as Kirzner recently stated: 'The ability to define usefully the terms used in theoretical economic discussion, turns out almost invariably to call for the very same insight into

---

[1] D. Ricardo, *On the Principles of Political Economy and Taxation*, ed. P. Sraffa and M. Dobb, *The Works and Correspondence of David Ricardo* (Cambridge: Cambridge University Press), I, 95.

[2] See L. M. Read, 'The measure of total factor productivity appropriate to wage-price guide-lines', *Canadian Journal of Economics*, I, May 1968, 349–58; T. K. Rymes, 'Professor Read and the measurement of total factor productivity', *ibid.*, 359–67.

economic processes that is required for the enumeration of theoretical propositions themselves.'[1]

In Chapter 2 I set forth definitions and the notation to be used and review certain aspects of traditional and recent capital theory. In Chapter 3, I set out and examine the main traditional measures of technological change and offer comments on and defence for the concepts of equilibrium and dynamics used in the main part of the book. In Chapter 4, I examine problems in the measurement of commodity capital. Chapter 5 sets out the main conclusions. Criticisms of the standard measures of technological progress examined in Chapter 3 are set out and established and support offered for the Harrod–Robinson capital input concept. In Chapters 6 and 7, several outcomes of the preceding analysis are examined: Solow's 'effective' capital is shown to be an empty concept and most contemporary measures of output are shown to be invalid. Chapter 8 sums up. It does so by critically examining the position of Professor Hicks and demonstrating how his search for a 'sophisticated' production function is satisfied by the concepts supported in this essay.[2]

Much of the dispute which emerged in the 1950s appeared to be concerned with aggregation problems and the fact that commodities can only be produced in a finite number of ways.[3] It is difficult in worlds of constant change and disequilibrium prices to attach much meaning to an aggregate stock of capital made up of such diverse commodities as door-knobs and blast furnaces. When the number of techniques is limited, then jumps among different input combinations will occur and ranges of input price indeterminacy result. This essay demonstrates, however, that such problems, while important, are not basic. One important by-product is, I think, to steer our thinking back to more critical problems in capital theory.

The essential point which must be remembered throughout the book is that I am considering capital as an input. I do not deal primarily with the theory of investment. I shall try to show, however, that, viewed correctly, the capital input concept stemming from my analysis satisfies both of Hicks' requirements for forward- and backward-looking concepts of capital and, as well, admirably serves Solow's concern with the social rate of return on investment.[4]

[1] I. M. Kirzner, *An Essay on Capital* (New York: A. M. Kelly, 1966), 1.
[2] Chapter 8 is a changed version of a talk I initially gave at Queen's University on 3 February 1969. I want to thank Professor Dan Usher for his comments at that time.
[3] See, for example, H. A. J. Green, *Aggregation in Economic Analysis: An Introductory Survey* (Princeton: Princeton University Press, 1964), esp. Part IV, The Measurement of Capital; and F. M. Fisher, 'The existence of aggregate production functions', *Econometrica*, XXXVII, 4, October 1969, 553–77.
[4] J. R. Hicks, 'The measurement of capital in relation to the measurement of other economic aggregates', ed. F. A. Lutz and D. C. Hague, *The Theory of Capital* (London:

INTRODUCTION

The notion of capital as a primary input has always been beset with difficulties. I discuss them in the context of the static theory of capital, demonstrate how the failure to develop the notion of capital as a truly primary input brings about theoretical difficulties when production analysis is concerned with dynamic economic systems and argue that the concept of capital as a primary input may be more persuasively developed in dynamic states. I confess to having some difficulty with the notion of the primary input called 'capital' in a static world of no technological progress. Strangely enough, I find the concept easier to grasp when technological progress is taking place.

Macmillan, 1961); R. M. Solow, *Capital Theory and the Rate of Return* (Amsterdam: North Holland Publishing, 1963), 16. See also Chapter 8.

2

THE TRADITIONAL THEORY OF CAPITAL

2.1 Introduction

I begin this chapter by setting out the main elements of the notation and concepts to be employed throughout the book. I then deal with the traditional theory of capital and some of the difficulties it encounters – even in a static framework of no technical change.

2.2 Definitions and notation

I shall be considering economies in which money plays no significant rôle. Quantities (flows and stocks) are primarily expressed in 'real' terms. Risk and uncertainty are not taken into account. I shall be dealing primarily with one- and two-sector models of economies exhibiting steady (i.e. unchanging) proportionate growth rates. These economies are *postulated* as being in unchanging general economic equilibrium. Economies exhibiting steady proportionate growth rates are those whose variables exhibit unchanging natural logarithmic proportionate growth rates. Economies could have changing growth rates but the equilibrium requirement then entails perfect foresight.[1] I shall not concern myself with problems of stability nor welfare. I largely ignore natural agents such as land.

In traditional neoclassical theory, it is argued that capital as an input in the process of economic production should be treated as a flow of the services of a primary input. Some authors consider the *flow* of the services of capital goods (e.g. a machine hour) as if they were comparable with the flow of the services of other primary inputs, such as the services of labour (e.g. a man-hour) and of land (e.g. hourly use of an acre).[2] Other authors, concentrating on the Böhm-Bawerk–Wicksell theory of capital, have dwelt on the stock aspect:

Whatever one thinks of capital as a productive agent or of the difficulties of regarding capital as an input element, it should not be difficult to agree on the

[1] J. Robinson, 'Pre-Keynesian theory after Keynes', *Collected Economic Papers*, III (Oxford: Blackwell, 1965).

[2] D. W. Jorgenson and Z. Griliches, 'The explanation of productivity change', *Review of Economic Studies*, XXXIV, July 1967, 249–84.

simple definition that capital as such is something which has the dimension 'quantity *at time t*' and not something 'per unit of time'. This applies to goods in process as well as to 'instruments'. Difficulties of measurement may have led to doubts about the possibility of a meaningful quantitative definition of capital. But that such a definition, whatever its nature, must have the dimensions of a stock is, I think, not a matter for controversy.[1]

In steady equilibrium, the flow of services emanating from capital goods is some constant proportion of the stock of such goods. Between the capital input viewed as a flow of services (e.g. the rentals on machines) or as a stock (e.g. the stock of the machines) rendering 'productive services by its presence in a production process',[2] there is, however, no fundamental difference. It is still the case that the stock of machines (and, consequently, the flow of services of the machines) has been built up to the steady-equilibrium state through capital accumulation, by a process of combining the services of primary inputs, such as the services of labour, and the services of intermediate inputs, such as machines. It is the intermediate input nature of capital inputs (in flow or stock form) which it is absolutely essential to remember. This is the central tenet of the capital theory of Böhm-Bawerk and Wicksell. The problem, as Haavelmo suggests in the previous quotation, has been to quantify this more fundamental capital input.

Essentially, then, I shall employ two definitions of capital. Commodity capital will mean the flow of services of machines and goods-in-process, and/or the stock of machines and goods-in-process, and/or the using-up of the machines or intermediate-input commodities during any time period in the process of production. *In short, commodity capital means commodity inputs, in flow or stock form.* Another concept of capital is 'real capital'. It is the measure for the capital input which is a primary agent of production 'on all fours' with labour as a primary input. It is defined by Mrs Robinson in the following way:

We can divide the value in terms of commodities of the stock of capital in any economy by the wage per man-hour in terms of commodities ruling in that economy and so obtain the quantity of capital in terms of labour time. This is in some ways the most significant way of measuring capital, for the essence of the productive process is the expenditure of labour time, and labour time expended at one date can be carried forward to a later date by using it to produce physical objects (or to store up knowledge) which will make future labour more productive, so that capital goods in existence to-day can be regarded as an embodiment of past labour time to be used up in the future.[3]

Since I deal in worlds postulated to be in equilibrium, the social accounts for such worlds portray equilibrium production relationships. By this

[1] T. Haavelmo, *A Study in the Theory of Investment* (Chicago: University of Chicago Press, 1960), 91. Haavelmo's emphasis.

[2] *Ibid.* 94.

[3] J. Robinson, *The Accumulation of Capital*, 3rd ed. (London: Macmillan, 1969), 121.

I mean that the amounts of any commodity or labour service being sold and purchased are not only always equal in the identity or social-accounting sense but are always equal in the behavioural sense.[1]

Since I shall be dealing primarily with one- and two-sector economies, the setting out of social accounts for such economies will illustrate the notation. Discussion of the notation will also help to clarify my definitions.

In the one-sector case, I have

$$Q \equiv \overline{W}L + RK + \Gamma K \qquad (2.1)$$

where the symbols are defined as

Q gross output of the commodity
$\overline{W}$ real wage per unit of labour input
L the flow of the labour input
R the net rate of return to the stock of commodity capital
K the number of pieces of commodity capital
Γ the rate of depreciation

I assume that the flow of labour as an input can be unambiguously defined and that, as a fraction of time available to any person, the time spent at work will be unchanging in steady-equilibrium situations where the growth rate of the real wage is constant.[2] The labour force is taken throughout as being homogeneous.

The rate of depreciation is taken for simplicity at present to be the rate of 'depreciation by evaporation'. Later, I shall consider 'depreciation by sudden death', which arises because capital goods are *assumed* to have finite physical lives. Both these assumptions are woefully unrealistic. The most realistic assumption of 'depreciation by obsolescence', which arises because capital goods are in a state of being continuously superseded by superior ones, implies technological progress and will be thoroughly dealt with later. By 'depreciation by evaporation' I mean that each piece of commodity capital is subject to a constant force of mortality or decay at the rate Γ. No matter when the stock of commodities was produced, a certain fraction of the stock will 'evaporate' each period. I introduce this assumption here for two reasons. In this chapter, it permits the existence of

---

[1] In simple macro-economic models used in the classroom where $I = \overline{I}$ is investment taken as exogenously determined, $S = S(Y)$ is savings functionally related to income, then $\overline{I} = S(Y)$ is an equilibrating relationship used to derive Y. In the social accounts, $I \equiv S$ by identity. *In* equilibrium, a reading of $\overline{I} \equiv S$ shows $\overline{I} = S(Y)$ exactly. Outside equilibrium, $I \equiv S$ but $\overline{I} \neq S(Y)$, and the social accounts tell us nothing about what is happening.

[2] G. Becker, 'A theory of the allocation of time', *Economic Journal*, LXXV, September 1965, 493–517. The assumption that the fraction of time available spent at work is completely inelastic with respect to the real-wage rate will be relaxed momentarily later when I discuss some of the forces determining the rate of accumulation.

a capital-good industry even in *stationary*-state equilibrium. In Chapter 5, it eases the demonstration of the inadequacy of the neoclassical concepts of technological change. As I show in Chapter 4, when the stock of commodity capital is considered to be subject to kinds of depreciation other than 'depreciation by evaporation', there will be many prices of the stock of capital goods and the rate of depreciation will be a function of the rate of technological change and the net rate of return to capital.

From identity (2.1), I have

$\overline{W}L$ as the real value of wages
RK as the real value of the net returns to commodity capital
ΓK as the real value of 'depreciation by evaporation'

Upper-case letters for all the elements of the social accounts represent levels. Lower-case letters represent proportionate natural logarithmic growth rates. Thus, where Q is defined as the level of gross output, $q[\equiv \mathrm{d}(\ln . Q)/\mathrm{d}t \equiv 1/Q . \mathrm{d}Q/\mathrm{d}t]$ is defined as the proportionate growth rate of gross output. These are instantaneous growth rates. The social accounts thus refer to arbitrary small chunks ('points') of time.

Identity (2.1) can be expressed as

$$1 \equiv \overline{W}A + RB + \Gamma B \qquad (2.2)$$

where $A \equiv L/Q$ and $B \equiv K/Q$. If $\overline{W}$ is factored out, I have

$$1/\overline{W} \equiv A + RJ + \Gamma J \qquad (2.3)$$

J is Mrs Robinson's 'real capital' per unit of gross output defined as $1/\overline{W} . K/Q$. 'Real capital' per unit of gross output equals $1 - \overline{W}A/\overline{W}(R+\Gamma)$, or the gross returns (measured in terms of commodities) per unit of output re-expressed in terms of labour capitalized at the ruling equilibrium gross rate of return to commodity capital.[1]

Finally, from identity (2.2), I define

$\overline{W}A \ (\equiv \alpha)$ to be the share of labour in gross output
$RB \ (\equiv \beta)$ the share of the net returns to commodity capital in gross output
$\Gamma B \ (\equiv \gamma)$ the share of depreciation in gross output

---

[1] The value of commodity capital per unit of gross output is $\overline{W}J \equiv 1 - \overline{W}A/R+\Gamma$, that is, the gross returns (measured in terms of commodities) per unit of gross output capitalized at the ruling equilibrium gross rate of return to commodity capital. When the labour force is heterogeneous, identity (2.1) becomes

$$Q \equiv \sum_{i=1}^{n} \overline{W}_i L_i + RK + \Gamma K \qquad (2.1\,(b))$$

or $1 \equiv \sum_{i=1}^{n} \overline{W}_i A_i + RB + \Gamma B$. If any real wage, say $\overline{W}_i$ is factored out, then 'real capital' per unit of gross output is measured in terms of labour type i. Thus 'real capital' measures will reflect the labour input chosen as numeraire.

The Greek letters are used for relative shares, and later in the analysis, as partial elasticities of production, they are allowed to vary exogenously. The share of labour in output net of depreciation, $\overline{W}L/Q - \Gamma K$, will be denoted α_N. Similarly for the other shares. From the definitions, it follows that

$$\alpha_N \equiv \frac{\alpha}{1-\gamma}$$

and

$$\beta_N \equiv \frac{\beta}{1-\gamma}$$

In the two-sector case, the social accounts will appear as:

$$P_C C \equiv WL_C + RP_K K_C + \Gamma P_K K_C \qquad (2.4(a))$$

$$P_K I \equiv WL_K + RP_K K_K + \Gamma P_K K_K \qquad (2.4(b))$$

where subscripts C and K are used to denote the consumption- and capital-good industries respectively. The flow of gross output of the consumption-good industry is C and its nominal price is P_C; for the capital-good industry it is I with a nominal price of P_K. W is the nominal wage rate.

If both identities are divided through by P_C, identity $(2.4(a))$ by C and $(2.2(b))$ by I, I then have

$$1 \equiv \overline{W}A_C + \frac{RP_K B_C}{P_C} + \frac{\Gamma P_K B_C}{P_C} \qquad (2.5(a))$$

$$\frac{P_K}{P_C} \equiv \overline{W}A_K + \frac{RP_K B_K}{P_C} + \frac{\Gamma P_K B_K}{P_C} \qquad (2.5(b))$$

The relative price, P_K/P_C, expresses commodity capital in terms of the consumption good and A_C, B_C, A_K and B_K refer to the respective input/output coefficients of technology expressed in physical units (e.g. $B_C \equiv K_C/C$).

Again, if the real-wage rate is factored out of identities (2.5), I have

$$\frac{1}{\overline{W}} \equiv A_C + RJ_C + \Gamma J_C \qquad (2.6(a))$$

$$\frac{P_K/P_C}{\overline{W}} \equiv A_K + RJ_K + \Gamma J_K \qquad (2.6(b))$$

where J_C and J_K are the ratios of 'real capital' per unit of gross output respectively in the two industries.

If there is more than one capital-good sector, I would have

$$1 \equiv \overline{W}A_C + R\sum_{i=1}^{n} \frac{P_{K_i}}{P_C} B_{iC} + \sum_{i=1}^{n} \Gamma_i \frac{P_{K_i}}{P_C} B_{iC} \qquad (2.7(a))$$

$$\frac{P_{K_j}}{P_C} \equiv \overline{W}A_j + R\sum_{i=1}^{n} \frac{P_{K_i}}{P_C} B_{ij} + \sum_{i=1}^{n} \Gamma_i \frac{P_{K_i}}{P_C} B_{ij} \qquad (2.7(b))$$

where B_{ij} represents the amount of commodity capital produced in the ith capital-good sector used per unit of gross output in the jth capital-good sector. Again, if the real-wage rate is factored out of identities (2.7), I have

$$\frac{\mathrm{I}}{\overline{W}} \equiv A_C + R \sum_{i=1}^{n} J_{iC} + \sum_{i=1}^{n} \Gamma_i J_{iC} \qquad (2.8\,(a))$$

$$\frac{P_{K_j}/P_C}{\overline{W}} \equiv A_j + R \sum_{i=1}^{n} J_{ij} + \sum_{i=1}^{n} \Gamma_i J_{ij} \qquad (2.8\,(b))$$

I ignore cases where there is more than one consumption-good sector. It is sometimes assumed that there is more than one consumption good but that they are produced and consumed in fixed proportions, an assumption which implies that the various consumption-good sectors are linearly combined into an aggregate consumption-good sector. These devices prevent any problems arising due to changes in the relative prices of consumption goods.

The multi-capital-good sector case largely complicates the story without strengthening the analytical content. Instead of there being one capital-good price in terms of the consumption good to consider, there are many. I shall largely ignore the multi-capital-good sector case.

With respect to the commodity-capital input, time enters in two essential ways. It takes time to produce commodity capital. If this were not so, an infinitely large capital stock could be produced in the 'twinkling of an eye', capital goods would not be scarce, and there would be no problem connected with the concept of the capital input. Capital goods do not last for ever. They are manufactured in such a way that a positive return to them occurs for only a finite period of time. When the return becomes zero, the capital good has no value, though its physical life could conceivably be infinitely long. (An abandoned rail embankment is the standard example.) Thus, capital goods as commodities have both 'periods of gestation' and 'periods of durability'. In equilibrium, the social-accounting price of a unit of new commodity capital will equal the present value of the streams of future gross returns expected to accrue to a unit of commodity capital over its 'period of durability', with the rate of discount being the equilibrium net rate of return to commodity capital. It is also equal to the compounded value of the direct and indirect labour used to produce such capital goods over its 'period of gestation', where labour is valued at the equilibrium wage rate and the rate of compounding is again the equilibrium net rate of return to commodity capital.

In each sector there will also be inventories or stocks of commodities of little durability in various states of completion, such as inventories of raw materials, goods-in-process and finished goods. There is obviously no *fixed* techological relationship between such commodity capital inputs and gross output. Such commodity-capital inputs are appropriate for a circulating-capital model, and their critical importance will be dealt with later.

In general, 'gestation and durability periods' are not given, but are part of the technology an economy adopts in equilibrium. In the traditional literature, one reads of a fall in the net rate of return to commodity capital leading to longer 'periods of production', lengthening of the 'period of investment' and increases in the 'roundaboutness' of capitalistic production. It seems better just to say that a description of equilibrium entails that each capital good will have its equilibrium periods of gestation and durability at the equilibrium net rate of return to capital. A different equilibrium, where a different net rate of return holds, entails different periods of gestation and durability for what appears to be the 'same' capital good. There need be no simple relationship, when two such equilibria are compared, between the different net rates of return and the different 'periods of production', 'periods of investment', and 'degrees of roundaboutness' of capitalistic production.

So much for the notation and the social-accounting relationships.

2.3 The capital input in a stationary economy

The notion of capital as a factor of production and the meaning which can be attached to the notion of a production function have been drawn up, until recently, within the context of a stationary state or in a world where, as Keynes assumed, the stock of capital is taken in the short run as part of the environment in which labour works.[1] By a stationary state I shall mean an economy in which output per unit of labour is constant. My concept of a stationary state includes therefore the classical stationary state with zero net accumulation of commodity capital and also a steady-growth state with zero technological progress and a positive rate of growth of net accumulation in forms of commodity capital equal to the rate of growth of the labour input. The classical stationary state is clearly a special case of the steady-state case with the rate of growth of labour set equal to zero.[2]

[1] J. M. Keynes, *The General Theory of Employment, Interest and Money* (London: Macmillan, 1936), 213–14.
[2] Suppose now, as a parenthetic footnote, that instead of comparing stationary states, I examine a given economy accumulating slowly over time. Output per unit of labour input can also be rising in economies where technological change is absent, by virtue of increases in the ratio of the stock of commodity capital to the labour input. Such increases, it is sometimes argued, are associated either with increased rates of accumulation with the labour input (or its rate of growth) held constant, which tends to cause the real-wage rate to rise and the net rate of return to commodity capital to fall, or with decreased work on the part of the labour force in the face of unchanged rates of accumulation of commodity capital, which again tends to cause wage rates to rise and the net rate of return to commodity capital to fall. As will be shown later, however, it is

Once technological change is introduced and output per unit of labour is rising, are the traditional notions of capital as an input and the production function affected? To answer such questions, one must have a clear grasp of what capital as a factor of production is in the stationary state.

I shall assume that perfect competition prevails and that returns to scale are constant. I also assume full employment. These are postulates. They are not meant to be realistic assumptions about any known economic system. Neoclassical analysis is most comfortable when such assumptions hold. *My main justification for using them is to show that, even when they hold, neoclassical analysis of capital accumulation and technical change is wrong.* I shall first assume that only one commodity is produced, which can be either consumed or stored for productive use. I shall then assume that there are two categories of final goods being produced, which are consumption goods and machines. The consumption-good and machine sectors are wholly integrated. Machines are built in the machine sector and sold or leased to the consumption-good sector. (The rental possibility is introduced only to permit reference to market rentals.) The population is assumed to be either homogeneous or composed of two homogeneous groups: workers who do not save and capitalists who do no work. For the one-commodity economy, the social accounts will appear, I have shown, as

$$Q \equiv \overline{W}L + RK + \Gamma K$$

$$\mathrm{I} \equiv \overline{W}A + RB + \Gamma B$$

$$\frac{\mathrm{I}}{\overline{W}} \equiv A + \left(\frac{R+\Gamma}{\overline{W}}\right) B \qquad (2.9)$$

The first assumption I shall make about technology is that there is only one way of producing commodities. Then, A and B are not only just equilibrium coefficients,[1] they are the unique coefficients of a fixed technology. What determines the real wage rate, $\overline{W}$, and the net return to commodity capital, R?

Is there some mechanism in the system that establishes the rate of profit so that, in given technical conditions, the real-wage rate emerges as a residual, or is there some mechanism that determines the behaviour of real wages, so that the rate of profit emerges as a residual?[2]

not necessarily the case that there is any predictable relationship between the ratio of commodity capital to the labour input and the ratio of the wage rate to the net rate of return to commodity capital. Furthermore, accumulation is probably affected by the labour supply, so it is not clear that decreases in work by the labour force necessarily lead to higher real-wage rates. In any event, the analysis of an economy in which the net rate of return is falling requires the perfect-foresight assumption if equilibrium analysis is to be used.

[1] J. R. Hicks, *Capital and Growth* (Oxford: Clarendon Press, 1965), 137.
[2] J. Robinson, 'A reconsideration of the theory of value', *Collected Economic Papers*, III (Oxford: Blackwell, 1965), 177.

Let me suppose that there are many economies with the same population, labour force, capital stock and technology. I would find some with high real wages and low net rates of return and others with low real wages and high rates of return. The maximum real wages to be earned is, of course, equal to output per unit of labour input as dictated by technology (i.e. $\overline{W}_{max} = 1/A - \Gamma B/A$). The maximum net rate of return is conversely where the real wage equals zero,[1] again dictated by technology (i.e. $R_{max} = 1/B - \Gamma$). Whatever combination of the real wage and the net rate of return to commodity capital is determined in any one economy, the combination must be along the factor-price line exhibited by the Panel (a) of Diagram 2.1. If the combination fell inside, the product being produced by the inputs K and L would be less than that made possible by technology and the competitive assumption. If the combination fell outside, the product would be greater than technically possible. Along the factor-price line, the actual input proportion, B/A, in any economy must be compatible with the technology. Panel (b) of Diagram 2.1 exhibits the relationships in the standard output/input format. It shows net (gross) output per unit of labour input, $1/A - \Gamma B/A$, $(1/A)$, related to commodity capital per unit of labour input, B/A. As Panel (b) of Diagram 2.1 graphically reveals, technology alone cannot determine factor prices. Whatever is the real wage, the balance of the technologically determined output per unit of labour input constitutes net return to capital per unit of labour input. As a proportion of the stock of commodity capital per unit of labour input, it represents the net rate of return.[2] When the social accounts are re-expressed as $1/A - \Gamma B/A \equiv \overline{W} + RB/A$, the net rate of return is shown as the slope of the line connecting output per unit of labour input and commodity capital per unit of labour input. From Panel (b), it can also be shown that the ratio of input prices is equal to the distance ON.[3] The production relationships can also be shown in terms of 'real capital' as the third part of identity (2.9) and Panel (c) of Diagram 2.1 shows. The ratio of 'real capital'

[1] The minimum stationary-state *equilibrium* wage could be zero only under the assumption that all members of the stationary population were capitalists and the net rate of return could be zero only if all members of the population were workers. Realistically, the possible wage and net rates of return would require to be bounded by Ricardian minima. See N. Kaldor, 'Alternative theories of distribution', *Essays on Value and Distribution* (London: Duckworth, 1960).

[2] In Diagram 2.1 (b), the net returns to capital per unit of labour input is shown as the distance on the vertical axis between, $\overline{W}$, the real wage rate, and net output per unit of labour input, $1/A - \Gamma B/A$. When expressed as a proportion of the stock of commodity capital, represented on the horizontal axis by the distance between the origin and capital per unit of labour input, B/A, the net rate of return to commodity capital is derived and shown, by similar triangles, as the tangent of the angle ϕ.

[3] The real wage is the distance $O\overline{W}$. With the help of the previous footnote, it can be seen that the net rate of return is equal to $O\overline{W}/ON$. Therefore, the ratio of the real wage to the net rate of return equals ON.

Diagram 2.1

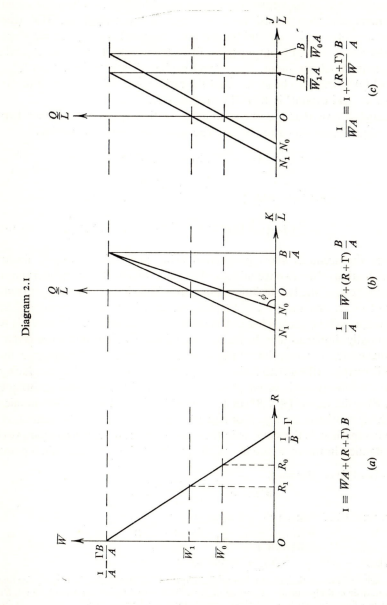

$$I \equiv \overline{W}A + (R+\Gamma)B$$

(a)

$$\frac{I}{A} \equiv \overline{W} + (R+\Gamma)\frac{B}{A}$$

(b)

$$\frac{I}{\overline{W}A} \equiv 1 + \frac{(R+\Gamma)}{\overline{W}}\frac{B}{A}$$

(c)

15

per unit of labour equals $1/\overline{W}.B/A$ and the net rate of return in Panel (c) of Diagram 2.1 is represented as $1/ON$,[1] with the ratio of the wage to the net rate of return to commodity capital equal to $\overline{W}/ON$. When the social accounts are re-expressed as $1/A - \Gamma B/A \equiv \overline{W}[1 + RB/\overline{W}A]$, $\overline{W}R$ (the product of the real wage and the net rate of return) is shown as the slope of the line connecting output per unit of labour input and 'real capital' per unit of labour input. Since 'real capital' has a 'price', then from Panel (c), it can also be shown that the ratio of the price of labour to the price of 'real capital' is $\overline{W}/\overline{W}R = 1/R$ or ON.

Suppose now that the one-commodity stationary economies have two techniques from which to choose. The social accounts now read as

$$1 \equiv \overline{W}[\lambda A + (1 - \lambda)A^*] + (R + \Gamma)[\lambda B + (1 - \lambda)B^*]$$

$$\frac{1}{[\lambda A + (1 - \lambda)A^*]} \equiv \overline{W} + (R + \Gamma)\frac{[\lambda B + (1 - \lambda)B^*]}{[\lambda A + (1 - \lambda)A^*]}$$

$$\frac{1}{\overline{W}} \equiv \left\{[\lambda A + (1 - \lambda)A^*] + \left(\frac{R + \Gamma}{\overline{W}}\right)[\lambda B + (1 - \lambda)B^*]\right\} \qquad (2.10)$$

where the accounts show production being undertaken as some linear combination of the two techniques.[2] The value which λ takes on determines whether one of the two techniques or both will be in use. As λ ranges from zero to one, first the (A^*, B^*) technique, then both and then the (A, B) technique will be used. This case is shown in Diagram 2.2. The analysis is essentially similar to that for the one-technique case. The difference is that at one critical combination of the wage and the net rate of return to commodity capital (the switch ratio, $\overline{W}_s/R_s$), any economy would be producing the commodity with equal profitability with either the first technique (A, B) or the second (A^*, B^*) or some combination of the two. If economies with input price ratios lower (or higher) than the switch ratio are examined, the comparison is the same as in the one-technique case. If I compare two economies, however, where in one the profit rate is above the switch point

---

[1] In Panel (b) of Diagram 2.1,
$$\overline{W}/ON = \frac{\overline{W}(1/A - \Gamma B/A)}{OB/A} = R.$$

In Panel (c) of Diagram 2.1, R is equal to
$$\frac{\overline{W}(1/A - \Gamma B/A)}{\overline{W}OB/\overline{W}A} \quad \text{and} \quad \frac{\overline{W}(1/A - \Gamma B/A)}{OB/\overline{W}A} = \overline{W}/ON.$$
Thus $\qquad\qquad \overline{W}R = \overline{W}/ON \quad \text{or} \quad R = 1/ON.$

[2] I exclude from consideration a second technique (A^*, B^*) such that its factor price line would lie entirely outside of, inside of, or coincident with that for technique (A, B). In the first case, such a technique would imply an improvement in techniques inconsistent with the classical stationary-state assumption; in the second case, a deterioration in techniques; and the third case would not represent a second technique at all.

Diagram 2.2

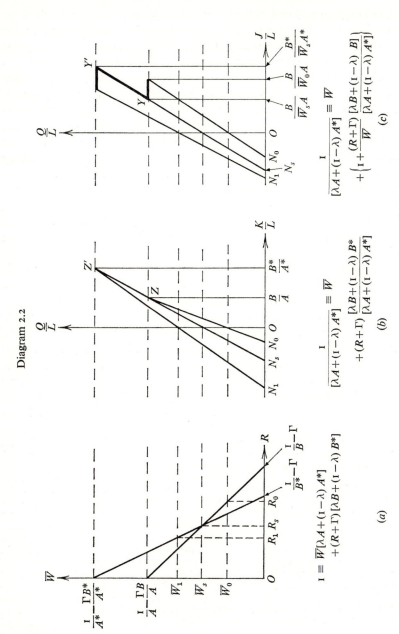

$$\frac{1}{[\lambda A + (1-\lambda)\,A^*]} \equiv \overline{W}$$

$$+ \left\{1 + \frac{(R+\Gamma)}{\overline{W}}\right\} \frac{[\lambda B + (1-\lambda)\,B]}{[\lambda A + (1-\lambda)\,A^*]}$$

(c)

$$\frac{1}{[\lambda A + (1-\lambda)\,A^*]} \equiv \overline{W}$$

$$+ (R+\Gamma) \frac{[\lambda B + (1-\lambda)\,B^*]}{[\lambda A + (1-\lambda)\,A^*]}$$

(b)

$$1 \equiv \overline{W}[\lambda A + (1-\lambda)\,A^*]$$

$$+ (R+\Gamma)\,[\lambda B + (1-\lambda)\,B^*]$$

(a)

(R_0 in Diagram 2.2) and in the other below (R_1 in Diagram 2.2), then the analysis is altered. Suppose in the two economies the differences in the rates of return were narrowed until they were equal at the switch point (R_s in Diagram 2.2). In the second economy, λ is one, and in the first, λ is zero. In the second, the *commodity-capital*/labour ratio will be higher than in the first. In the second, the '*real-capital*'/labour ratio will be higher than in the first.[1] The proportionate differences between the commodity-capital/labour and 'real-capital'/labour ratios will be identical since in the comparison of the two economies there is no proportionate difference in the relative input prices at the switch point. Along the flat (denoted by ZZ' in Diagram 2.2(*b*) and by YY' in Diagram 2.2(*c*)), it is clear that the traditional elasticity of substitution would be infinite. If we compare economies whose input price ratios are below and above the 'switchpoint', then in terms of commodity capital the elasticity of substitution will be positive, less than infinity and will, as the difference between the input price ratios becomes large, approach zero. For 'real capital' on the other hand, at the set of input prices ($\overline{W}_1$, R_1) the 'real-capital'/labour ratio might well be greater, equal to, or less than that for the input prices ($\overline{W}_0$, R_0).[2] The case where it is less is illustrated in Diagram 2.2(*c*).

Suppose now that there are many techniques. If there are an infinite number of possible techniques, the equi-profitable range of each of the linear relationships between output per unit of labour input and commodity capital per unit of labour input becomes smaller and smaller until, taken altogether, they merge into the standard neoclassical production function. There is still only one commodity being considered and the time which it takes to produce such commodities is being neglected. If gestation

---

[1] It must be remembered that I am comparing economies in their stationary states and not considering *one* economy engaged in commodity accumulation, since such behaviour would violate the stationary-state assumption.

[2] Samuelson finds the (normal) behaviour of the relationship between the input price ratio and the commodity-capital/labour ratio more appealing (in what way he did not make clear) than the 'lightning' relationship exhibited in the 'real capital' case. He states, in discussing Mrs Robinson's 'real capital', that it 'gives another example where a labour theory of value can help to make the analysis more complicated. Faced with a heterogeneous model in which there are terrible index number problems involved in measuring any aggregate, some modern economists fall back on despair on wage units as a best approximation for measurement, including the measurement of some kind of an aggregate of capital itself.' This illustrates the confused beliefs that the concept of 'real capital' involves the labour theory of value and that Mrs Robinson's structures were mainly concerned with index number and aggregation problems. See P. A. Samuelson, 'Parable and realism in capital theory: the surrogate production function', *Review of Economic Studies*, XXIX, June 1962, 193–206, esp. 203–4, reprinted in ed. J. E. Stiglitz, *The Collected Scientific Papers of Paul A. Samuelson*, I (Cambridge: M.I.T. Press, 1967), 325–38. See also D. C. Champernowne, 'The production function and the theory of capital: a comment', *Review of Economic Studies*, XXI(2), 1953–4, 112–35.

periods for the commodity were taken into account, there would exist, at any moment of time, commodities in various states of completion and the one commodity assumption would be violated. This is the 'capital as putty' concept often found in the literature. The social accounts for such an economy will now read

$$I \equiv \overline{W} \frac{L}{Q(L, K)} + (R + \Gamma) \frac{K}{Q(L, K)}$$

$$\frac{Q(L, K)}{L} \equiv \overline{W} + (R + \Gamma) \frac{K}{L}$$

$$\frac{Q(L, K)}{\overline{W}L} \equiv I + (K + \Gamma) \frac{J}{L} \qquad (2.11)$$

where $A \equiv \dfrac{L}{Q(L, K)}$, and $B \equiv \dfrac{K}{Q(L, K)}$.

For any one economy in stationary-state equilibrium, only one combination of the commodity-capital/labour ratio and the wage-rate/net-rate-of-return ratio will prevail. Whatever the determinants of $\overline{W}$ or R in each economy, it is assumed that a commodity-capital/labour ratio exists such that full employment holds.[1] This case is illustrated in Diagram 2.3.

[1] Elementary neoclassical 'growth' theory can be introduced at this moment to display the properties of the production function commonly assumed. First, the production function is assumed to be linear and homogeneous in its arguments so that

$$Q = Q(L, K) = LQ\left(I, \frac{K}{L}\right) = LF \frac{K}{L}$$

or gross output per unit of labour input may be expressed as a function of the commodity-capital/labour ratio. Net output (i.e. gross output less depreciation) per unit of labour input is then

$$\frac{Q}{L} - \Gamma \frac{K}{L} = F \frac{K}{L} - \Gamma \frac{K}{L}$$

and, in order for the economy to be technically viable, it is assumed that there exists at least one commodity-capital/labour ratio where net output is positive (or, at best, non-negative). Second, in neoclassical economics, it is commonly assumed that all individuals are alike, supplying an nth part of the labour input, owning and renting an nth part of the commodity capital stock and all saving the same fraction, S, of their income. The change in the commodity-capital/labour ratio in stationary states is zero. Then, the equilibrium capital/labour ratio, K/L^*, is found from

$$\frac{d}{dt}\left(\frac{K}{L}\right) = \frac{L \frac{dK}{dt} - K \frac{dL}{dt}}{L^2} = \frac{SQ}{L} - \Gamma \frac{K}{L} = SF\left(\frac{K^*}{L}\right) - \Gamma \frac{K^*}{L} = 0$$

Third, it is assumed that a positive stationary state capital/labour ratio exists and this is ensured by assuming that the production function has the following additional properties: $F'(K/L) > 0$; $F''(K/L) < 0$; $F'(0) = \infty$; and $F'(\infty) = 0$. The first and second order partial derivatives ensure that technology is subject to generalized diminishing returns, the third ensures that low saving rates would not see the economy accumulate commodity capital below its technologically given rate of 'depreciation by evaporation' and the fourth ensures that there is some upper limit to the stationary

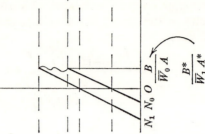

Diagram 2.3

$\dfrac{Q}{L} = f(B/A)$

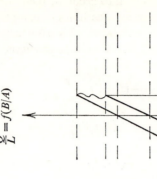

$F(I/A, B/A) \equiv 0$

(b)

$F\left(\dfrac{1}{A}, \overline{W}, \dfrac{B}{A}\right) \equiv 0$

(c)

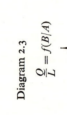

$F(\overline{W}, R) \equiv 0$

(a)

20

A comparison between the different economies reveals proportionate differences in input price ratios and in commodity-capital/labour ratios. The ratios of such differences are measures of the traditional elasticity of substitution. That the traditional elasticity of substitution can be so measured is based on the assumptions that production functions are characterized by constant returns to scale and that the various economies have identical technologies. Consider the following traditional isoquant diagram for an economy with a given labour force and at various stages of stationary-state equilibria. The proportionate change in commodity capital per unit of labour is

$$\left[\frac{OK_1}{K_1 C} - \frac{OK_0}{K_0 A}\right] \bigg/ \frac{OK_0}{K_0 A} = \left[\frac{OK_1}{O\bar{L}} - \frac{OK_0}{O\bar{L}}\right] \bigg/ \frac{OK_0}{O\bar{L}} = \frac{OK_1 - OK_0}{OK_0}$$

similar to $\left[\dfrac{OB_1}{A_1} - \dfrac{OB_0}{A_0}\right] \bigg/ \dfrac{OB_0}{A_0}$ in Diagram 2.2(b). The proportionate changes in the ratio of input prices are given by the proportionate changes in the slope of the isocost lines. By the assumption of constant returns to scale, the marginal rate of substitution (the input price ratio) between labour and commodity capital is the same at B as at C. Assume that B, on the factor ratio line OC, lies on the same isoquant as A. Then the change in the slope of the factor ratio line from OA to OB is equal to the proportionate change in commodity capital per unit of labour accompanied by increases in the level of output. Since the elasticity of substitution is the ratio of the proportionate change in the factor ratio line divided by the proportionate change in the slope of the isocost line, we can also assess the elasticity of substitution by considering the proportionate change in the ratio of commodity capital to labour input for any level of output, and as Diagram 2.4 also shows, for any level of labour input. The state of the industrial arts in the economies being compared must be the same. If not, special assumptions must be made about the way the factor price frontiers and production functions have 'shifted' to ensure that the same constant-returns-to-scale isoquant map is being discussed.

In each economy a measure of 'real capital' is obtained by 'deflating' the stock of commodity capital by the real wage prevailing in that economy. If the traditional elasticity of substitution is greater than, equal to or less

commodity-capital/labour ratio. Neoclassical 'growth' theory consists essentially of amending the differential equation to allow for the labour force to grow in either natural or efficient units and then again finding the stationary value of the suitably adjusted commodity-capital/labour ratio. See R. M. Solow, 'A contribution to the theory of economic growth', *Quarterly Journal of Economics*, LXX, February 1956, 65–94, reprinted in eds. J. E. Stiglitz and H. Uzawa, *Readings in the Modern Theory of Economic Growth* (Cambridge: M.I.T. Press, 1969).

than unity then, as higher and higher real-wage-rate/rate-of-return-to-capital ratios are considered, there will be evidenced higher, unchanged or lower 'real-capital'/labour ratios.

I shall suppose now that the economy produces two goods in two sectors: one consumption good and one capital good – called a machine. I shall assume first that in each sector there is but one technique available and that

Diagram 2.4

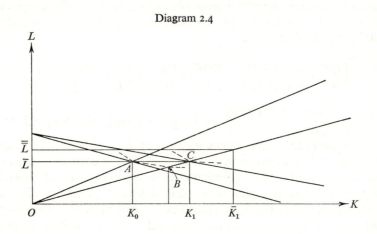

machines are sold, not rented, to the consumption-good sector. The social accounts are then:

$$P_C C \equiv WL_C + RP_K K_C + \Gamma P_K K_C$$

$$P_K I \equiv WL_K + RP_K K_K + \Gamma P_K K_K \tag{2.12}$$

In the standard notation and re-expressed in terms of a traditional *net* input/output table, the social accounts are

		Sectors		Net output		
		C	I	C	I	Total output
Sectors	C			I		I
	I	$\Gamma \dfrac{P_K}{P_C} B_C$	$\Gamma \dfrac{P_K}{P_C} B_K$			$\dfrac{P_K}{P_C}$
Primary input	L	$\overline{W} A_C$	$\overline{W} A_K$			$\overline{W}(A_C + A_K)$
	K	$R \dfrac{P_K}{P_C} B_C$	$R \dfrac{P_K}{P_C} B_K$			$R \dfrac{P_K}{P_C} (B_C + B_K)$
Total input		I	$\dfrac{P_K}{P_C}$		I	(2.13)

22

where total outputs are all normalized at the unit level and the table is expressed in terms of the consumption good. Given R, the 'prices' may be expressed as

$$\left[\overline{W}\ \frac{P_K}{P_C}\right] \equiv [\mathrm{I}\ \ \mathrm{o}]\begin{bmatrix}A_C & A_K \\ (R+\Gamma)B_C & (R+\Gamma)B_K\end{bmatrix} - \begin{bmatrix}\mathrm{o} & \mathrm{o} \\ \mathrm{o} & \mathrm{I}\end{bmatrix}^{-1}$$

There are now three 'prices' to determine: the real consumption-good wage rate, the net rate of return to commodity capital and the price of the machine in terms of the consumption good. Again, it is necessary to introduce preferences to determine either $\overline{W}$ or R. I shall assume that R is determined exogenously. Then, from (2.13)

$$\overline{W} \equiv \frac{\mathrm{I}-(R+\Gamma)B_K}{A_C[\mathrm{I}-(R+\Gamma)\,B_K]+A_K(R+\Gamma)\,B_C}$$

and

$$\frac{P_K}{P_C} \equiv \frac{A_K}{A_C[\mathrm{I}-(R+\Gamma)\,B_K]+A_K(R+\Gamma)\,B_C} \qquad (2.14)$$

Define $m \equiv \dfrac{A_K}{A_C}\Big/\dfrac{B_K}{B_C}$, a coefficient to express the relative machine- to labour-intensity of the consumption to the capital-good sector. Then the price equations may be written as

$$\overline{W} \equiv \frac{\mathrm{I}-(R+\Gamma)\,B_K}{A_C+A_C B_K(R+\Gamma)(m-\mathrm{I})}$$

and

$$\frac{P_K}{P_C} \equiv \frac{A_K}{A_C+A_C B_K(R+\Gamma)(m-\mathrm{I})} \qquad (2.15)$$

If $m = \mathrm{I}$, the techniques in the two sectors are identical, and the model collapses to the one-commodity case where $\overline{W} = \mathrm{I}-(R+\Gamma)B_K/A_C$ for a given R, $\mathrm{d}\overline{W}/\mathrm{d}R = -B_K/A_C < \mathrm{o}$, $\mathrm{d}^2\overline{W}/\mathrm{d}R^2 = \mathrm{o}$, and $P_K/P_C = A_K/A_C$. The labour theory of value holds.

From the definition of m, it follows that $m > \mathrm{I}\ (< \mathrm{I})$ implies that the consumption-good (the capital-good) sector is relatively machine-intensive. If technology across all economies is such that the consumption-good sector is relatively capital-intensive, then, as I compare economies having high wages and low net rates of return (high input price ratios) with those having low wages and high net rates of return (low input price ratios), the price of machines in terms of the consumption good will be higher in the former than in the latter and, as a consequence, the stock of capital per unit of labour in terms of consumption goods will also be higher. However, if the capital-good sector is relatively capital intensive, the price and the stock of capital in terms of consumption goods will both be lower. In the first case there is a positive, while in the second case there is a negative, Wicksell *price* effect. From the set of seven equations

$$C = \frac{L_C}{A_C} = \frac{K_C}{B_C}$$

$$I = \frac{L_K}{A_K} = \frac{K_K}{B_K} = \Gamma K$$

$$L_C + L_K = \overline{L} \qquad \text{(the labour force being exogenously determined)}$$

$$K_C + K_K = K$$

for any economy, given $\overline{L}$, it is possible to determine from technology alone what the solution of the variables C, I, L_C, L_K, K_C, K_K and K will be. For instance, the labour employed in the capital-good sector in stationary equilibrium will be

$$L_K = \frac{B_C \Gamma \overline{L}}{1 + \Gamma \overline{L} B_K (m-1)}$$

which, when $m = 1$, is $B_C \Gamma$. In the one-technique case the distribution of the labour force over the two sectors is determined entirely by technology.

Introduction of the two accounting relationships shown in identities (2.15) produces three more variables to determine, $\overline{W}$, R, and P_K/P_C. It should be noted that the assumption that all wages and net returns are consumed is already given in the previous set of equations (namely, $I = \Gamma K$), and so prices still remain undetermined as the setting of the level of R exogenously implies.

In the two-commodity two-sector case, I have the following relationship between $\overline{W}$ and R and P_K/P_C and R.

$$\frac{d\overline{W}}{dR} = \frac{-B_K m}{[1 + B_K(R+\Gamma)(m-1)]^2}$$

and

$$\frac{d^2\overline{W}}{dR^2} = \frac{2B_K^2 A_C m(m-1)}{[1 + B_K(R+\Gamma)(m-1)]^3}$$

and

$$\frac{d(P_K/P_C)}{dR} = \frac{-A_K B_K(m-1)}{[1 + B_K(R+\Gamma)(m-1)]^2}$$

and

$$\frac{d^2(P_K/P_C)}{dR^2} = \frac{2A_K B_K^2 A_C(m-1)^2}{[1 + B_K(R+\Gamma)(m-1)]^2}$$

The denominator cannot be less than zero, for if it were I should have

24

negative real-wage rates. A matrix, portraying the signs of these relation-ships for different values of m, may be set out as follows

	$\dfrac{d\overline{W}}{dR}$	$\dfrac{d^2\overline{W}}{dR^2}$	$\dfrac{d(P_K/P_C)}{dR}$	$\dfrac{d^2(P_K/P_C)}{dR^2}$
$m > 1$	< 0	> 0	< 0	> 0
$m = 1$	< 0	0	0	0
$m < 1$	< 0	< 0	> 0	> 0

These results are also set out in Diagram 2.5. As Diagram 2.5 reveals, when R reaches its maximum, $(1/B_K) - \Gamma$, the price of machines in terms of consumption goods is equal to the relative machine-intensities of the two sectors. The above analysis shows that while the aggregate number of machines is determined by the technical conditions and the supply of

Diagram 2.5

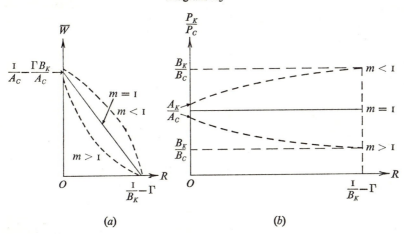

(a)   (b)

labour assumed, the value of the stock of machines in terms of consump-tion goods will be greater or less, for different levels of the net rate of return, depending upon the relative machine-intensities. If, for a lower rate of profits, the consumption-good sector is the more machine-intensive, the value of the total stock of machines in terms of the consumption good will be higher and a *positive price Wicksell 'effect'* is said to be holding.

On the other hand, in terms of 'real capital' per unit of labour, the relationship between aggregate real capital per unit of labour input and the ratio of primary-input prices is just as it was in the one-industry case.

I indicated earlier that 'real capital' could be computed in terms of the consumption-good or the machine wage. At the aggregate level, as different

25

economies are compared, in the two-sector one-technique case the stock of capital measured in terms of consumption goods is less high (more low) proportionally compared to the increase (decrease) in the real wage as lower (higher) net rates of return are considered. From the price equations, it can be seen that

$$\frac{\overline{W}}{P_K/P_C} = \frac{W}{P_K} = \frac{1-(R+\Gamma)B_K}{A_K} \quad \text{and} \quad \frac{d\left(\frac{\overline{W}}{P_K/P_C}\right)}{dR} = \frac{-B_K}{A_K} < 0$$

Whereas with a lower rate of return, the value of the stock of commodity capital may be higher or lower, the stock of real capital must be lower. Again, it must be remembered that the gestation period of the machines is being ignored. Suppose, however, that a second capital-good industry, again with one technique, were introduced. A comparison of economies with different input price ratios would show that the value of the aggregate stock of capital (two different kinds of machines) in terms of consumption goods would again depend upon the various capital-intensities, and an *aggregate* traditional elasticity of substitution in this sense would be meaningless.[1]

[1] Again, I would have in the three-sector case

$$C = \frac{L_C}{A_C} = \frac{K_{1C}}{B_{1C}} = \frac{K_{2C}}{B_{2C}}$$

$$I_1 = \Gamma_1(K_{1C}+K_{11}+K_{12}) = \frac{L_{K1}}{A_{K1}} = \frac{K_{11}}{B_{K11}} = \frac{K_{21}}{B_{K21}}$$

$$I_2 = \Gamma_2(K_{2C}+K_{21}+K_{22}) = \frac{L_{K2}}{A_{K2}} = \frac{K_{12}}{B_{K12}} = \frac{K_{22}}{B_{K22}}$$

$$L_C+L_{K1}+L_{K2} = L$$

$$K_{1C}+K_{11}+K_{12} = K_1$$

$$K_{2C}+K_{21}+K_{22} = K_2$$

fourteen equations to determine the fourteen unknowns (C, I_1, I_2, L_C, L_{K1}, L_{K2}, K_{1C}, K_{11}, K_{12}, K_{2C}, K_{21}, K_{22}, K_1 and K_2). The distribution of the labour force would be determined strictly by technology and the relationship between real capital per unit of labour input and input price ratios would continue to be monotonic as shown in the text. If I add the social-accounting identities

$$\left[\overline{W} \; \frac{P_{K1}}{P_C} \; \frac{P_{K2}}{P_C}\right] = [1 \; 0 \; 0] \left[\begin{pmatrix} A_C & A_1 & A_2 \\ (R+\Gamma_1)B_{1C} & (R+\Gamma_1)B_{11} & (R+\Gamma_1)B_{12} \\ (R+\Gamma_2)B_{2C} & (R+\Gamma_2)B_{21} & (R+\Gamma_2)B_{22} \end{pmatrix} - \begin{pmatrix} 0 & 0 & 0 \\ 0 & 1 & 0 \\ 0 & 0 & 1 \end{pmatrix}\right]^{-1}$$

I still require an additional exogenous relationship to determine $\overline{W}$, P_{K1}/P_C, P_{K2}/P_C and R.

In general, in the one-technique, one-consumption-good, n-capital-good-sector case, there will be $2+4n+n^2$ technical and supply relationships to determine the $2+4n+n^2$ outputs, sector inputs and total amounts of the n capital goods, given the supply of labour. There will be $n+1$ social-accounting relationships in $n+2$ unknowns and the rate of return, R, must still be determined exogenously.

In my view this aggregate case clearly relegates the traditional concept of the elasticity of substitution to the compound of partial equilibrium. At the level of the individual industry, then, the elasticity of substitution must be calculated for each machine and kind of labour, since the aggregate stock used in each industry can only be summarized in terms of a numéraire. This case shows clearly that the traditional concept of the elasticity of substitution, drawn up in terms of 'labour' and 'commodity capital', cannot be employed when any aggregate or empirically-oriented general-equilibrium analysis is in mind.

If more than one technique exists in each sector, the behaviour of real-wage rates and, especially, the price of machines in terms of a consumption good, as economies are compared in which different input price ratios prevail, can in general be very complex.

I shall initially return to the assumption that there are two sectors, each with only two possible techniques, but that over all techniques the capital good remains physically unchanged. Even if the machine sector changes its technique, the machine remains identifiably the same. I shall assume that the consumption good also remains unchanged. For the whole economic system, there would appear to be four possible techniques: (A_C, B_C, A_K, B_K), (A_C^*, B_C^*, A_K, B_K), (A_C, B_C, A_K^*, B_K^*), and $(A_C^*, B_C^*, A_K^*, B_K^*)$. The importance of assuming the identifiability of the capital good may now be seen. If the capital-good sector 'switches' its process from (A_K, B_K) to (A_K^*, B_K^*), the capital/output ratio in the consumption-good sector remains identifiable. There will now be four possible relationships between $\overline{W}$ and R and between P_K/P_C and R. If no one of the four techniques dominates over the whole range of $\overline{W}$ and R, and providing they are, in fact, different processes, then there should be at least three intersections of the $(\overline{W}, R)$ factor price line and of the $(P_K/P_C, R)$ price line at which the sectors will 'switch' processes. There may be other intersections but, though important, as I shall show, they will be dominated by the 'switch' intersections. This case is shown in Diagram 2.6 which is comparable to Diagram 2.5. In Diagram 2.6, the four $(\overline{W}, R)$ lines have three 'switch' intersections, as do the four $(P_K/P_C, R)$ lines. If higher and higher net rates of return are considered, it will be seen from Diagram 2.6 that the system 'switches' from the first technique, where the capital-good sector is the most capital-intensive $(m_1 < m_2)$, to the second, where its capital-intensity is reduced $(m_2 < 1)$, to the third, where relative intensities are equal $(m = 1)$, to the fourth, where the consumption-good sector becomes relatively capital-intensive $(m > 1)$. At each 'switch' point, the price of the capital good in terms of the consumption good is the same for both techniques. There is then for each 'switch' point, a set of prices $(\overline{W}, R, P_K/P_C)$ common to both techniques. Moreover, from Diagram 2.6, the *value* of the stock of capital per man in terms of consumption goods can be derived. At the first 'switch' point, denoted $(\overline{W}, R, P_K/P_C)$, the maximum possible wage rate, $\overline{W}_{\max 1}$, is equal to the intercept of the technique line $m_1 < m_2$ with the $\overline{W}$ axis. This is the maximum consumption or net output (net of depreciation necessary to preserve the stationary stock of commodity capital) per unit of the labour force which can be achieved with that technique. The actual wage rate is $\overline{W}_1$, and, as a consequence

Diagram 2.6

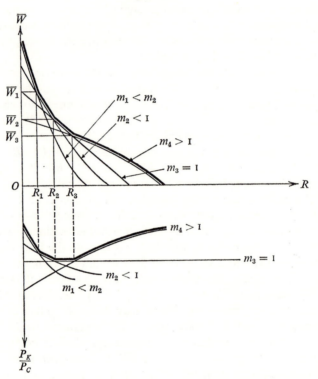

profit per man equals $\overline{W}_{\max 1} - \overline{W}_1$. The value of the stationary state stock of capital, in terms of the consumption good, equals then $\dfrac{\overline{W}_{\max 1} - \overline{W}_1}{R_1}$. At the first 'switch' point, however, the system 'switches' to the technique $m_2 < 1$, whose maximum net output is $\overline{W}_{\max 2}$ with profits per man of $\overline{W}_{\max 2} - \overline{W}_1$. Since $\overline{W}_{\max 2}$ is lower than $\overline{W}_{\max 1}$, the value of capital per man associated with the second technique is lower than that for the first technique. This will be true for all techniques, and so the value of capital per man and the maximum potential consumption per man becomes lower and lower as higher and higher net rates of return are considered.

Could there be more than three 'switch' intersections? Could two $(\overline{W}, R)$ relationships intersect twice? Not, as it turns out, in this case. This result rests, however, on the assumption that the capital good remains identifiably the same, that is, there is *only* one capital good. At each 'switch' point, the same rate of return holds. Consider any two techniques. For each the equal rates of profit will be, from identity (2.15)

$$R = \frac{1 - \overline{W}A_C}{B_K[1 + \overline{W}A_C(m-1)]} - \Gamma$$

When I examine consecutive 'switch' points, I have

$$\frac{1 - \overline{W}A_C}{B_K[1 + \overline{W}A_C(m_1 - 1)]} = \frac{1 - \overline{W}A_C}{B_K^*[1 + \overline{W}A_C(m_2 - 1)]}$$

$$\frac{1 - \overline{W}A_C}{B_K^*[1 + \overline{W}A_C(m_2 - 1)]} = \frac{1 - \overline{W}A_C^*}{B_K^*[1 + \overline{W}A_C^*(m_3 - 1)]}$$

$$\frac{1 - \overline{W}A_C^*}{B_K^*[1 + \overline{W}A_C^*(m_3 - 1)]} = \frac{1 - \overline{W}A_C^*}{B_K[1 + \overline{W}A_C^*(m_4 - 1)]}$$

For the first and third cases, the numerators cancel, and I am left with a linear relationship for $\overline{W}$ in terms of the techniques: hence the pairs of techniques being considered can only intersect once. For the second case, cross-multiplication shows that again a linear relationship in $\overline{W}$ results and hence the pairs of techniques intersect once. Therefore, no two $(\overline{W}, R)$ relationships can intersect twice. This will be true for as many techniques as may be considered.[1]

I may thus assume that the capital good, while it retains its identity, is produced under conditions similar to those postulated for the one-commodity case when the neoclassical production function was developed. I may also assume that the consumption-good sector is also characterized by the standard neoclassical production function. Thus, I would have

$$\left.\begin{aligned} 1 &= \overline{W}\frac{L_C}{C(K_C, L_C)} + (R+\Gamma)\frac{P_K}{P_C}\frac{K_C}{C(K_C, L_C)} \\ \frac{P_K}{P_C} &= \overline{W}\frac{L_K}{I(K_K, L_K)} + (R+\Gamma)\frac{P_K}{P_C}\frac{K_K}{I(K_K, L_K)} \end{aligned}\right\} \quad (2.16)$$

and the standard neoclassical two-sector story may now be told.[2]

[1] M. Bruno, E. Burmeister, and E. Sheshinski, 'The nature and implications of the reswitching of techniques', Paradoxes in Capital Theory: A Symposium, *Quarterly Journal of Economics*, LXXX, November 1966, 536.

[2] For details, see F. H. Hahn and R. C. O. Matthews, 'The theory of economic growth: a survey', *Economic Journal*, LXXIV, December 1964, I. 8 Two-sector models, 812–21.

It is obvious, however, that the assumption that the capital good remains identifiably the same over all techniques should be replaced with a more realistic one. Three different assumptions, leading to the same result, may be made. First, it can be assumed that there is a different capital good appropriate to each process adopted in the capital-good sector.[1] Second, it can be assumed that for each technique there is more than one capital good. Third, 'gestation periods' required in the constructing of capital goods may be brought back into the story, which, of course, insures that for each technique there will be more than one capital good (completed machines and uncompleted machines). I shall assume that for each technique there are two capital goods. A change in technique will occur when any sector 'switches' processes. If a 'switch' point exists between two techniques, then, at the same real-wage rate, the same rate of profit and the same set of relative prices for the two capital goods will hold. The $(\overline{W}, R)$ line will for any technique take on the shape seen for the one capital good case and there will be two $(\overline{W}, R)$ lines to consider, one for each technique. In this case, the $(\overline{W}, R)$ lines may intersect twice, so that for two techniques there are two 'switch' points in the positive ranges of $\overline{W}$ and R. If there are three capital goods and two techniques, there may be three 'switch' points. The more capital goods, the more the possible number of 'switch' points.[2] The two capital-good two-technique case is shown in Diagram 2.7.

Inspection of Diagram 2.7 reveals two important things. First, if we compare two economies, each employing in stationary-state equilibrium two capital goods and with two viable techniques at their disposal, and if the rate of return is allowed to range over the two 'switch' points, then as the rate becomes higher and higher in one economy compared with the other, the high-rate economy will initially be seen to have a lower *value* of capital per man, $(\overline{W}_{\max 2} - \overline{W}_1)/R_1$ is less than $(\overline{W}_{\max 1} - \overline{W}_1)/R_1$, but at higher rates it will have higher *value* of capital per man, $(\overline{W}_{\max 1} - \overline{W}_2)/R_2$ is

[1] This problem is dealt with in Chapter 6.

[2] The 'switching' controversy is based upon P. Sraffa, *Production of Commodities by Means of Commodities* (Cambridge: Cambridge University Press). From page 26, n.1, it can be shown that for a given R and two techniques (a 'switch' in any one of the columns of the technology matrix will produce two techniques), and two capital goods, a second degree equation in $\overline{W}$ results which may have two positive roots. For three capital goods, given the net rate of return, there will be a third degree equation in $\overline{W}$ and for n capital goods, an n degree equation in $\overline{W}$ with n possible positive roots. In a more general analysis, Bharadwaj has shown that the maximum number of 'switches' between the techniques is equal to the number of what Sraffa has called basics, i.e. commodities which enter directly and indirectly into the production of every other commodity, and non-basics, which 'use up' some of themselves in their own production. 'Switches' related to non-basics, however, do not affect the relative prices among the basics. See K. Bharadwaj, 'On the maximum number of switches between two production systems' (Cambridge University, mimeo, n.d.).

greater than $(\overline{W}_{\max 2} - \overline{W}_2)/R_2$. There no longer exists a monotonic relation between the rate of return to capital and the value of capital per man. As can also be readily seen from Diagram 2.7, the maximum possible consumption per unit of labour will also no longer be in a monotonic relation with the rate of return. That is, an economy with a high rate of interest

Diagram 2.7

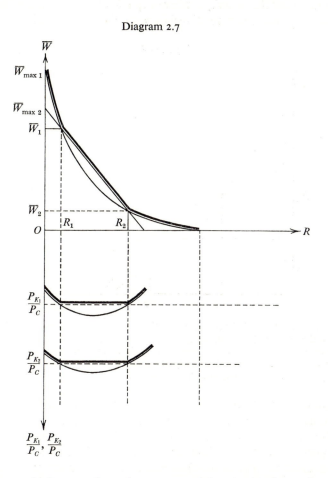

may have a high rate of maximum potential consumption, whereas an economy with a low rate may have a low potential consumption. The same 'perverse' relationship holds with respect to the rate of profit and the capital/net-output ratios, expressed in terms of the consumption good. These are the surprising results which have emerged from recent discussion on the 'reswitching' of techniques. Second, the $(P_K/P_C, R)$ lines for any *one* technique will not display a monotonic relation. In Diagram 2.7, the second technique was deliberately chosen to ensure equal input-intensities in all the sectors, so that where the second technique holds, the prices of the two capital goods are invariant to changes in the rate of return, being dictated by the relative labour input requirements only. Because relative prices must be the same at each 'switch' point, the $(P_K/P_C, R)$ for each capital good for the technique where capital-intensities are not equal will not show a monotonic relationship with the rate of return. That is,

Diagram 2.8

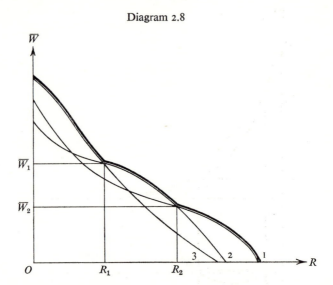

Note. There may be 'switch' points below the frontier but these represent false switch points in the sense that, though the wage rates and profit rates are equal, relative prices for the techniques will not be the same. These false switch points occur when a comparison is drawn between two techniques, where at least two commodities have experienced a change in the way they are produced.

variations of the rate of return, in an economy with two capital goods, will not produce monotonic variations in the relative prices of the capital goods. This fact can again be extended to the world of many capital goods, with many possible 'switches' in the behaviour of relative prices with respect to the rate of return. I shall use these results more extensively in Chapter 4.

Where 'reswitching' can take place, then the same perversity with respect to the relationships between the rate of return and the value of capital per unit of labour, the maximum potential consumption per unit of labour, and the value of capital per unit of net output, can occur even though no technique 'comes back'. This case is illustrated in Diagram 2.8. In Diagram 2.8, one of the 'double switch' points for $(\overline{W}, R)$ lines 2 and 3 is dominated by the technique represented by $(\overline{W}, R)$ line 1. No technique is in use along two segments of the envelope of the $(\overline{W}, R)$ lines. Yet still, as higher and higher rates of return are considered, the economic system at first adopts techniques which imply lower values of capital per man, but then techniques entailing higher values of capital per man are employed. This illustrates the importance of 'switch' points which are dominated.[1]

The three sectors can be assumed to have the standard neoclassical production functions with each capital good being a different kind of perfectly malleable substance, and being the product and input of any one of a large number of techniques. So the assumption of capital malleability – that is, the ability of each capital good to be produced and used in a very large number of techniques – is not a critical assumption, at least for this problem. One still gets the 'reswitching' phenomenon.[2] How do all these findings affect the traditional theory of capital?

2.4 Behavioural assumptions behind the stationary economy

Many economists have traditionally asserted that the wage rate is the price of non-leisure and the net rate of return is the price of non-consumption or abstinence.[3] In terms of a 'real cost' theory of production in a stationary state (with a positive rate of return), the price of any commodity is said to be resolvable into its direct and indirect unit 'labour' and 'waiting' costs. The resources of the steady state economy are made up of so much labour and stock of 'waiting'. Put another way, the stock of 'waiting' is seen as a Consumption Fund. An economy with given labour might add to that Fund by saving – by giving up (i.e. abstaining from the production of) a part of the flow of consumption 'today', $C_0 - \overline{C}_0$, with the result that 'tomorrow's' larger Fund would result in an additional flow of consumption 'tomorrow' $\overline{C}_1 - C_1$, larger than would have been the case had the abstinence not occurred. Conversely, by dissaving – by consuming part of the Fund 'today' – an economy would reduce the size of the Fund and 'tomorrow' the smaller Fund would result in a flow of consumption lower than would have been the case if the dissaving had not occurred. Let the decrease (increase) in the flow of consumption 'today' be $C_0 - \overline{C}_0 = \Delta C_0$,

---

[1] L. L. Pasinetti, 'Changes in the rate of profit and switches in techniques', Paradoxes in Capital Theory: A Symposium, *Quarterly Journal of Economics*, LXXV, November 1966, 515–16.

[2] If the number of techniques approaches infinity so that smooth production functions prevail, then since marginal products relate to unique input/output ratios, 'reswitching' cannot take place (M. Bruno *et al.*, 'Nature and implications', 545–6). The question then arises, however, of the meaning of the marginal product of incomplete capital goods in long-period equilibrium.

[3] With money present, a distinction must be drawn between the net rate of return and the rate of interest. If the price of the consumption good is rising (falling), the rate of return will equal the rate of interest less the rate of increase (decrease) of the price of the consumption good.

and the increase (decrease) in the flow of consumption 'tomorrow' be $\bar{C}_1 - C_1 = \Delta C_1$. Define a number R, such that

$$(1 + R_1)(C_0 - \bar{C}_0) = \bar{C}_1 - C_1 \quad \text{or} \quad R_1 = \frac{\Delta C_1}{\Delta C_0} - 1$$

The number R_1 may be called the marginal product of investment, or the 'one period' rate of return.[1] It was further postulated that for a given technology, additional saving (dissaving) 'today' would be associated with a smaller (larger) addition to (subtraction from) the flow of consumption 'tomorrow'. Define the number R_2 such that

$$(1 + R_2)(\bar{C}_0 - \bar{\bar{C}}_0) = \bar{\bar{C}}_1 - \bar{C}_1 \quad \text{or} \quad R_2 = \frac{\Delta \bar{C}_1}{\Delta \bar{C}_0} - 1$$

so that where

$$\Delta C_0 = \Delta \bar{C}_0, \quad \Delta C_1 > \Delta \bar{C}_1 \quad \text{and} \quad R_1 > R_2.$$

The decreasing marginal product of investment was postulated to be the result of 'hard' technological facts. If the relationship between 'today's' and 'tomorrow's' consumption was

$$F(C_0, C_1) = 0$$

then, if it is also assumed that the first and second order derivatives exist, it is postulated that

$$\frac{\partial F}{\partial C_0} \quad \text{and} \quad \frac{\partial F}{\partial C_1} > 0 \quad \text{and} \quad \frac{\partial F}{\partial C_0^2} \quad \text{and} \quad \frac{\partial^2 F}{\partial C_1^2} > 0 \quad \text{and} \quad \frac{\partial^2 F}{\partial C_0 \partial C_1} < 0.[2]$$

To the relation $F(C_0, C_1) = 0$, there must be added the initial Consumption Fund, K_0, the supplies of 'time' in the two periods and the terminal Consumption Fund, K_1, though the horizon can be extended as far into the 'future' as desired by subdividing 'tomorrow' as many times as required. The analysis remains substantially the same. In traditional theory, it was also postulated that a preference relation between consumption

---

[1] Solow, *Capital Theory*, Chapter 1.

[2] The technology set made up of C_0 and C_1 is concave. In terms of the sets of prices which, given the technology, permit a maximum F, I have the inequalities

$$P_{C_0} C_0 + P_{C_1} C_1 > P_{C_0} \bar{C}_0 + P_{C_1} \bar{C}_1$$
$$\bar{P}_{C_0} \bar{C}_0 + \bar{P}_{C_1} \bar{C}_1 > \bar{P}_{C_0} C_0 + \bar{P}_{C_1} C_1$$

If P_{C_0} and $\bar{P}_{C_0}$ are set equal to 1, and P_{C_1} and $\bar{P}_{C_1}$ are 'discount prices', then the inequalities may be re-expressed as

$$C_0 - \bar{C}_0 + P_{C_1}(C_1 - \bar{C}_1) > 0$$
$$0 > (C_0 - \bar{C}_0) + \bar{P}_{C_1}(C_1 - \bar{C}_1)$$

so that
$$(P_{C_1} - \bar{P}_{C_1})(C_1 - \bar{C}_1) > 0$$

or
$$(R_1 - R_0)(C_1 - \bar{C}_1) > 0$$

Concavity ensures that if $C_1 \gtrless \bar{C}_1$ then $R_1 \gtrless R_0$.

'today' and 'tomorrow' existed. Such a relation was defined either for a single person (e.g. Robinson Crusoe) or as a Bergsonian social welfare function. On the preference relation, an increasing marginal rate of substitution was also defined.[1] The preference function can also be suitably amended to include initial and terminal Consumption Funds as well as the demands for 'time', again with the horizon being extended as far into the 'future' as desired. One of the Pareto conditions is the equality between the marginal rate of transformation between consumption 'today' and consumption 'tomorrow' (what I have called the marginal product of investment) and the marginal rate of substitution between consumption 'today' and consumption 'tomorrow'. A price, the rate of interest, emerges in equilibrium, and is said to be equal to these two rates. Such may be said to be the traditional theory of capital, yet strangely enough there has been no mention of capital as an input nor has there been any mention of the marginal product of capital.[2]

In an appraisal of traditional theory, it must be remembered that there are two 'runs' in which the analysis is conducted. There is the Marshallian short period, when all the stocks of capital instruments are given and, similarly to Ricardo's different qualities of land, earn quasi-rents. The rents are quasi because – and here the 'run' changes from the short to the long – capital accumulation would occur, it is argued, until quasi-rents were eliminated in every line of economic activity and a ruling rate of return held in final equilibrium. It is also argued that capital accumulation

---

[1] Given the preference relation $U (C_0, C_1)$, it was assumed that the first and second order partial derivatives exist such that $\partial U/\partial C_0$ and $\partial U/\partial C_1 > 0$, and $\partial^2 U/\partial C_0^2$ and $\partial^2 U/\partial C_1^2 < 0$ and $\partial^2 U/\partial C_0 \partial C_1 > 0$. The preference set made up of C_0 and C_1 is convex. In terms of the set of prices which, given the preferences, permit a maximum U, I have the inequalities

$$P_{C_0} C_0 + P_{C_1} C_1 < P_{C_0} \overline{C}_0 + P_{C_1} \overline{C}_1$$
$$\overline{P}_{C_0} \overline{C}_0 + \overline{P}_{C_1} \overline{C}_1 < \overline{P}_{C_0} C_0 + \overline{P}_{C_1} C_1.$$

These may again be re-expressed as

$$C_0 - \overline{C}_0 + P_{C_1}(C_1 - \overline{C}_1) < 0$$
$$0 < C_0 - \overline{C}_0 + \overline{P}_{C_1}(C_1 - \overline{C}_1)$$

so that

$$(P_{C_1} - \overline{P}_{C_1})(C_1 - \overline{C}_1) < 0$$

or

$$(R_1 - R_0)(C_1 - \overline{C}_1) < 0$$

Convexity ensures that if $C_1 \gtrless \overline{C}_1$ then $R_1 \lessgtr R_0$.

[2] My brief statement of traditional theory is a paraphrase of the argument found in Rae and Fisher. In its more modern guise it is found in Solow, *Capital Theory*; E. Malinvaud, 'Capital accumulation and efficient allocation of resources', *Econometrica*, XXI, 1953, 233–68, revised in AEA, *Readings in Welfare Economics* (London, 1969); E. Malinvaud, 'The analogy between atemporal and intertemporal theories of resource allocation', eds. J. E. Stiglitz and H. Uzawa, *Readings in the Modern Theory of Economic Growth* (Cambridge: M.I.T. Press, 1969); and Hicks, *Capital and Growth*, Ch. XX–XXII.

would occur in the event that the marginal product of capital was greater than the rate of return and would reduce it until it was equal to the rate of return.

Now it was always recognized that, in the long run, capital – in terms of a stock of intermediate inputs – was not a primary input in any fundamental sense. As Malinvaud argues

The question of whether there are two or three primary factors of production has been much debated. However, the answer seems to be fairly clear. Considering any one period there are indeed three factors. But if economic development as a whole, past, present, and future is considered, capital cannot be considered a primary factor.[1]

Careful writers always recognized that capital could not be defined as an agent of production *independent* of the rate of return. There was no economically meaningful way of adding together heterogeneous commodities except in terms of prices which, since prices were resolvable into their direct and indirect unit primary input costs, *including the rate of return*, meant that the rate of return was already included in the calculation of something (capital) to the determination of which its marginal product was supposed to contribute. Wicksell admitted that the 'period of production', either as an aggregate or as an average concept, could not be defined independently of the rate of interest. Mrs Robinson's 'real capital' is a function of the rate of return. Dorfman's concept encounters the same 'problem'.[2] Malinvaud *defines*[3] the marginal product of capital as

$$\frac{p^1(x-x^1)}{p^1(c-c^1)}$$

where p^1 is a vector of prices for any efficient program of capital accumulation, x and x^1 are the vectors of the net outputs for the comparison and efficient programs and c and c^1 are the vectors of the stock of capital for the comparison and efficient programs. This is clearly not a physical concept, as Pasinetti has pointed out.[4] However, if all elements save one of the vector of net outputs are equal to zero and all elements of the capital vector save the *same* one are also equal to zero, then there exists a marginal physical product of capital. The one-commodity one-sector model examined previously is just this case. As Malinvaud goes on to say, however, if the element of the capital vector which is non-zero is different, the

[1] Malinvaud, 'Capital accumulation', rev. AEA *Readings in Welfare Economics*, 648 n. 4.
[2] R. Dorfman, 'Waiting and the period of production', *Quarterly Journal of Economics*, LXXIII, August 1959, 351–72.
[3] Malinvaud, 'Capital accumulation', rev. AEA *Readings in Welfare Economics*, 674.
[4] L. L. Pasinetti, 'Switches of technique and the "rate of return" in capital theory', *Economic Journal*, LXXIX, September 1969, 508–31.

marginal product of capital is, of course, the marginal physical product of a particular commodity-capital input, multiplied by the ratio of the price of the product to the price of the commodity input. If I consider a stationary-state equilibrium with many capital goods, there will be many marginal physical products for *each* of the commodity-capital inputs. Whether or not technology is 'smooth' is neither here nor there: the important thing is the assumption of convexity, for it ensures that the marginal physical product of each identifiable capital good will be decreasing in the sense I have discussed. If individual capital goods cannot be identified, however, then the aggregation which will be required runs afoul, as I have shown, of the 'double switching' problem. As Pasinetti has pointed out, one can no longer argue from convexity alone that there will be a monotonic inverse relationship between the rate of return, which, once more than one capital good is in the vector of capital inputs, is a *value* concept, and the *value* of the stock of commodity capital. Strictly speaking, however, the neoclassical position need only deal with vectors of capital inputs and the many implied marginal physical products of each one of the commodity-capital inputs.

Yet all this is somewhat by the way. Traditional theory never told us how the equilibrium marginal physical products of the many capital goods were to be determined. Nor did traditional theory tell us how the equilibrium relative prices were to be determined. Yet Walrasian economics, if it tells us anything, tells us what relative quantities and prices in equilibrium will be. What is left out of the traditional argument, however, is any convincing theory of the determination of the equilibrium rate of return – what the product of the marginal physical products of the commodity-capital inputs and the relative output/input prices were all supposed, in long period equilibrium, to equal. The basic problem is related to the argument that the rate of return is fundamentally a dynamic concept.[1] The equilibrium marginal product of accumulation, the marginal rate of transformation and of substitution between consumption 'today' and consumption 'tomorrow' are determined by propensities to engage in net accumulation and net saving – essentially dynamic concepts. Strangely enough, traditional analysis has made little headway with the theory of accumulation. In most neoclassical growth models, for example, there is no separate propensity to accumulate: it is assumed that all savings are automatically (or with the help of an omniscient monetary authority) accumulated.[2] There are no entrepreneurs deciding upon additions to their stocks of

[1] '…the static theory of equilibrium does not, and cannot, have anything satisfactory to say about the rate of interest, while dynamic theory is still undeveloped.' Sir Roy Harrod, *Money* (London: Macmillan, 1969), 193.
[2] J. E. Meade, *A Neo-classical Theory of Economic Growth*, 2nd ed. (London: Allen and Unwin, 1968), and *The Growing Economy* (London: Allen and Unwin, 1968).

commodity capital.[1] I shall comment further on the dynamic accumulation function in the next chapter. The theory of investment, even in the static context of no technological progress, has always been unsatisfactory. Before examining that problem in the context of the traditional theory of capital, there is one further problem to be handled. In traditional economic theory, it has been assumed that, *ceteris paribus*, an increase in the rate of saving would lead to an increase in the rate of accumulation. If I consider the two-commodity two-sector infinite-techniques case dealt with in the previous section, the shift for one period, of a unit of labour from the consumption-good sector would entail a reduction in the flow of consumption of $\partial C_0/\partial L \ (= C_0 - \bar{C}_0)$. The output of machines would rise by the amount $\partial \Delta K/\partial L$ where $\partial \Delta K/\partial L$ is the marginal product of labour in the capital-good sector. The increase in the value of machines,

$$P_K/P_C \cdot \partial \Delta K/\partial L,$$

where P_K/P_C is the consumption-good price of a machine, would be equal to the present value of the extra stream of consumption 'tomorrow' which results when the new machines accompany the unit of labour back to the consumption-good sector

$$\frac{\partial \Delta K}{\partial L} \frac{\partial C_1}{\partial \Delta K} \bigg/ 1 + R \left(= \frac{\bar{C}_1 - C_1}{1 + R} \right)$$

Thus, I would have

$$\frac{\partial C_0}{\partial L} = \frac{P_K}{P_C} \frac{\partial \Delta K}{\partial L} = \frac{\partial C_1}{\partial L} \bigg/ 1 + R$$

or

$$R = \left(\frac{\partial C_1}{\partial L} \bigg/ \frac{\partial C_0}{\partial L} \right) - 1$$

$$= \frac{\bar{C}_1 - C_1}{C_0 - \bar{C}_0} - 1$$

More formally, in stationary equilibrium, the flow of returns to any machine will not be expected to go on forever but will be expected to fall at the rate Γ. The present value, expressed in terms of the consumption good, of a machine in the capital good-industry will then be

$$\frac{1}{B} \int_{K_0}^{\infty} \left(\frac{P_K}{P_C} - \overline{W} A_K \right) e^{-(R+\Gamma)t} dt \quad \text{or} \quad \frac{(P_K/P_C - \overline{W} A_K)}{B_K (R + \Gamma)}$$

---

[1] Harrod's problem of the 'knife edge' arose not because of his supposed assumption of fixed coefficients technology but rather because of possible discrepancies between the 'warranted' rate of growth (determined by propensity to accumulate) and the 'natural' rate of growth (the growth path where all markets are cleared optimally). The fixed coefficients assumption gives rise to the possibility that a steady rate of growth, given the technology and the proportional rate of saving, will not exist. This is not the same problem as the 'knife-edge'.

In the consumption-good industry, it will equal

$$\frac{1}{B}\int_{C_0}^{\infty}(1-\overline{W}A_C)e^{-(R+\Gamma)t}dt \quad \text{which equals} \quad \frac{1}{B_C}\frac{(1-\overline{W}A_C)}{(R+\Gamma)}$$

These present values are of course, identical. In a survey by D. Usher in *Review of Economic Studies*,[1] the equality between the present value of an additional machine in the capital-good industry,

$$\frac{P_K/P_C-\overline{W}A_K}{B_K(R+\Gamma)}, \quad \text{and its supply price,} \quad P_K/P_C$$

[or, alternatively, the present value of an additional machine in the consumption-good industry,

$$\frac{1-\overline{W}A_C}{B_C(R+\Gamma)}, \quad \text{and its supply price,} \quad P_K/P_C]$$

is expressed as a marginal input/output equation. Thus, one finds

$$\int_{0}^{\infty}\Delta C_0(t)e^{-\int r(t)dt}dt = \int_{-\infty}^{0}\Delta C_i(t)e^{-\int_t r(t)dt}dt$$

where $\Delta C_0(t)$ is the period flow of additional consumption good accruing to the marginal machine and $\Delta C_i(t)$ is the period flow of consumption goods foregone during its construction. Usher allows for changes over time in rates of return. The argument, though more exact, tells us nothing more than the simple case.

It is clear that I am merely repeating definitions set out before.[2] There is no statement of how this real saving is supposed, in *laissez-faire* systems, to be embodied in new machines under conditions of full employment. The traditional argument would have it that an increase in the propensity to save would lead to an increase in capital accumulation by generating a lower rate of interest through its effects in the capital markets. This argument Keynes destroyed. Earlier I pointed out that I was not going to concern myself with money. Traditional theory, however, requires an integration of the theory of relative and absolute price levels and I shall abandon my self-denying ordinance momentarily to reveal the special nature of that integration.

In some of the modern literature, it is argued that perfectly competitive capitalistic economies will automatically equilibrate at full employment

---

[1] D. Usher, 'Traditional capital theory', *Review of Economic Studies*, XXXII, April 1965, 169–86.

[2] The difference that is involved is that the price of the machine in terms of the consumption good has also been introduced. As I have shown, movements of the labour input across the two sectors will be associated with Wicksell price effects – i.e. changes in P_K/P_C which prevent uniqueness of equilibrium.

and that a higher rate of savings will be associated with a higher rate of investment. I refer to the 'real balance effect' associated with the concept of outside money.[1] Yet if I consider a truly *laissez-faire* economy, as in strict logic I must, the real balance effect disappears. Under conditions of *laissez-faire* production of money which has no commodity content, the marginal private cost of producing money will be very low, approaching zero, owing to enormous economies of scale in the banking industry. Under perfectly competitive rules of behaviour, the supply of money will approach infinite levels, the price level in terms of money will likewise approach infinite levels and either a monopoly must come to characterize the banking industry (so that the perfectly competitive assumption on which the argument rests has to be abandoned) or the economy will retreat to the use of commodity money with positive and rising short run costs of production (so abandoning a superior technology associated with costless or near costless money and accordingly falling below the traditionally assumed Pareto-optimal position).

I should argue that where money is privately produced the price level is indeterminate. If I consider a full-employment equilibrium with an *assumed* money-wage rate and price level, the slightest disturbance will lead to price-level indeterminacy. Consider an increased propensity to save. Even if we assume money-wage-rate and price-level flexibility, the resultant fall in price levels will not generate any 'real balance effect'. The decreased money profits will cause households and firms to be unable to meet interest payments and amortization schedules couched in fixed money terms. Banks will find that the loans and bonds which they hold, and the creation of which led to their deposit liabilities, are being defaulted upon and will accordingly restrict their deposit liabilities. As a consequence, the supply of money will be reduced *pari passu* with the price level. It is sometimes argued that in these circumstances the rate of interest will also fall, although the immediate impact of a financial crisis is surely an increase in the level of interest rates. Even if rates do fall, as Keynes pointed out, there is no reason to believe either that they will fall far enough to do any good, or, if they do fall significantly, that expenditures will be sufficiently interest-rate elastic for the original increase in savings to be offset.[2] Theoretically, there is no bottom stop to the price level.

[1] D. Patinkin, *Money, Interest and Prices*, 2nd ed. (New York: Harper and Row, 1965).
[2] With a given state of expectations about the future flows of quasi-rents accruing to capital goods, the demand price of capital goods depends on the rate of interest. The lower the rate of interest, the higher this demand price and, as will be argued later, the higher the level of investment (see A. Leijonhufvud, *On Keynesian Economics and the Economics of Keynes* (Oxford: Oxford University Press, 1968), Ch. III, 3). It is unreasonable, however, to expect changes in the rate of interest to be associated with an unchanged marginal efficiency of investment. Indeed, Keynes himself went on to

Similarly, a decrease in savings would lead to an upward spiral in money-wage rates and prices which, providing expectations were sufficiently elastic, would lead to an indeterminate Wicksellian cumulative expansion. An inside-money model, where inside money means the perfectly competitive *laissez-faire* production of non-commodity money, is characterized by indeterminacy in the money-wage rate and price level and the absence of any automatic equilibrating device to ensure full employment.[1] The introduction of outside money, where money is produced by the state (or by a monopoly banking system whose monopoly profits, it is said, are taxed away through the requirement that the banking system must hold non-, or low-, interest-bearing debt instruments of the state)[2] in effect means that the state determines the rate of capital accumulation. Yet this is what the *laissez-faire* model was supposed to determine. The contention that, in a perfectly competitive *laissez-faire* economy, an increased propensity to save would lead, through a reduction in interest rates, to an increase in the rate of commodity-capital accumulation, was surely demolished by Keynes.

The introduction of outside money, that is, money which is an 'obligation' of the public sector, to demonstrate that there exists a set of money-wage rates and prices at which the economic system would be at full-employment equilibrium, would appear to be self-defeating. While the price level becomes determinate, it does so at a rate of capital accumulation, and therefore at a rate of profit, determined by the public sector.

A vital issue is thus joined. If, as Sraffa suggested,[3] the rate of profit is determined outside the 'real' economy, in the 'monetary' sector, then, as Keynes in fact showed, in a *laissez-faire* economy the rate of interest need

argue that an increase in liquidity preference, which would moderate any fall in the rate of interest due to lower income levels, would tend to be associated with a fall in the marginal efficiency of new investment. See J. M. Keynes, 'The general theory of employment', *Quarterly Journal of Economics*, LI, February 1937, 209–23, reprinted as 'The general theory: fundamental concepts and ideas' in R. W. Clower, *Monetary Theory: Penguin Modern Economic Readings* (Harmondsworth: Penguin, 1970), 220–7.

[1] As Patinkin admitted in *Money, Interest and Prices*, 303 and Note E.

[2] Banks earn profits for many other services apart from the 'production of money'. If *laissez-faire* banks carried the production of money to the point where price equalled marginal cost, the price of money would be zero and the price of commodities infinitely high. Central banks limit this process and prevent the economic system retreating back to the use of commodity money, which has a rising marginal cost and is thereby associated with a determinate price level but a sub-optimum technology. Costless (or near costless) money permits the economy to operate at higher levels of consumption per head. Banks, under the control of a central bank, make profits even after the 'taxes' levied by the central bank in requiring them to hold non-interest bearing deposits (i.e. reserves) with it. There is no efficiency justification at all for allowing banks to earn returns to capital on the 'production' of money. The suggestions sometimes found in the literature, that the central bank should pay interest on deposits of banks with it in order to restore economic efficiency, seem rather wide of the mark.

[3] Sraffa, *Production of Commodities*, 33.

not, in long period equilibrium, be equal to Wicksell's natural rate of interest or rate of profit. Hence I still lack a theory for the determination of the rate of profit.[1]

I have finished the digression on money and now return to the discussion of the static theory of accumulation. I remarked that the theory was unsatisfactory. The main problem arises out of Keynes's theory of accumulation, and his argument that the level of investment was inversely related to the rate of interest. Lerner, Haavelmo and Witte have all argued that the rate of investment is indeterminate or infinitely elastic with respect to the rate of interest.[2]

There is a straightforward sense in which this is true. In traditional analysis, the long-run-equilibrium level of output of the perfectly competitive firm, producing with constant-returns-to-scale technology, is indeterminate.[3] This means that its rate of commodity-capital accumulation is also

---

[1] See R. M. Solow, 'On the rate of return: reply to Pasinetti', *Economic Journal*, LXXX, June 1970, 423–8, and L. L. Pasinetti, 'Again on capital theory and Solow's "rate of return"', *ibid.*, 428–31.

[2] A. P. Lerner, *The Economics of Control* (New York: Macmillan, 1944), Ch. 25; Haavelmo, *A Study in the Theory of Investment*, 215; and J. G. Witte, Jr., 'The micro foundations of the social investment function', *Journal of Political Economy*, LXXI, October 1963, 441–56.

[3] This is well known, of course. For the perfectly competitive representative firm in the one-commodity infinite-number-of-techniques economy, the short run problem is to maximize

$$\Pi = Q - \overline{W}L \quad (\equiv (R_Q + \Gamma)\overline{K}) \quad + \lambda[Q - Q(L, K)]$$

where Π is profits, defined to equal quasi-rents, the rate of short run profit, R_Q, times the fixed stock of commodity capital, $\overline{K}$, and the other variables are as previously defined. First order conditions for a maximum and solution of Π are

$$\frac{\partial \Pi}{\partial Q} = 1 + \lambda = 0$$

$$\frac{\partial \Pi}{\partial L} = -\overline{W} + \lambda \left[-\frac{\partial Q}{\partial L} \right] = 0$$

$$\frac{\partial \Pi}{\partial \lambda} = Q - Q(L, K) = 0$$

and

$$(RQ + \Gamma)\overline{K} = Q - \overline{W}L$$

Four equations are found to solve four unknowns: Q, L, R, and λ. Second order conditions must be inspected to test for other properties of the solution. The long run problem is to maximize

$$\Pi = Q - [\overline{W}L + (R + \Gamma)K] + \lambda[Q - Q(L, K)]$$

where R is now the ruling rate of return. The first order conditions and solution for Π are

$$\frac{\partial \Pi}{\partial Q} = 1 + \lambda = 0$$

$$\frac{\partial \Pi}{\partial L} = -\overline{W} + \lambda \left[-\frac{\partial Q}{\partial L} \right] = 0$$

indeterminate.[1] The essential problem is that the size of the firm is indeterminate. It was this problem which led at one time to the abandonment of

$$\frac{\partial \Pi}{\partial K} = -(R+\Gamma)+\lambda\left[-\frac{\partial Q}{\partial K}\right] = 0$$

$$\frac{\partial \Pi}{\partial \lambda} = Q - Q(L, K) = 0$$

$$\Pi = Q - [\overline{W}L + (R+\Gamma)K] = 0.$$

There are five equations to solve for Q, L, K, and λ and the system is overdetermined with an infinity of possible solutions for Q, L, and K. The problem arises once it is specified that long run profits must be zero. If they are not, then either the adding up theorem is falsified, or the assumption about technology is maintained but an unexplained variable, such as management efficiency or economies of scale, is introduced, which immediately implies that there is some input the firm cannot ever vary – i.e. there is no long run. The argument is customarily concluded by postulating entrepreneurs who will enter any line of activity in which profits are being earned, thus ensuring that, in long run equilibrium, a set of long run prices and determinate *industry* levels of outputs and inputs will exist. See Paul A. Samuelson, *Foundations of Economic Analysis* (Cambridge: Harvard University Press, 1953), 78–9 and his 'The monopolistic competition revolution', ed. R. E. Kuenne, *Monopolistic Competition Theory: Studies in Impact*, Essays in Honour of Edward H. Chamberlin (New York: Wiley, 1967), 114–15. The argument suffers, however, from indeterminacy with respect to the rate of accumulation which ensures long run equilibrium.

[1] For the perfectly competitive firm in the one-commodity infinite-number-of-techniques economy, the long run maximization problem may be more formally put. The problem is to maximize the firm's net worth, i.e.

$$\text{Max } V = \int_t^\infty \{(Q_t - \overline{W}_t L_t - \Delta K_t)e^{-Rt} + \lambda_0(t)(Q_t - Q_t(L_t, K_t)) + \lambda_1(t)[\dot{K}_t - \Delta K_t + \Gamma K_t]\}\,dt$$

where $Q_t - \overline{W}_t L_t - \Delta K_t$ represents the gross returns to capital in any period, less the firm's expenditures on commodity capital in that period, and the two constraints are (i) the standard production function and (ii) the technical 'fact' that additions to the stock of commodity capital in any period, K_t, are equal to gross accumulation of that period less 'depreciation by evaporation'. This may be re-expressed as

$$\text{Max } V = \int_t^\infty [Q_t(L_t, K_t) - \overline{W}_t L_t - (\dot{K}_t + \Gamma K_t)]e^{-Rt}\,dt$$

where it is a functional of the form

$$\int_t^\infty F(L_t, K_t, \dot{K}_t)\,dt$$

The Euler equations for the first order conditions of a maximum are

$$\frac{\partial V}{\partial L_t} = \left(\frac{\partial Q_t}{\partial L_t} - \overline{W}_t\right)e^{-Rt} = 0$$

$$\frac{\partial V}{\partial K_t} - \frac{d}{dt}\frac{\partial V}{\partial \dot{K}_t} = \left[\frac{\partial Q_t}{\partial K_t} - (\Gamma + R)\right]e^{-Rt} = 0.$$

Thus, solutions for L_t and K_t ($t = 1, 2, \ldots$) may be obtained (and consequently $\dot{K}_t$). The value of Q_t is determined from $Q_t = Q_t(L_t, K_t)$ and ΔK_t from $\Delta K_t = K_t + \Gamma K_t$. Jorgenson's recent demonstration that the long run equilibrium is determinate suffers, I believe, from the assumption that the price level is necessarily changing – i.e. capital gains and losses are introduced to bring about determinacy. I say something about this in Chapter 3. See D. W. Jorgenson, 'The theory of investment behaviour', ed. R. Ferber, *Determinants of Investment Behaviour* (New York: Columbia University Press for NBER, 1967).

the assumption of perfect competition in traditional analysis. If that particular line of thought is set aside (see Chapter 3), what then determines the rate of *gross* accumulation in stationary states?

The comparison of various stationary states can no longer be used to solve this problem. The question now is, what holds a given economy at its stationary level? There is a sense in which this question cannot be answered, for, once equilibrium has already been specified, any assumed further accumulation must determine a different equilibrium stationary position. For any given two-sector economy in stationary equilibrium, the amount of gross capital accumulation being undertaken by entrepreneurs is just making good the 'depreciation by evaporation'. Given the technology, this determines the sectoral distribution of the labour force. The ruling rate of profit is such that entrepreneurs are satisfied with their gross accumulation programme and the consumption out of profits is such that at the ruling consumption-good wage rate the labour force is content to work as long and as hard as the technical conditions require. In the short run, any attempt in such an economy to expand the operations of the capital-good sector would result in a rise in the short run price of the capital good in terms of the consumption good. The elasticity of this short run supply curve depends upon the usual conditions of the short run elasticity-of-utilization function in that sector. Yet it is clear that any attempted accumulation also results in a shift of the curve, as the wage rate measured in terms of the consumption good is reduced by any change in the distribution of the labour force between the two sectors. Should there be some reduction in the consumption out of returns to capital,[1] the change in the real wage and the extent of the shift of the curve would be minimized. If there were no possibility of increasing the degree of utilization of existing commodity-capital stock in the capital-good sector, or if there were no possibility of reducing the consumption-good real-wage rate and changing the distribution of the labour force, then any attempted accumulation would be completely thwarted. It seems reasonable to assume, though, the presence of some elasticity in the system and the existence of a less-than-perfectly inelastic short run supply curve for gross capital accumulation. All this may be illustrated by reference to a one-commodity infinite-number-of-techniques case. Short run accumulation will be possible only if there is some excess capacity – i.e. if there is some unemployment. The concept of capacity is a nebulous concept, depending as it does on the extent to which entrepreneurs are prepared to incur rising marginal user

---

[1] To postulate increases in the entrepreneurs' propensity to save out of profits (or out of wages) in response to the same set of expectations (i.e. a higher expected marginal product of accumulation) imparts an unwonted homogeneity to the population of the economy. I have already shown how, in a *laissez-faire* system, the money markets serve to do little but impart indeterminacy to the money-wage rate and price level.

costs, the extent to which a fully employed labour force is prepared to vary the intensity of its work, the rate at which various members of the population participate in the labour force and so forth. However, the supply price, when expressed in terms of wage units in the context of the one-commodity assumption, will, in the short run, tend to rise with any attempted increase in accumulation, and it is this rise in the short run price which restrains the short run rate of accumulation.

In the standard one-commodity infinite-number-of-techniques model, there is assumed to be a 'representative firm' which maximizes short run profits with the constraint of a given stock of commodity capital. That is, the problem is

$$\text{Max } \Pi = Q - \overline{W}L + \lambda_1[Q - Q(L, \overline{K})]$$

The first order conditions and the quasi-rent equations are

$$\frac{\partial \Pi}{\partial Q} = 1 + \lambda_1 = 0 \qquad \frac{\partial \Pi}{\partial L} = -\overline{W} + \lambda_1\left[-\frac{\partial Q}{\partial L}\right] = 0$$

$$\frac{\partial \Pi}{\partial \lambda_1} = Q - Q(L, \overline{K}) = 0 \quad \text{and} \quad \Pi = (R_Q + \Gamma)\overline{K} = Q - WL$$

where Π is profits, R_Q is the rate of quasi-rent and $\overline{K}$ is the given stock of capital.

The 'representative worker' is assumed to maximize a utility function, subject to the constraints that all his income is consumed and that he has only so many hours in any time period.

$$\text{Max } Z_W = U_W(Q_W, H) + \lambda_2[\overline{W}L - Q_W] + \lambda_3[L - (\overline{T} - H)]$$

where Q_W is workers' consumption, H is hours of time 'reserved', L is hours of time worked and $\overline{T}$ is total time available.

The first order conditions are

$$\frac{\partial Z_W}{\partial Q_W} = \frac{\partial U_W}{\partial Q_W} - \lambda_2 = 0 \qquad \frac{\partial Z_W}{\partial H} = \frac{\partial U_W}{\partial H} - \lambda_3 = 0 \qquad \frac{\partial Z_W}{\partial L} = \lambda_2\overline{W} + \lambda_3 = 0$$

$$\frac{\partial Z}{\partial \lambda_2} = \overline{W}L - Q_W = 0 \qquad \frac{\partial Z}{\partial \lambda_3} = L - (\overline{T} - H) = 0$$

The 'representative capitalist' also maximizes a utility function, subject to the constraint that all income, in the form of dividends received on the stock of commodity capital, is consumed. That is, the problem is

$$\text{Max } Z_C = U_C(Q_C) + \lambda_4[R_P\overline{K} - Q_C]$$

where R_P is the rate of 'dividend' earned by the capitalists on their given stock.

The first order conditions are

$$\frac{\partial Z_C}{\partial Q_C} = \frac{\partial U_C}{\partial Q_C} - \lambda_4 = 0 \qquad \frac{\partial Z}{\partial \lambda_4} = R_P\overline{K} - Q_C = 0$$

Entrepreneurs take two decisions in the short run: they determine the level of short run accumulation and the rate of dividends to be paid to capitalists, a function of the rate of quasi-rent and the rate of gross accumulation. That is

$$\Delta K = \Delta \bar{K} \quad \text{and} \quad R_P = R_P(R_Q, \Delta K)$$

such that $\qquad\qquad R'_{P_1} > 0 \quad \text{and} \quad R_{P_2} < 0$

This is a system in fifteen unknowns and fourteen equations. The commodity-market-clearing equation

$$\overline{WL} + (R_Q + \Gamma)\bar{K} = Q_W + Q_C + \Delta K$$

provides a determinate system. Note that the usual Keynesian result applies, viz., the labour market is not necessarily cleared – the whole point of the model is to show the possibility of a rate of gross accumulation in excess of the rate of depreciation, with unemployment and higher levels of short run net accumulation possibly being associated with lower levels of the real-wage rate. Inspection of the commodity market equilibrium equation shows

$$R_Q - R_P = \frac{\Delta K}{K} - \Gamma$$

That is, in short period equilibrium, a positive rate of net accumulation will yield positive quasi-rents, with a rate of quasi-rents in excess of the rate of dividend. If entrepreneurs, in deciding to undertake gross accumulation at a rate higher than the rate of depreciation, set a lower rate of dividend, the resulting rate of quasi-rent will be lower. A more complicated model would show that if capitalists increased their consumption in the face of a reduced rate of dividend, on the expectation that the value of the stock of commodity capital, being augmented out of the quasi-rents retained by the entrepreneurs, would be increased, then the rate of quasi-rent would be higher; as a consequence, the rate of dividend would also be higher than if the capitalists had spent their dividends and nothing more. I have already shown that the money markets, in a *laissez-faire* model, cannot bring about equilibrium in the labour market. They will produce a set of short run rates of *yields* on equities and rates of interest on bonds. Fundamentally, though, it would appear that the short run rate of gross accumulation determines the rate of quasi-rents and rates of dividend and so forth, and that the rate of interest is determined by the rate of accumulation rather than the other way round. Inspection of the model shows that higher rates of accumulation will eventually lead to a situation in which full employment and rising short run supply functions, in terms of wage-units, render the achievement of still higher rates impossible.

2.5 A steady-growth state with no technical change

Nothing in the foregoing is fundamentally altered by the assumption that the labour force, instead of being constant, is steadily growing. The comparisons are then drawn amongst economies in steady-state-of-growth equilibrium. 'Switching' problems will arise, there will still be problems in determining the relative price of commodity capital in terms of the consumption good among the various economies, and there will be all the difficulties involved in determining the rate of accumulation. The assumption of a growing labour input tells us nothing new. There is, moreover, no conclusive evidence to suggest that, in models of growth of advanced economies, the supply of labour can be meaningfully introduced endogenously into the discussion.

2.6 Conclusion

Even in the static case, it is clear that rentals, machine services, machine stocks, etc., are intermediate inputs and cannot be considered primary in any sense. The list of economists who recognized this (Ricardo, Marx, Senior, Böhm-Bawerk, Wicksell, Robinson) is long and distinguished, but agreement as to what *is* the non-labour primary input is not general. In particular, the Austrian 'period of production' concept, which was supposed to be a capital input concept, was shown by Wicksell to be a function of the rate of return to capital – something which the concept was supposed to help to explain. Mrs Robinson's concept of 'real capital' is equally dependent on the rate of interest though, in her argument, 'real capital' can in no sense be a determinant of the rate of return to capital. Yet it is clear that the Ricardian, Austrian and Robinson concepts go beyond the intermediacy of the neoclassical concept of commodity capital. In this chapter I have shown that any complete description of equilibrium technology involves a large number of gestation and durability periods. Any different equilibrium would presumably involve a different set of such periods. There seems to be little point in attempting to summarize such information into an 'average period of production', a concept of 'real capital', an aggregate commodity-capital/output ratio or what have you.[1] As this study will demonstrate, however, the economists I call the Ricardians are striving after a valid concept. One need not necessarily have any aggregate concept in mind, but we should expect to find a capital concept which, as an input, is independent of the rate of interest: we should want inputs to be defined independently of prices.

[1] See D. Dewey, *Modern Capital Theory* (New York: Columbia University Press, 1965), Ch. 12, and C. G. Uhr, *Economic Doctrines of Knut Wicksell* (Berkeley and Los Angeles: University of California Press, 1960), Ch. v.

3

SOME COMMENTS ON THE THEORY OF GROWTH AND THE TRADITIONAL MEASURES OF TECHNICAL CHANGE

The short period is here and now, with concrete stocks of means of production in existence. Incompatibilities in the situation – in particular between the capacity of equipment and expected demand for output – will determine what happens next. *Long-period equilibrium is not at some date in the future*; it is an imaginary state of affairs in which there are no incompatibilities in the existing situation, here and now.

> J. Robinson, '*The General Theory* after twenty-five years', *Collected Economic Papers*, III, 101. My italics.

...a golden age is a logical construction without history, in which there is no distinction between the future and the past.

> J. Robinson, 'Comment on Samuelson and Modigliani', *Review of Economic Studies*, XXXIII, October 1966, 308.

3.1   The equilibrium context

In this chapter, I outline the traditional concepts and measures of technological progress, which I shall be discussing in Chapters 5 and 6. I make some comments about the theory of growth, which are offered as a defence of the methodology employed throughout this essay. With respect to the latter point, I shall plead the case for the steady state, as the epigraphic introduction to this chapter would suggest. I do this not because I find equilibrium analysis realistic but for two reasons. First, I can see at present no satisfactory way around Harrod's problem of instability in a *laissez-faire* world of many capital goods. Second, changes (from one equilibrium to another) in the net rate of return to capital involve a tremendous muddle so far as the measurement of capital and technological change is concerned.[1] Thus I feel compelled, at present, to venture no further than the confines of steady-state analysis. Yet if, in the steady-state world, I can

---

[1] 'Once we leave the steady state all is chaos and confusion.' Hahn and Matthews, 'Theory of economic growth', 824.

prove the neoclassical distinction between commodity-capital accumulation and technical change to be wrong, I conjecture that it must be *a fortiori* wrong in 'the real world'.

Some confusion has emerged as to what is meant by steady-state equilibrium. Surely it is nothing more than Pigou's thoroughgoing stationary state,[1] with or without exogenous technological change. Any analysis dealing with *levels* can be adequately conducted with technological change shut off. Switching problems, for instance, arise in a comparison of classical stationary states with different positive rates of interest.[2] As Harrod insists, dynamic analysis, eschewing levels, must be conducted in *rates of change*:

Dynamics would be concerned with an economy in which the rates [i.e. levels] of output are changing; we should have as the correspondent concept of velocity in Physics a *steady* rate of change (of increase or of decrease) in the rate of output per annum; acceleration (or deceleration) would be a change in this rate of change.[3]

Again:

I regard the fundamental concept in dynamic economics as the rate of increase, just as the state of rest is that of statics. It is the rate of increase that obtains *at a given point of time*, given the fundamental determinants. In dynamics, or at least in Part I of dynamics – and I do not think that we can yet get beyond that – we are not, according to my view, concerned with a succession of events through time. The analogy with mechanics is, surely, precise. There we seek to determine the velocity of a particle in consequence of the forces acting upon it at a particular instant. Thereafter it may become subject to new forces. The dynamic determinants of economic progress change from time to time, and the consequence of such changes will have to be considered in due course. But, to begin with, we need to determine the rate of increase at one point. This is but applying in the realm of dynamics the procedure so well known, and, I would say, fruitful, in the theory of static equilibrium. *It has always been recognised that the determinants of that equilibrium (desires of individuals, etc.) are constantly changing; none the less, it has been found serviceable to establish the equilibrium pattern required by a given set of determinants.* I am convinced that we must do this in dynamics also, as an essential prelude to all else. Edgeworth once said of general value theory that 'the path is short, but very slippery'. If this is true of dynamics also, as is surely the case, we must proceed carefully, step by step. One consequence of this method of initial approach to dynamics is that time-lags do not appear in the equations.[4]

As I understand it, this implies no less than that expectations at any

[1] A. C. Pigou, *The Economics of Stationary States* (London: Macmillan, 1935), Chap. 2–3.
[2] In Chapter 4, I examine such problems and argue that they have little *direct* relevance to the subject matter of this study.
[3] Sir Roy Harrod, *Towards a Dynamic Economics* (London: Macmillan, 1948), 4 (my italics).
[4] Sir Roy Harrod, 'Second essay in dynamic theory', *Economic Journal*, LXX, June 1960, 279 (second emphasis mine).

time must be such that no transactor (consumer or producer) expects the net rate of return to commodity capital to be changing.[1]

In Harrod's second essay, after he had set out dynamic relationships in which: (i) the natural rate of interest equalled the natural rate of growth *per caput*, divided by the elasticity of marginal utility of income (= consumption in equilibrium), designated by him as $r_n = \dfrac{P_O G_n}{e}$ or Equation I; and (ii) the required capital coefficient was inversely related to the natural rate of interest, designated by $C_r = f(r_n)$ or Equation II, he said:

> This article is concerned with a **steady** shift of the 'production function' outwards from the origin. It is not implied that the successive functions, moving outwards with time, are parallel to each other; the analysis has been consistent with innovations being neutral, labour saving or capital saving. Some students of growth have laid stress on the phenomenon of a movement *along* the productivity function in consequence, not of innovations, but of a rise in the ratio of capital to other factors due to the accrual of fresh saving. Such a movement implies a falling rate of interest (by Equation (II)). A falling natural rate of interest implies a falling natural rate of growth *per caput* (by Equation (I)), save in the event of *e* increasing, which seems improbable. Thus a shift along the production function, as distinct from a movement outwards of the production function, should occur only in periods when the rate of technical progress is falling. Such a shift may ensure that the rate of growth *per caput* does not fall as quickly as the rate of technical progress. None the less, it is essentially a phenomenon of a falling natural rate of growth.[2]

It is not clear from his writings whether Harrod's equilibrium, or natural, rate of interest can be taken both as the rate of interest earned by savers and as the expected rate of profit on new investments envisaged by entrepreneurs. Following the discussion on savings in his original lectures, in later works he discusses the optimum rate of accumulation as being determined by the rate of interest desired by entrepreneurs.[3]

I can find only one reference in Harrod's writings which suggests that

---

[1] If it is changing, the changes in it must be perfectly foreseen. Thus, Mrs Robinson says: 'The assumption of continuous equilibrium is very exacting. For instance, when the path that the economy is following entails a falling rate of profit on capital over the future, investment which is being made today in long-lived installations will be designed for a more mechanised technique than would have been chosen if today's rate of profit were going to continue, while very short-lived investments will be appropriate to nearly today's current rate.' (J. Robinson, 'Equilibrium Growth Models', *Collected Economic Papers* III (Oxford: Blackwell, 1965), 19.) If capital goods are perfectly malleable, the perfect foresight assumption is not necessary. Since, as I shall argue in Chapter 4, the assumption of 'depreciation by obsolescence' is much the most realistic assumption to make, i.e., that perfect malleability is not the rule, the requirements for an economy, experiencing a changing rate of interest, to be in equilibrium, seem very exacting indeed.

[2] Harrod, 'Second Essay', 285 (my emphasis bold).

[3] Harrod, *Money*, 193 ff.

he was dealing with changes in rates of change at a point in time.[1] He says, in *Towards a Dynamic Economy*:

It is, however, possible that when we have a well-developed corpus of dynamic principles the most important part of the theory of expectations will be found to lie in the dynamic field. The determinant in a dynamic system will not be the existence of a certain expectation or a once-over change in that expectation, but a rate of change of expectation.[2]

Thus, the concept of steady state used here is what I shall call the Ricardian–Marshallian–Harrodian 'long period' equilibrium. It does not refer to a world where, years from now, the economy has settled down to some steady-state line of development. If the fundamental determinants of dynamic (static classical stationary-state) equilibrium are altered 'tomorrow', the *equilibrium* rates of change will also be changed 'tomorrow'. How an *actual* economy moves from one to the other is a far harder story to tell. I have nothing to say about it. The difficulties would appear to be formidable enough. While what I have to say can most effectively be said in worlds of steady equilibria, it may be that the analysis can be carried over into worlds of disequilibria; albeit with much confusion and imprecision of measurement.

The main reason why I wish to keep my analysis within the strait jacket of the steady state is the fact that in Chapter 5, which is the central chapter, I shall be dealing with changes in the price of capital goods in terms of the consumption good. In order for Harrod-neutrality to hold in the aggregate and at the individual-sector level, the 'marginal products of commodity capital' in terms of consumption goods must remain unchanged. Expressed in terms of physical units, however, the 'own marginal product of capital' may vary in any direction so long as the movement is offset by changes in the price of capital in terms of consumption goods. As I have suggested, this is a stiff equilibrium requirement, particularly in the context of the assumption of 'depreciation by obsolescence'. In order to retain a many-capital-good model in Harrod equilibrium, then, it is necessary that the capital/output ratios expressed in terms of consumption goods should remain unchanged.

There has been a long discussion in the literature on Harrodian stability in the context of a one-commodity model. As always, global instability depends strictly on the specifications of the reaction function of entrepreneurs and households in their investment decisions.[3] To my knowledge,

---

[1] For a contrary view, see A. Asimakopulos and J. C. Weldon, 'A synoptic view of some simple models of growth', *Canadian Journal of Economics and Political Science*, XXXI, February 1965, 55.

[2] Harrod, *Towards a Dynamic Ecomomics*, 8.

[3] See Asimakopulos and Weldon, 'A synoptic view', especially section I, and Hahn and Matthews, 'Theory of Economic Growth', 805–9.

there is no reason to believe that a fairly simple set of behavioural assumptions can be set up to ensure stability in two-sector and many-capital-good models.[1] I exclude the case where entrepreneurs can be cajoled into thinking alike.[2]

Recently, the conditions for uniqueness of momentary equilibrium and stability in a more-than-one-capital-good environment have been investigated.[3] Once more than one capital good is postulated, the problem would appear to be how to specify the demand conditions for additions to the various stocks of capital goods. This is linked to expectations about the course of relative prices.[4] What Hahn showed was the following: For *laissez-faire* economies with more than one capital good, there exists no mechanism which ensures that the distribution of savings over the many capital goods in a way which is consistent with the fulfilment of short run expectations will necessarily lead to balanced growth. If relative prices of capital goods are changing and the whole course of such relative prices is known over future time, then, in order for rates of return to be equalized over all capital goods, a particular course of capital/labour ratios must hold. There is no reason to expect a balanced growth configuration, where the capital/labour ratios, with labour measured in efficiency units, will all be constant. It is possible, for instance, for the price of one of the capital goods to fall to zero.[5] More importantly, what mechanism is there to ensure, in Harrod's sense, that, in the face of changing relative prices, the

---

[1] The literature which deals with the uniqueness of momentary equilibrium, determinateness and stability of a steady-state solution for two-sector models is examined by F. H. Hahn in 'On two-sector growth models', *Review of Economic Studies*, XXXII, October 1965, 339–45. For well-behaved production functions, where k is the capital–labour ratio and μ is the wage-rental ratio, a rise in the ratio μ will lead to a heightened k if (i) a constant fraction of nominal income is consumption, so that the real product of the capital-intensive sector rises relatively, or (ii) if workers buy relatively more capital-intensive goods than capitalists, in which case a rise in μ raises the nominal proportions of income spent on the goods whose relative price is falling. Thus, if steady-state equilibrium implies that $s/k^* = n$ in the neoclassical case, there exists an μ (between $\mu = 0$ and $\mu = \infty$) such that $k = k^*$ (between $k = 0$ and $k = \infty$). Hahn also considers cases where k takes on values such that $s/k^* \neq n$ in steady-state equilibrium but one factor is free. See also J. Robinson, 'Harrod's knife-edge', *Collected Economic Papers*, III. As Hahn subsequently states, however, there is not the slightest reason to suppose that the sectoral intensities will be of the order required for unique momentary equilibrium. See F. H. Hahn, 'On the stability of growth equilibrium', Memo from Institute of Economics, University of Oslo, 19 April 1966.
[2] Sir Roy Harrod, 'Are monetary and fiscal policies enough?', *Economic Journal*, LXXIV, December 1964, 903–15.
[3] F. H. Hahn, 'Equilibrium dynamics with heterogeneous capital goods', *Quarterly Journal of Economics*, LXXX, November 1966, 633–46.
[4] *Ibid.*, and P. A. Samuelson, 'Indeterminacy of development in a heterogeneous-capital model with constant saving propensity', ed. K. Shell, *Essays on the Theory of Optimal Economic Growth* (Cambridge: M.I.T. Press, 1967).
[5] K. Shell and J. E. Stiglitz, 'The allocation of investment in a dynamic economy', *Quarterly Journal of Economics*, LXXXI, November 1967, 592–609.

warranted capital/output ratios will be equal to the actual capital/output ratios? There is no reason to expect momentary equilibrium to exist, let alone to be unique.

The course of relative capital-goods prices over time will be largely a function of the rates of technological advance in the various capital-good sectors. The rates of technological advance will themselves be functions of the rates of accumulation in the various sectors. A theory of the rate of accumulation is lacking. For these reasons, I *postulate* steady states.

3.2 The traditional concept and measurement of technological progress

The traditional concept of technological change is clearly that developed by Hicks.

although an invention must increase the total Dividend, it is unlikely at the same time to increase the marginal products of all factors of production in the same ratio. In most cases, it will select particular factors and increase the demand for those factors to a special extent. If we concentrate on two groups of factors, 'labour' and 'capital', and suppose them to exhaust the list, then we can classify inventions according as their initial effects are to increase, leave unchanged, or diminish the ratio of the marginal product of capital to that of labour. We may call these inventions 'labour-saving', 'neutral', and 'capital-saving' respectively. 'Labour-saving' inventions increase the marginal product of capital more than they increase the marginal product of labour; 'capital-saving' inventions increase the marginal product of labour more than that of capital; 'neutral' inventions increase both in the same proportion.[1]

This definition has, of course, been taken over by neoclassical economists. Hicks later made a distinction between two kinds of capital, a distinction which is crucial. He distinguishes between backward-looking and forward-looking concepts.[2] The backward physical concepts would seem to represent Hicks' attempt to retain the validity of the neoclassical production function. In Chapter 8, I shall show that Hicks is uneasy with the neoclassical constructs.[3] Hicks' earlier ideas have been most baldly taken over by Professor J. E. Meade[4] and I use his development of them as the most clearcut statement of the neoclassical position.

The Hicks–Meade concept of technological progress takes on three possible variants – or what appear to be three possible variants. It is alternatively product-augmenting (sometimes written as $Q = Ae^{at}F(K, L)$),

[1] J. R. Hicks, *The Theory of Wages*, 2nd ed. (London: Macmillan, 1963), 121–2.
[2] Hicks, 'The measurement of capital in relation'; 'Commentary: Inventions', in *Theory of Wages*; and *Capital and Growth*, Ch. xxiv, The Production Function.
[3] In particular, I show that the concepts for which he is struggling are the ones advanced and advocated here. Seen clearly, Hicks' new position is a considerable 'volte face' from *The Theory of Wages*.
[4] Meade, *Neo-classical Theory of Economic Growth*. See also his *Growing Economy*, 56–62.

labour-augmenting ($Q = F(K, Le^{l't})$) or capital-augmenting ($Q = F(Ke^{k't}, L)$) technological progress, or a mixture of the three.[1] Product-augmenting technological progress may also be called disembodied, while capital-augmenting may be embodied. In Chapter 6, I demonstrate that there is *no* difference between the capital- and product-augmenting variants. In Chapter 5, I demonstrate that capital- or product-augmenting technological progress has no theoretical meaning. I show that Harrodian technological progress is the only valid general-equilibrium concept. In addition, I show in Chapter 5 (with analysis based on Read's work) how the Harrodian concept is to be made operational.

Exactly what is meant by Hicks–Meade technological progress? Following Hicks's definition already quoted, Meade states that 'growing technical knowledge would enable more to be produced by the same amount of factors'.[2] Robinson considers changes in technique in two categories, 'those which arise from inventions and discoveries and those which are due to changes in wages relatively to profits in a given state of technical knowledge',[3] which would imply that inventions and discoveries can be lumped together and called technological advance. She would not now,[4] however, accept Meade's description of growing technological knowledge. Salter also distinguishes between advances in techniques of production and changes amongst techniques in response to changed factor prices.[5] Brown suggests that an abstract technology is characterized by: (i) the efficiency of the technology; (ii) the degree of economies of scale technologically determined; (iii) the degree of capital-intensity of a technology, measured in terms of the rate of input substitution and; (iv) the elasticity of substitution.[6] It can thus be seen that most authors

---

[1] In *Growing Economy*, 57, Meade employs a technical wizard who says:
  (i) 'Let there be a need for 100 units of labour wherever there would have been a need for 102, had I not waved this wand', or, what is called labour-expanding or augmenting technological progress;
  (ii) 'Let there be a need for 100 units of capital wherever there would otherwise have been a need for 103', or, what is called capital-expanding or augmenting technological progress; and
  (iii) 'Let there be 104 units of output wherever there would have been 100, had I not waved this wand', or, what is called output-expanding or augmenting technological progress.

[2] Meade, *Neo-classical Theory of Economic Growth*, 10. By factors, Meade means human effort, natural resources and man-made instruments.

[3] Robinson, *Accumulation of Capital*, 2nd ed., 70.

[4] Though clearly she would have at the time when she developed the same argument as Hicks. See J. Robinson, 'The Classification of inventions', *Review of Economic Studies*, v, 1937–8, 139–42 reprinted in AEA, *Readings in the Theory of Income Distribution* (New York: Blakiston, 1949).

[5] W. E. G. Salter, *Productivity and Technical Change* (Cambridge: Cambridge University Press, 1960), Chapters II and III.

[6] M. Brown, *On the Theory and Measurement of Technological Change* (Cambridge: Cambridge University Press, 1966), Ch. 2.

would attempt to distinguish between improvements in techniques and changes amongst techniques caused by changes in relative factor prices though some authors have argued that the distinction is impossible.[1] How is this done in practice?

Since I shall argue that the Harrodian measure of technological progress is superior and shall be subjecting the Hicks–Meade version of technological progress to severe criticism in Chapter 5, I shall, for the purposes of this chapter, set out the latest version of the latter which I know. There are virtually dozens of possible choices.[2] I have chosen a recent paper by Jorgenson and Griliches[3] as exemplifying the traditional approach, for two reasons.

First, their results throw much cold water on the various estimates in the U.S.A. of the importance of technical advance as a contributor to economic growth.[4] Jorgenson, at least, while stressing that there are still enormous differences among competing neoclassical measures of total factor productivity, now admits that his earlier conclusions about the unimportance of technical change must be revised.[5]

[1] Kaldor argues that it is impossible to distinguish shifts in the production function from movements along it. N. Kaldor, 'Capital accumulation and economic growth', ed. F. A. Lutz and D. C. Hague, *The Theory of Capital*, 205.

[2] The pioneering article, in terms of its impact, would be, in my estimation, R. M. Solow, 'Technical change and the aggregate production function', *The Review of Economics and Statistics*, XXXIX, August 1957, 312–20. Solow's later work is discussed in Chapter 6 below. Equally new at the time was M. C. Urquhart, 'Capital accumulation, technological change and economic growth', *Canadian Journal of Economics and Political Science*, XXV, November 1959, 411–30. Recent important studies are J. W. Kendrick, *Productivity Trends in the United States* (Princeton: Princeton University Press for NBER, 1961); Brown, *Theory and Measurement of Technological Change*; and Salter, *Productivity and Technical Change*. At the more extensive 'sources of growth' level are the works of E. F. Denison, *The Sources of Economic Growth* (New York: Committee for Economic Development, 1962), and (with J. P. Poullier) *Why Growth Rates Differ* (Washington: Brookings Institutions, 1967). In Canada, there is the work of my colleague, N. H. Lithwick, *Economic Growth in Canada* (Toronto: University of Toronto Press, 1967), and my own work in N. H. Lithwick, G. Post, and T. K. Rymes, 'Postwar production relationships in Canada', ed. M. Brown, *The Theory and Empirical analysis of Production* (New York: Columbia University Press for NBER, 1967). See, in particular, my Technical Appendix to that paper.

[3] D. W. Jorgenson and Z. Griliches, 'The explanation of productivity change', *The Review of Economic Studies*, XXXIV, July 1967, 249–83, reprinted in *Survey of Current Business*, XLIX, May 1969, 31–64.

[4] Denison, arguing within the traditional neoclassical context, has demonstrated that many of the Jorgenson–Griliches findings are questionable and, in some cases, erroneous. In particular, he questions their capital utilization adjustment procedure. Denison does not, of course, criticize the neoclassical theory underpinning not only their estimates but his own as well. See Edward F. Denison, 'Some major issues in productivity analysis: an examination of estimates by Jorgenson and Griliches', *Survey of Current Business*, XLIX, May 1969, 1–30.

[5] L. R. Christensen and D. W. Jorgenson, 'US real product and real factor input, 1929–1967', *Review of Income and Wealth*, XVI, 1, March 1970, 19–50.

Second, the Jorgenson–Griliches approach, baldly stated, implies that a correctly deflated set of national economic accounts yields measures of total factor productivity or technical advance. The question is: What is the correct way of measuring 'real' factor inputs? Their concept is still the traditional one and accordingly invalid.

Suppose I were dealing with a one-sector economy in growing equilibrium. At any point in time, the level of the social accounts for that economy would appear as

$$PQ \equiv WL + PRK + \Gamma PK \tag{3.1}$$

where P is introduced to represent the nominal price level. Using the notation set out in Chapter 2, I may rewrite this in what is called Divisia index number form

$$p + q \equiv \alpha(w+l) + \beta(r+p+k) + \gamma(\hat{\imath}+p+k)$$

or as
$$q - [\alpha l + \beta k + \gamma(\hat{\imath}+k)] \equiv [\alpha w + \beta(r+p) + \gamma p] - p \equiv t \tag{3.2}$$

What do the left-hand and right-hand sides of identities (3.2) represent? The growth rate of total output is represented by q and the growth rates of the appropriately weighted *quantities* of the inputs by $[\alpha l + \beta k + \gamma(\hat{\imath}+k)]$. Hence the difference must represent, in some sense, the growth rate of the efficiency or technology of the economic system. The appropriately weighted growth rate of the *prices* of the inputs is $[\alpha w + \beta(r+p) + \gamma p]$ and the growth rate of the price of output is p. Again, the difference must be equal to the growth rate of the efficiency or technology of the economic system. In the context of the social accounts, the appropriate weights are, of course, the 'shares' of the inputs in total output (e.g. $\alpha \equiv WL/PQ$).[1]

---

[1] These relationships may be expressed in the more familiar index number form. Identity 3.1 can be re-written as
$$PQ \equiv \Sigma p_i q_i,$$

where p_i and q_i are the price and quantity of the ith input. Now

$$\frac{P_1 Q_1}{P_0 Q_0} \equiv \frac{P_0 Q_1}{P_0 Q_0} \frac{P_1 Q_1}{P_0 Q_1} = \frac{P_1 Q_0}{P_0 Q_0} \frac{P_1 Q_1}{P_0 Q_1}$$

and
$$\frac{\Sigma p_{i1} q_{i1}}{\Sigma p_{i0} q_{i0}} \equiv \frac{\Sigma p_{i0} q_{i1}}{\Sigma p_{i0} q_{i0}} \frac{\Sigma p_{i1} q_{i1}}{\Sigma p_{i0} q_{i1}} = \frac{\Sigma p_{i1} q_{i0}}{\Sigma p_{i0} q_{i0}} \frac{\Sigma p_{i1} q_{i1}}{\Sigma p_{i1} q_{i0}}$$

That is, I have the familiar social accounting relationship that a value index can be decomposed into the product of Laspeyres quantity (price) and Paasche price (quantity) indexes. Thus, I may express the measure of economic efficiency in index number form as

$$\frac{P_0 Q_1}{P_0 Q_0} \bigg/ \frac{\Sigma p_{i0} q_{i1}}{\Sigma p_{i0} q_{i0}} \equiv \frac{\Sigma p_{i1} q_{i1}}{\Sigma p_{i0} q_{i1}} \bigg/ \frac{P_1 Q_1}{P_0 Q_1}$$

using the Laspeyres quantity and Paasche price indexes, or as

$$\frac{P_1 Q_1}{P_1 Q_0} \bigg/ \frac{\Sigma p_{i1} q_{i1}}{\Sigma p_{i1} q_{i0}} \equiv \frac{\Sigma p_{i0} q_{i1}}{\Sigma p_{i0} q_{i0}} \bigg/ \frac{P_1 Q_0}{P_0 Q_0}$$

using the Laspeyres price and Paasche quantity indexes.

Thus, the left-hand side of identities (3.2) is nothing more than the correctly deflated Jorgenson–Griliches set of national economic accounts expressed in terms of proportionate rates of change. The right-hand side of the identity is, of course, the prices analogue of the deflated accounts,[1] again expressed in terms of proportionate rates of change. All of the measures of technological change, 'Residual', or call it what you will, are based on some version of identities (3.2).

The left-hand side can be used to express 'sources of growth'. That is, it may be rewritten as

$$I \equiv \frac{\alpha l}{q} + \frac{\beta k}{q} + \frac{\gamma(\hat{\imath}+k)}{q} + \frac{t}{q}$$

or the growth rate of output may be broken into percentage components, showing labour's contribution to growth, $\alpha l/q$, etc. The expression $\alpha l/q$ is taken in the literature as labour's share in national product (e.g. 0·75) multiplied by the growth rate of the labour force (e.g. 0·02) divided by the growth rate of output (e.g. 0·04) and is said to represent the fact that labour contributed 0·015 'points' toward a growth rate of output of 0·04, or a 'percentage contribution' of 37·5 %. This exercise, which is merely an *ex post* accounting and says nothing about the causes of growth, may be done for as many kinds of labour and as many kinds of capital as the data permit.[2] If all these percentage contributions do not add up to 100 %, the rest (the Residual) is said to be due to technical chagne or the advance of knowledge. Again, the left-hand side of the identity may be re-expressed as

$$q-l-[\beta(k-l)+\gamma(\hat{\imath}+k-l)] \equiv t$$

where $\hat{\imath}$ is the growth rate of the rate of depreciation. If I assume that it is constant, then I have

$$q-l-[(\beta+\gamma)(k-l)] = t$$

or, the growth rate of technology is the difference between the growth rate of output per unit of labour and the growth rate of capital per unit of labour input.[3] In later work by Solow, it is suggested that identity (3.1) should be rewritten as

$$PQ \equiv WL+RP^*K^*+\Gamma P^*K^* \tag{3.1a}$$

---

[1] These matters are sorted out in the Technical Appendix of Lithwick, Post and Rymes, 'Postwar production relationships in Canada'.

[2] See, for instance, Denison, 'Some major changes'. Denison, of course, seeks to break the Residual down into further components.

Even in the traditional format, Denison's approach suffers, I believe, from a haziness with respect to the treatment of depreciation and from the incorrect use of the gross stock, rather than the net stock, as a measure of the capital input. This latter point is dealt with in Chapters 4 and 6.

[3] See, for example, Solow, 'Technical change'. Some authors then compare $q-l-t$, i.e. the growth rate of output per unit of labour input 'deflated' for technical change with the growth rate of capital per unit of labour to learn 'something about the production function'.

where an asterisk means 'effective' capital and hence, identity (3.2) should be

$$q - [\alpha l + \beta k^* + \gamma(\hat{\imath} + k^*)] \equiv \alpha w + \beta(r + p^*) + \gamma p^* - p \equiv t^* \quad (3.2a)$$

If I again make the assumption that the growth rate of the rate of depreciation is zero and compare the left-hand sides of identities (3.2) and (3.2a), I have

$$q - [\alpha l + (\beta + \gamma)k] = t$$

$$q - [\alpha l + (\beta + \gamma)k^*] = t^*$$

Obviously, if $k^* > k$, that is, if 'effective' capital is said to be more rapidly growing than commodity capital, the capital accumulation will appear to be a more important 'source of growth'. As I shall show in Chapter 6, however, the distinction between 'effective' and commodity capital is false.

The right-hand side of identities (3.2) expresses the growth rate of economic efficiency in terms of the growth rates of prices and of inputs and outputs. It is sometimes suggested that this formulation escapes the problem of measuring capital.[1] This is incorrect. The growth rate of the net return to commodity capital cannot be estimated until the growth rate of the price of commodity capital (either the growth rate of the price of the stock of existing capital or the price of the flow of new capital goods) is known. Indeed, since an identity is involved, the problem of measuring capital cannot be escaped. The use of the prices approach does, however, highlight one thing – the measurement of technical change is the measurement of increases in the real prices of the primary inputs and throws light on the distribution of the fruits of technical change. There are virtually endless number of questions which can be raised about all of these measures.[2] I shall be concentrating only on the concept of capital input involved, not on matters such as whether gross or net stocks should be used or how depreciation is to be handled, which, while important, are not fundamental.

The fact that measures of technological progress are identical to a *correctly*[3] deflated set of national accounts means that it does not matter how many labour or capital inputs are being considered or how detailed a sectoral disaggregation in 'real' terms is required: the process must always be the same. It will also be remembered that, in Chapter 1, I

---

[1] See, for instance, H. Lydall, 'On measuring technical progress', *Australian Economic Papers*, VIII, June 1969, 1–12.

[2] For a useful review, see M. Abramovitz, 'Economic growth in the United States', *American Economic Review*, LII, September 1962, 762–82.

[3] What 'correctly' means will be shown in Chapter 5. It does not, of course, mean measurement which is free of error in the normal sense. It means conceptual correctness.

mentioned that the measurement of capital and technological progress were *ex post* problems. Here is the connection with the deflated national accounts. Just as it was very important in the static accounts to implement Keynes's identity between investment and savings, so too it is important to record technological progress correctly in the dynamic version of the accounts – the deflated accounts which record changes in economic efficiency over time.

Regardless of whether estimates of Hicksian technical change are derived along simple Kendrick–Denison or more econometric Brown–Solow lines, I regard them as variants of the same basic concept – as Jorgenson and Griliches indicate. They are all subject to many problems, such as aggregation. More important, they are all subject to one basic and fundamental fallacy, as Chapter 5 will show.

3.3 Conclusion

In this chapter I have set out the basic concepts of technical change which I wish to attack and have offered some comments defending the postulated choice of the environment – Harrod's steady-state equilibrium – in which I wish to make my critique. If the neoclassical case is strong, it must be strongest in steady-state equilibrium. If it can be shown to be fundamentally wrong in such a favourable context, then it must, *a fortiori*, be wrong elsewhere.

4

THE MEASUREMENT OF THE FLOW AND STOCK OF COMMODITY CAPITAL

4.1 Introduction

For the purposes of my argument, a precise statement of some of the theoretical problems associated with the *measurement* of commodity capital is necessary. The basic measurement problems have not been set out in one place as rigorously and as exhaustively as I should like.[1] In this chapter, I deal with measurement in terms of physical units.

The chief *practical* difficulty in commodity capital measurement is the massive process of imputation necessitated by the fact that, in the real world, there is a lack of meaningful prices for existing pieces of commodity capital.[2] I shall continue to assume conditions of perfectly competitive equilibrium for a steadily *progressive* economy: that is, knowledge and foresight such that all present and future prices are known and held with certainty. I assume that the nominal price of new commodities remains constant, since this simplifies the arithmetic.[3] I shall consider a number of assumptions about the kind of depreciation taking place. It turns out that one of the assumptions, that of 'depreciation by obsolescence', is closely

[1] There are many discussions available which deal with the practical aspects of capital measurement. There are all the problems of data which, to a great extent, determine the choice of the method of measurement. The most common is known as the Perpetual Inventory Method. Most of the practical problems associated with such a method in the Canadian context (and for other methods as well) are discussed in a study I did for Canada. See Dominion Bureau of Statistics, *Estimates of Fixed Capital Flows and Stocks, Manufacturing, Canada, 1926–1960.*

[2] Hicks, 'The measurement of capital in relation', 19.

[3] By this assumption I mean three things. For a consumption good whose physical characteristics remain unchanged, its nominal price remains unchanged. This elimination of monetary inflation is in line with my initial decision to ignore the rôle of money. Second, in a one-commodity model, since the good can play the rôle of either a consumption good or a new capital good, the nominal price of a new capital good also remains unchanged. Third, in a model where capital goods are made obsolete, *new* capital goods have a constant nominal price level. Since, in this latter case, new capital goods have their physical characteristics changed as time passes, the meaning of constancy in nominal price requires further explanation, which is provided in Chapter 6. That chapter also deals with the question of changes over time in the physical characteristics of the consumption good.

related to the so-called 'embodied', or capital-augmenting technical progress. I shall also return to the 'double switching' problem, this time in the Sraffian context of the time which it takes to produce commodity capital.

My consideration of measurement problems is thus devoted to the theoretical problems involved in knowing precisely what is meant by the capital input in a world in which disequilibrium phenomena, such as changing rates of return, index-number difficulties, acceleration and deceleration in technological progress, etc., are ruled out. The Dominion Bureau of Statistics Reference Paper, *Estimates of Fixed Capital Flows and Stocks, Manufacturing, Canada, 1926–1960*, is adequate, I believe, as a survey of the measurement problems involved in the ugly real world of 'chaos and confusion'.[1]

4.2 No depreciation

I assume that pieces of commodity capital remain in productive service forever and can, therefore, continuously and costlessly be transferred from association with older techniques of lower output per unit of labour input to newer techniques with higher output per unit of labour input. Thus, all pieces of commodity capital are forever 'new'. At any given moment, t, the value of the stock of capital, will be $\sum_{i=1}^{m} P_i K_i(t)$ where K_i is the ith piece of commodity capital and P_i is the equilibrium price at time t.

In conditions of steady growth a constant flow of gross returns to capital, V_i, will be expected to accrue to each additional ith piece of commodity capital.[2] The equilibrium price of the commodity capital is therefore

$$P_i = V_i \int_t^{t+n} e^{-R(\hat{t}-t)}\,d\hat{t} \qquad (4.1)$$

or

$$P_i = \frac{V_i}{R}[1 - e^{-Rn}], \qquad (4.2)$$

where R is, as previously indicated, the net rate of return to commodity capital.[3]

Clearly

$$\lim_{n\to\infty} P_i = \lim_{n\to\infty} \frac{V_i}{R}[1 - e^{-Rn}] = \frac{V_i}{R}$$

In conditions of positive steady growth, the flow of gross returns to capital

[1] Hahn and Matthews, 'Theory of economic growth', 824.
[2] The flow of gross returns to capital, V_{it}, is defined as the flow of total proceeds per period, Q_{it}, less the flow of total prime costs per period, $W_t L_{it}$.
[3] Since $\int_t^{t+n} e^{-R(\hat{t}-t)}\,d\hat{t} = \left[\dfrac{e^{-R(\hat{t}-t)}}{-R}\right]_t^{t+n} = \dfrac{1}{R}[1 - e^{-Rn}].$

expected to accrue to each piece of commodity capital is assumed to remain constant, owing to offsetting influences of competitive accumulation and technological progress.

It follows then that the value of the stock of commodity capital at time t will be

$$\sum_{i=1}^{m} P_i K_i(t) = \int_1^m \int_{t-n}^t \frac{V_i}{R} I_i(t) \, e^{-g(t-\tau)} dt \, di \qquad (4.4)$$

$$\sum_{i=1}^{m} P_i K_i(t) = \int_1^m \frac{V_i}{Rg} I_i(t) [1 - e^{-gn}] di \qquad (4.5)$$

which as $n \to \infty$ equals

$$\int_1^m \frac{V_i}{Rg} I_i(t) \, di \qquad (4.6)$$

where $I_i(t)$ is the number of ith pieces of commodity capital born during time t and g is the growth rate. The social accountant would have no difficulty in valuing the stock of commodity capital at any time period. He would merely count the number of ith pieces of commodity capital at any time t and multiply by the ith piece price at time t.[1] Given the assumption about depreciation, the values of the gross and net stocks are identical.

4.3 'Depreciation by evaporation'

With 'depreciation by evaporation', commodity capital is subject to a constant force of mortality, Γ, but, again, existing pieces of commodity capital can be costlessly reassociated with the latest techniques. Each piece of commodity capital, regardless of its age, has the same foreseen discounted collection of gross returns to capital and, therefore, its price at time t is

$$P_i = V_i(t) \int_t^{t+n} e^{-(\Gamma+R)(\tau-t)} d\tau \qquad (4.7)$$

or

$$P_i = V_i(t) \frac{1}{\Gamma+R} [1 - e^{-(\Gamma+R)n}] \qquad (4.8)$$

where Γ is the rate of 'depreciation by evaporation'. Further

$$\lim_{n \to \infty} P_i = \lim_{n \to \infty} V_i(t) \frac{1}{\Gamma+R} [1 - e^{-(\Gamma+R)n}]$$

$$= V_i(t) \frac{1}{\Gamma+R} \qquad (4.9)$$

[1] Given the assumptions, the current-price value of the stock in (say) the period $t+k$ in $t+k$ period prices is the same as the constant-price value of the stock in the period $t+k$ in t period prices.

In conditions of steady-state growth, the value of the stock of commodity capital at time t will be

$$\sum_{i=1}^{m} P_i K_i(t) = \int_1^m \int_{t-n}^t \frac{V_i(t)}{\Gamma+R} I_i(t) e^{-(g+\Gamma)(t-\tau)} d\tau \, di \qquad (4.10)$$

or

$$= \int_1^m \frac{V_i(t)}{(\Gamma+R)} \frac{I_i(t)}{(g+\Gamma)} [1 - e^{-(g+\Gamma)n}] di \qquad (4.11)$$

which as $n \to \infty$ equals

$$\sum_{i=1}^{m} P_i K_i(t) = \int_1^m \frac{V_i}{(\Gamma+R)} \frac{I_i(t)}{(g+\Gamma)} di \qquad (4.12)$$

Since each ith piece of commodity capital, regardless of its age, will have the same equilibrium value, it follows that the value of the gross and net stocks of capital will again be the same. Depreciation and replacement will be identical and the value of depreciation in any period, t, under conditions of steady growth, will be

$$\sum_{i=1}^{m} P_i \Gamma K_i(t) = \int_1^m \int_{t-n}^t \frac{V_i(t)}{\Gamma+R} I_i(t)(1 - e^{-\Gamma}) e^{-(g+\Gamma)(t-\tau)} d\tau \, di \quad (4.13)$$

or

$$= (1 - e^{-\Gamma}) \int_1^m \frac{V_i I_i(t)}{(\Gamma+R)(g+\Gamma)} di \qquad (4.14)$$

such that the ratio of depreciation to the net stock is

$$\frac{P_i \Gamma K_i(t)}{P_i K_i(t)} = 1 - e^{-\Gamma} \simeq \Gamma \qquad (4.15)$$

The social accountant would value the stock of commodity capital in the same way as he did in the case of no depreciation and would value depreciation in any time period t at time-period t prices merely by counting the ith pieces of commodity capital vanishing during the period and multiplying by the price at time t.

Commodities which have a rate of 'depreciation by evaporation' equal to one – i.e. are completely 'used up' in the process of economic production within one time period – are intermediate inputs. The value of their flow is determined in exactly the same way as the value of the stock of commodity capital subject to a less rapid rate of 'depreciation by evaporation'.

4.4 'Depreciation by sudden death'

'Depreciation by sudden death' assumes that pieces of commodity capital last a finite predictable period of time (say T), but again the costless transferability assumption still holds. In this case, the equilibrium price of a piece of ith capital at time t with T period to live will be

$$P_i T(t) = V_i(t) \int_t^{t+T} e^{-R(\tau-t)} d\tau \tag{4.16}$$

$$P_i T(t) = \frac{V_i(t)}{R} [1 - e^{-RT}] \tag{4.17}$$

That of a piece with $T-1$ periods to live will be

$$P_i T - 1(t) = V_i(t) \int_t^{t+(T-1)} e^{-R(\tau-t)} d\tau \tag{4.18}$$

$$= \frac{V_i(t)}{R} [1 - e^{-R(T-1)}] \tag{4.19}$$

and that of a piece with one period to live will be

$$P_i 1(t) = \frac{V_i(t)}{R} [1 - e^{-R}] \tag{4.20}$$

Finally, the piece of commodity capital just approaching the end of its life will have the value of

$$P_i 0(t) = \frac{V_i(t)}{R} [0] = 0 \tag{4.21}$$

In a steady-state growth situation, it follows that the value of the *net* stock of commodity capital at time t in time t prices will be

$$\sum_{i=1}^{m} P_i K_i(t) = \int_1^m \frac{V_i(t)}{R} I_i T(t) \int_{t-T}^t (1 - e^{-R[(\tau-t)-T]}) e^{g(\tau-t)} d\tau \, di \tag{4.22}$$

$$= \int_1^m \frac{V_i(t)}{R} I_i T(t) \left[\left(\frac{1}{g} - \frac{e^{-gT}}{g} \right) - \left(\frac{e^{-RT}}{g-R} - \frac{e^{-gT}}{g-R} \right) \right] di \tag{4.23}$$

Since a piece of commodity capital falls in value as it ages, the value at time t in time t prices of the gross stock will be greater than the net stock, given in (4.23). The value of the gross stock[1] at time t will be

$$P_i K_i(t) = \int_1^m \frac{V_i(t)}{R} I_i T(t)[1 - e^{-RT}] \int_{t-T}^t e^{g(\tau-t)} d\tau \, di \tag{4.24}$$

[1] It follows from (4.23) and (4.25) that at time t in period t prices, the ratio of the net to the gross stock in steady-state growth will be

$$\frac{P_i K_i(t)}{P_i T(t) K(t)} = \frac{[(1-e^{-gT})/g] - [(e^{-RT}-e^{-gT})/g-R]}{(1-e^{-RT})[(1-e^{-gT})/g]} \frac{1}{1-e^{-RT}}$$

$$= \frac{e^{-gt}(e^{(g-R)T}-1)}{g-R} \frac{g}{e^{-gT}(e^{gT}-1)} \frac{1}{1-e^{-RT}}$$

$$= \frac{1}{1-e^{-RT}} - \frac{1}{(R-g)T} \frac{g^T}{e^{gT}-1} \frac{1-e^{-(R-g)T}}{1-e^{-RT}}$$

or
$$P_i T(t) K_i(t) = \int_1^m \frac{V_i(t)}{R} I_i T(t)[1 - e^{-RT}]\left(\frac{1}{g} - \frac{e^{-gT}}{g}\right) di \qquad (4.25)$$

The value of depreciation during the period t in period t prices will then be

$$D_t = \int_1^m \frac{V_i(t)}{R} I_i T(t)[e^R - 1]\int_{t-T}^t e^{-R[(\tau-t)+T]+g(\tau-t)}\,d\tau\,di \qquad (4.26)$$

$$= \int_1^m \frac{V_i(t)}{R} I_i T(t)[e^R - 1]\left(\frac{e^{-RT}}{g-R} - \frac{e^{-gT}}{g-R}\right) di \qquad (4.27)$$

and the ratio of depreciation to the net stock is

$$\frac{D_t}{P_i T(t) R_i(t)} = \frac{1 - e^R}{1 - \dfrac{e^{gT} - 1}{gT}\dfrac{(R-g)\,T}{1 - e^{-(R-g)T}}} \qquad (4.28)$$

The ratio of depreciation to the gross stock is

$$\frac{D_t}{P_i K_i(t)} = \frac{-(1 - e^R)(1 - e^{-(R-g)T})}{(R-g)T}\frac{gT}{(1 - e^{-RT})(e^{gT} - 1)} \qquad (4.29)$$

The value of replacement during the period t in period t prices will be

$$R_t = \int_1^m \frac{V_i(t)}{R}[1 - e^{-RT}]I_i T(t)e^{-gT}\,di \qquad (4.30)$$

and hence the ratio of replacement to depreciation[1] is

$$\frac{R_t}{D_t} = \frac{-(R-g)\,1 - e^{-RT}}{[1 - e^R][1 - e^{-(R-g)T}]} \qquad (4.31)$$

In the case of 'depreciation by evaporation' there was a simple relationship between the value of depreciation and the value of the gross and net stocks of commodity capital. In the case of 'depreciation by sudden death', the relationship, though constant, is fairly complicated.

The social accountant may value the gross stock in existence at time t in period t prices by multiplying the number of ith pieces with the time-period t price of brand new ith pieces. To value the net stock he must

This is the formula which appears in J. Robinson, 'Some problems of definition and measurement of capital', *Collected Economic Papers*, II (Oxford: Blackwell, 1960), 202. The formulae for the zero-growth steady-state situation in the limiting case when g approaches zero, is found in the above source and also in 'The value of invested capital', an appendix by D. C. Champernowne and R. F. Kahn in Robinson, *Accumulation of Capital* (3rd ed.).

[1] The ratio Rt/Dt is greater than o and, ignoring powers of the exponents of greater than one in the expansion for e, I have when $g = 0$

$$\frac{Rt}{Dt} = 1 \quad \text{and} \quad \frac{Rt}{Dt} = \frac{1 + (R-g)T}{1 + RT} < 1$$

when $g > 0$.

65

classify ith pieces of capital by their respective ages and multiply by the respective vintage prices. To obtain the value of depreciation in time-period t in time-period t prices, he must take into account the various pieces of ith commodities passing over various ages and multiply by their respective declines in vintage prices.

The 'depreciation by sudden death' assumption can be modified by applying more continuous survival functions. That is, instead of assuming that a bundle of jth commodities born in time-period t *all* die in time-period $t+T$, it can be assumed that fractions will die in $t+1, t+2, ...,$ $t+2T$, etc., so that the collection of the deaths over the periods $t+1, ...,$ $t+2T$, etc. will equal the commodities born in time-period t. This variant of the 'depreciation by sudden death' assumption should not be confused with the assumption of 'depreciation by evaporation'. This variant of the 'depreciation by sudden death' assumption implies that the expected mean life of a batch of new ith pieces added to the stock in time-period t is T periods and that the expected mean life of the survivors in the time-period $t+1$ is less than T periods. In the case of 'depreciation by evaporation', the expected mean life of the original additions in the period t and of the survivors in the period $t+1$ remains unchanged.

4.5   Depreciation by obsolescence

In the real world, it is highly unlikely that commodity capital falls to or approaches a zero value merely because it has aged ('depreciation by sudden death') or disappeared through decay ('depreciation by evaporation'). Much more likely is that the assumption of malleability or costless transferability of existing capital goods is unrealistic. Indeed, it would appear safe to assert that pieces of commodity capital are malleable only under conditions of sharply rising short run costs. It is the emergence of new pieces of commodity capital, which can be associated with techniques of production giving improved output per unit of labour input at lower cost than older pieces, that eventually brings about the disappearance of the older pieces.[1] Within the context of models of steadily progressive

[1] Commodity capital is 'putty clay'. See E. S. Phelps, 'Substitution, fixed proportions, growth and distribution', *International Economic Review*, IV, September 1963, 265–88. Technically, any degree of *ex post* substitutability between labour and existing pieces of commodity capital is possible, but short run rising supply prices (see Chapter 2) set a maximum level to the amount of labour optimally concerned with taking apart and reassembling 'meccano sets' and fix the *ex post* degree of substitutions below its *ex ante* counterpart. Steady neutral technological progress will, in the face of steadily rising wage rates, permit the same rate of taking apart and reassembling 'meccano sets' in such a way that a constant *ex post* degree of substitutability is preserved. An increase in the degree of *ex post* substitutability requires an increase in the rate of capital renovation – a form of capital accumulation which encounters the constraints confronting short run accumulation set out in Chapter 2.

economies, the stream of gross returns accruing to any piece of commodity capital under conditions of 'depreciation by obsolescence' is expected to decline steadily over future time periods. I shall assume initially that no transferability is possible. As before, I define the flow of additional gross returns expected to accrue to an additional piece of ith commodity capital at any time period t to be

$$V_i(t) \equiv P(Q_t - \overline{W}_t L_t) \tag{4.32}$$

where Q_t is the amount of output associated with the ith piece of new commodity capital and $\overline{W}_t$ is the real wage rate to be paid to the amount of associated labour input, L_t. If the piece of ith commodity capital at time t is associated with unchanging techniques of production, then

$$V_i(t) = P_t Q_t [1 - \overline{W}_t A_t] \tag{4.33}$$

where A_t is the fixed-labour-input-per-unit-of-output technique. Under steady-state assumptions, $\overline{W}_t$, the real-wage rate, will be rising at the same rate as output per unit of labour input, under the assumption that the nominal price of all new commodities remains constant. Then as $\overline{W}_t$ approaches the value of output per head, $1/A_t$, the flow of gross returns approaches zero.[1]

The price of the ith piece of new commodity capital in time-period t will be

$$P_i(t) = V_i(t) \int_t^{t+n} e^{-\delta(\tau-t)-R(\tau-t)} d\tau \tag{4.34}$$

or

$$P_i(t) = \frac{V_i(t)}{\delta+R}[1 - e^{-(\delta+R)n}] \tag{4.35}$$

where δ is the rate at which gross returns to a given period's investment in commodity capital is expected to fall.

Again,

$$\lim_{n \to \infty} P_i(t) = \lim_{n \to \infty} \frac{V_i(t)}{\delta+R}[1 - e^{-(\delta+R)n}] = \frac{V_i(t)}{\delta+R} \tag{4.36}$$

The rate δ at which nominal gross returns fall is related to the rate at which the wage rate (i.e. input per head) rises. From

$$V_i(t) = P_t Q_t(1 - \overline{W}_t A_t)$$

[1] Capital goods will be scrapped when $1 - \overline{W}_t A_t$ equals zero. In the case of completely fixed coefficients, a capital good, which when new had a gross return associated with it equal to $(1 - \overline{W}_{t-v} A_{t-v})$, will be scrapped when $1 - \overline{W}_t A_{t-v}$ equals zero. The flow of gross returns will be falling at the rate δ because the real-wage rate is rising at the rate t_R, the rate of Harrodian technological progress to be discussed in Chapter 5. Thus, the capital good is scrapped when $1 - \overline{W}_{t-v} e^{t_R v} A_{t-v} = 0$. In steady-state equilibrium, t_R is known and hence v, the lifetime of capital goods is

$$\frac{\log 1 - \log \overline{W}_{t-v} A_{t-v}}{t_R} = v$$

it follows that

$$V_i(t+1) = P_t Q_t[1 - \overline{W}_t e^{t_R} A_t] = P_t Q_t[1 - \overline{W}_t A_t] e^{-\delta}$$

where t_R is the growth rate of output per labour input. Then

$$e^{-\delta} = \frac{1}{1-\alpha} - \frac{\alpha}{1-\alpha} e^{t_R} \quad \text{and} \quad \alpha = \overline{W}_t A_t$$

Ignoring powers of the exponents greater than one in the expansion, I have

$$\delta = \frac{\alpha t_R}{1-\alpha}$$

Since α, the share of labour in the initial first period quasi-rents accruing to any new ith piece of commodity capital, will remain constant in steadily progressive economies, the rate at which output per head will be rising will be constantly related to the rate at which quasi-rents will be expected to decline. The assumption of zero *ex post* substitutability between labour and existing pieces of commodity capital implies that A, the given labour input/output ratio, remains constant. Clearly, a greater than zero degree of *ex post* substitutability could be introduced by assuming that A falls at a rate such that

$$V_i(t+1) = P_t Q_t[1 - \overline{W}_t e^{t_R} A_t e^{-s}] = P_t Q_t[1 - \overline{W}_t A_t] e^{-\delta^*}$$

such that

$$e^{-\delta^*} = \frac{1}{1-\alpha} - \frac{\alpha}{1-\alpha} e^{t_R - s}$$

where approximately

$$\delta^* = \frac{\alpha(t_R - s)}{1-\alpha}$$

Clearly, $\delta^* < \delta$ and $\delta^* = 0$ where $t_R = s$ or where *ex post* and *ex ante* substitutability are the same.

Where there exists no *ex post* substitutability, the entrepreneur, considering investment programmes per unit of labour input, will be maximizing

$$-k + \int_0^v (f(k) - \overline{W} e^{t_R t}) e v^{-Rt} dt$$

where k is investment per man and $f(k)$ is not a function of time – that is to say, once the optimum investment per man is selected, it cannot be varied over the life of the investment. The conditions for a maximum are

$$R = f'(k)(1 - e^{Rt})$$

where $f'(k)$ is $\partial f(k)/\partial k$ and

$$\frac{\log f(k) - \log(\overline{W})}{t_R} = v,$$

where again v is the age at which machines are scrapped. This is the same as in footnote 1 on page 67 since $f(k)$ equals $1/A$. Where there exists some *ex post* substitutability, the entrepreneur will, in selecting the optimum investment per unit of labour input, take it into account. As the real wage rate rises, the entrepreneur will be able to reduce the number of men associated with the investment thus lengthening the life of the capital good. If *ex post* substitutability is too great, the conditions for a maximum do not exist.[1] It appears, however, that again the determinateness of the rate of accumulation is to be derived from the short run supply, not from the short or long run demand, conditions.

In conditions of steady progressive growth, the total flow of additional gross returns

$$\int e^{-\delta(\tau-t)}d\tau$$

remains constant for each additional new superior piece of commodity capital, owing to the offsetting influences of competitive accumulation and neutral technological progress. The competitive price of a one-time-period-old piece of commodity capital is, however, at time t

$$P_{i-1}(t) = V_i(t)e^{-\delta}\int_t^{t+n} e^{-\delta(\tau-t)-R(\tau-t)}d\tau \tag{4.37}$$

or
$$\lim_{n\to\infty} P_{i-1}(t) = \frac{V_i(t)e^{-\delta}}{\delta+R} \tag{4.38}$$

The competitive price of an n-time-period-old piece of commodity capital is

$$P_{i-n}(t) = V_i(t)e^{-n\delta}\int_t^{t+n} e^{-\delta(\tau-t)-R(\tau-t)}d\tau \tag{4.39}$$

or
$$\lim_{n\to\infty} P_{i-n}(t) = 0 \tag{4.40}$$

Hence, the value of a steadily growing *net* stock of commodity capital is

$$P_{i_{N(t)}}K_i(t) = \int_1^m \frac{V_i(t)}{\delta+R}I_i(t)\int_{t-n}^t e^{(\delta+g)(\tau-t)}d\tau di \tag{4.41}$$

or
$$P_{i_{N(t)}}K_i(t) = \int_1^m \frac{V_i(t)}{\delta+R}I_i(t)\frac{1}{\delta+g}[1-e^{-(\delta+g)n}]di \tag{4.42}$$

and, as $n\to\infty$,
$$\int_1^m \frac{V_i(t)}{\delta+R}I_i(t)\frac{1}{\delta+g}di \tag{4.43}$$

where $I_i(t)$ is the additional ith piece of commodity capital born in time period t. The value of a steadily growing gross stock of commodity capital is

$$P_i(t)K_i(t) = \int_1^m \frac{V_i(t)}{\delta+R}I_i(t)\int_{t-n}^t e^{g(\tau-t)}d\tau di \tag{4.44}$$

[1] See C. Bliss, 'On putty clay', *Review of Economic Studies*, xxxv, April 1968, 105–32.

or
$$P_i(t)K_i(t) = \int_1^m \frac{V_i(t)}{\delta+R} I_i(t) \frac{1}{g} [1 - e^{-ng}] di \qquad (4.45)$$

and, as $n \to \infty$
$$\int_1^m \frac{V_i(t)}{\delta+R} \frac{I_i(t)}{g} di \qquad (4.46)$$

The ratio of the values of the net and the gross stock in time period t in time-period t prices is
$$\frac{C_t}{K_t} = \frac{P_{i_N}(t)K_i(t)}{P_i(t)K_i(t)} = \frac{g}{\delta+g} \qquad (4.47)$$

The value of depreciation in time period t in time-period t prices is
$$D_t = \int_1^m \frac{V_i(t)}{\delta+R} I_i(t)[1-e^{-\delta}] \int_{t-n}^t e^{(\delta+g)(\tau+t)} d\tau \, di \qquad (4.48)$$

or
$$D_t = \int_1^m \frac{V_i(t)}{\delta+R} I_i(t)[1-e^{-\delta}] \frac{1}{\delta+g} [1 - e^{-(\delta+g)n}] di \qquad (4.49)$$

and
$$\lim_{n \to \infty} D(t) = \int_1^m \frac{V_i(t)}{\delta+R} I_i(t) \frac{[1-e^{-\delta}]}{\delta+g} di \qquad (4.50)$$

such that the ratio of depreciation to the net stock is
$$\frac{D_{(t)}}{P_{i_{N(t)}}K_{i(t)}} = \frac{[1-e^{-\delta}]}{\delta+g} \cdot \delta+g = [1 - e^{-\delta}] \simeq \delta^{1} \qquad (4.51)$$

and the ratio of depreciation to the gross stock is
$$\frac{D_{(t)}}{P_{i(t)}K_{i(t)}} = \frac{g}{\delta+g} [1 - e^{-\delta}] = \frac{g}{\delta+g} \qquad (4.52)$$

The fact that, in the case of 'depreciation by obsolescence', the ratio of the *value* of depreciation to the *value* of the net stock is approximately equal to δ will mean that the results in Chapters 5 and 6, which hold in the case of 'depreciation by evaporation' (where the ratio of *physical* depreciation to physical stock equalled approximately Γ) can be used, *providing consistent aggregation is possible*. Aggregation means, however, the use of prices. Indeed, as I have shown, the rate of 'depreciation by obsolescence' is fundamentally a value construct.

The value of replacement in time period t in time-period t prices is
$$R_t = \int_1^m \frac{V_i(t)}{\delta+R} I_i(t) e^{-gn} [1 - e^{-(\delta+R)n}] di \qquad (4.53)$$

$$\lim_{n \to \infty} R_t = 0 \quad \text{and therefore the ratio} \quad \lim_{n \to \infty} \frac{D_t}{R_t} = 0 \qquad (4.54)$$

[1] In the case where *ex post* and *ex ante* substitutability are the same (i.e. $\delta = 0$), then $C_t = K_t$, $D_t = 0$ and the case collapses back to the assumption of infinitely long-lived pieces of commodity capital.

At first blush, this is a surprising result. Reflection indicates, however, that the assumption of 'depreciation by obsolescence' implies that the resource cost of replacement of a piece of commodity capital which is just disappearing from the stock is, in fact, zero. Of course, the commodity capital is vanishing from the stock because of the advent of newer improved capital goods, which do have a resource cost. However, the replacement cost of the completely obsolete capital as capital is zero. This will also be true in the case where the labour coefficient for vintage capital goods is being reduced as they become more and more obsolete. Consequently, if one tried to obtain, in this case, a measure of the value of replacement, it would be zero as well. If one seeks a measure of replacement the output no longer produced by the totally obsolete piece of capital, then one is, of course, in the fixed coefficients case, measuring output and not capital. In the variable coefficients case, the output of the totally obsolete machine is zero. I conclude that the value of replacement of capital goods in the case of 'depreciation by obsolescence' is zero.

The 'depreciation by obsolescence' assumption, which is the most realistic in my view, can be modified by assumptions as to decay and ageing.

It is interesting to compare the results found here for 'depreciation by obsolescence' with those of Solow.[1] Before I do so, however, I should point out that, when technological advance is said to take place in such a way that only new capital goods are associated with new techniques of production and the flow of gross returns associated with old capital goods begins to fall, one is, in fact, confronted in measuring the stock of commodity capital – gross and net commodity capital formation and depreciation over time – in comparable terms with what social accountants would call the phenomenon of 'quality change'. If the new machines are associated with new techniques of production, then presumably the new machines are different from the old. How are they to be compared?[2]

If the social accountants are performing their tasks properly, however, the resulting capital measures over time will properly reflect the occurrence of technological prorgess, showing up in the phenomenon of 'depreciation by obsolescence', with the result that, at least in steady-state configurations, *the rate of growth of the net stock of commodity capital will be equal to the rate of growth of a stock of commodity capital in which technological*

---

[1] R. M. Solow, 'Investment and technical progress', eds. K. J. Arrow *et al.*, *Mathematical Methods in the Social Sciences, 1959* (Stanford: Stanford University Press, 1960).

[2] Salter apparently believed that problems associated with the measurement and addition of different kinds of *stocks* of capital goods could be evaded by dealing with an *ex ante* production function or investment function. The problem is, however, merely thrown forward on to a comparison of investments in different time periods or different economies. See Salter, *Productivity and Technical Change*, 17 ff.

progress is being embodied in new vintages. The fact that part of the technological progress may not be showing up in the phenomenon of 'depreciation by obsolescence' simply means that the rate at which the gross returns
accruing to pieces of commodity capital fall as they age is reduced relative
to that at which they would fall, were technological progress solely of the
type which gives rise to 'depreciation by obsolescence'. This mixed case,
along with possible (but unlikely) cases of 'depreciation by sudden death'
or 'depreciation by evaporation', offer no difficulties in principle to the
measurement of commodity capital flows and stocks in comparable terms
over time. I deal with this matter conclusively in Chapter 6. As a consequence, there is no difference between the standard net stock of commodity capital and Solow's effective capital. Further, as I show in Chapter 6,
there is no difference between disembodied and embodied technological
advance.

I ignore Solow's assumption of a constant rate of 'depreciation by
evaporation'. Instead of assuming that the amount of labour associated
with each vintage piece of commodity capital is fixed, Solow allows it to
fall as technological progress occurs, so that the total supply of labour
(constant or growing) is shuffled at a steady rate from all ages of old to new
pieces of commodity capital.[1] However, the output which is associated
with older pieces of commodity capital falls as it loses labour, because it is
assumed that vintage pieces of commodity capital do not share in technological progress, and, under standard neoclassical assumptions, the marginal
and average physical products of vintage pieces of commodity capital fall
over time.[2] This is merely a trivially different description of the process of
technological progress. Solow has attempted to show that, under his
assumptions, 'provided the capital stock were measured not by a count of
machines [meaningless anyway where machines differ in their productive

---

[1] The output associated with vintage of commodity capital v is, in Solow's well-known
terms,
$$Q_v(t) = Be^{\lambda v}L_v(t)^\alpha K_v(t)^{1-\alpha}$$
so that if $\qquad L_v(t+1) < L_v(t), \qquad Q_v(t+1) < Q_v(t)$

In my analysis, labour is shuffling from pieces of commodity capital just reaching zero
value to new pieces. Solow's assumptions preserve the existence of marginal physical
products; mine do not, but everything of substance is the same.

[2] That is, instead of writing
$$V_i(t+1) = P_t Q_t[1 - \overline{W}_t e^{t_R} A_i] = P_t Q_t[1 - \overline{W}_t A_i]e^{-\delta}$$

I may write, as an illustration of Solow's method, as before,
$$V_i(t+1) = P_t Q_t[1 - \overline{W}_t e^{t_R} A_i] = P_t Q_t e^{-\delta}[1 - \overline{W}_t e^{t_R} A e^{-s}]$$

a reformation which clearly indicates that, in terms of the valuation of the stock of
capital, Solow gets the same results as given above in the assumption of the 'depreciation by obsolescence' case.

capacities] but by the real market value of the stock of capital...'[1], then it would follow (using Solow's notation) that[2]

$$A(t) = e^{-\sigma t} J(t) \qquad (4.55)$$

where $\sigma = \lambda^s/(1-\alpha)$, with λ^s being Solow's rate of 'embodied' technological progress, α being the partial elasticity of output with respect to labour, $A(t)$ the value of the net stock of commodity capital at time t in time-period t prices, and $J(t)$ the value of the 'effective' stock of commodity capital at time t in time-period t prices. To compare the two results further, it should be noted that Solow ends up with three stock concepts. In terms of his notation, where the rate of 'depreciation by evaporation' is zero, Solow's three concepts are:

First, the net stock of commodity capital

$$A(t) = e^{-\sigma t} \int_{-\infty}^{t} e^{\sigma v} I(v) \mathrm{d}v \qquad (4.56)$$

second, the gross stock of commodity capital

$$K(t) = \int_{-\infty}^{t} I(v) \mathrm{d}v \qquad (4.57)$$

and, third, the effective stock of commodity capital

$$J(t) = \int_{-\infty}^{t} e^{\sigma v} I(v) \mathrm{d}v \qquad (4.58)$$

In steady-state conditions, commodity-capital formation will be growing at the rate g. Hence, in time period t in time-period t prices, Solow's net stock will be

$$A(t) = \frac{I(-\infty)e^{gt}}{g+\sigma} \qquad (4.59)$$

and the gross stock will be

$$K(t) = \frac{I(-\infty)e^{gt}}{g} \qquad (4.60)$$

where $I(-\infty)$ is investment in the year $-\infty$, so that

$$\frac{A(t)}{K(t)} = \frac{g}{g+\sigma} = \frac{g}{g+[\lambda^s/(1-\alpha)]} \qquad (4.61)$$

How does this compare with the ratio of the value in time period t in time-period t prices of the net to the gross stock of commodity capital, as found above under the assumption of 'depreciation by obsolescence'? That is, does

$$\frac{g}{g+[\lambda^s/(1-\alpha)]} = \frac{g}{\delta+g} \qquad (4.62)$$

[1] Solow, 'Investment and technical progress', 100. My insert.
[2] As indicated, I have excluded the rate of 'depreciation by evaporation' from Solow's definition of σ.

hold true? It is shown in Chapter 5, that, in steady-state conditions, the neoclassical rate of technological progress is equal to the rate of growth in the real wage rate (assuming homogeneous labour), multiplied by the partial elasticity of production with respect to labour. That is

$$\lambda^s = \alpha t_R \tag{4.63}$$

When this finding is substituted into (4.62), it is readily seen that the ratio of the value of Solow's net to gross stocks is identical to the ratio found under the assumption of 'depreciation by obsolescence'.[1] Solow's effective stock will appear to be

$$J(t) = I\frac{(-\infty)e^{(g+\sigma)t}}{g+\sigma} \tag{4.64}$$

so that
$$\frac{A(t)}{J(t)} = e^{-\sigma t} \quad \text{and} \quad \frac{K(t)}{J(t)} = e^{-\sigma t}\frac{g+\sigma}{g} \tag{4.65}$$

Under conditions of steady-state growth, it would appear to follow that

$$\frac{\dot{A}(t)}{A(t)} = -0+\frac{\dot{J}(t)}{J(t)} = \frac{-\lambda^s}{1-\alpha}+\frac{\dot{J}(t)}{J(t)} = -t_R+\frac{\dot{J}(t)}{J(t)} \tag{4.66}$$

where in this case $\dot{A}(t)$ represents $dA(t)/dt$, etc. That is, Solow's stock of 'effective' capital will be growing at a rate in excess of that of the net stock of commodity capital.

As I earlier indicated, Solow's 'effective' stock of capital raises the conceptual difficulty generally known among social accountants as the problem of the measurement of 'quality change'. Solow's formulation would suggest that a new piece of commodity capital is, in some sense, superior to an old piece. As I have indicated, this suggestion can be drawn up in terms of the changing labour-per-unit-of-output relationships associated with the different vintages of pieces of commodity capital and, under the assumptions employed in the foregoing analysis, the exact effects on the evaluation of the stock (particularly, the net stock) of commodity capital can be drawn out. It would *appear* to be the case, however, that, confronted with the fact that the nominal price of new pieces of commodity capital were remaining unchanged over time and that pieces of commodity capital were said to be improving in some sense, the social accountant must produce price indexes for new capital goods which would be declining. From my analysis in Chapter 6, it would *appear* to follow that a new piece of commodity capital would be worth e^δ more than the piece produced a year ago, for the cost of producing a new piece of com-

[1] Since $\delta = \alpha t_R/(1-\alpha)$, then $g/(\delta+g) = g/[(\alpha t_R/1-\alpha)+g]$. Since $\lambda^s = \alpha(t_R)$, then $g/\delta+g = g/[(\lambda^s/1-\alpha)+g]$ as argued in the text.

modity capital under current conditions of technology is $e^{-\delta}$ that of producing it under conditions of older technology. It then would appear to follow that I can easily amend the theoretical statements about the value of the net and gross stocks of commodity capital under the assumption of 'depreciation by obsolescence' accordingly. For I merely assume that 'effective' commodity-capital formation is growing at the rate $g+\delta$ rather than, as before, at the rate g. I then have, in place of (4.43),

$$\lim_{n\to\infty} C_t^e = \int_1^{\cdot m} \frac{V_i(t)}{\delta+R} I_i(t) \frac{1}{g} di \qquad (4.67)$$

and in place of (4.46),

$$\lim_{n\to\infty} K_t^e = \int_1^{\cdot m} \frac{V_i(t)}{\delta+R} \frac{I_i(t)}{-\delta+g} \qquad (4.68)$$

where C_t^e and K_t^e are 'effective' net and gross commodity-capital stocks respectively. Note that the ratio of

$$\frac{P_{i_{N(t)}} K_{i(t)}}{C_t^e} = \frac{1/(\delta+g)}{1/g} = \frac{g}{\delta+g} \qquad (4.69)$$

may be compared with the ratio

$$\frac{A(t)}{J(t)} = e^{-\delta t} \qquad (4.70)$$

for, having shown that Solow's net stock is comparable with that of (4.43), I may rewrite (4.45) as

$$A(t)e = \frac{I(-\infty)e^{(g+\delta)t}}{g+\delta} \qquad (4.71)$$

This is the same as

$$J(t) = I(-\infty)\frac{e^{(g+\sigma)t}}{g+\sigma} \qquad (4.64)$$

since, as I have shown, Solow's σ equals my δ.

Hence, Solow's 'effective' stock of commodity capital is exactly equivalent to my net stock of commodity capital under the assumption of 'depreciation by obsolescence', when the growing flow of commodity-capital formation is said to incorporate the improving quality of pieces of commodity capital. Thus, it would seem that Solow's 'effective' stock of commodity capital merely requires that the social accountant uses correct capital-goods' price indexes for its implementation.[1]

---

[1] For incorrect conclusions about Solow's effective capital and the net stock of commodity capital, see B. G. Hickman, *Investment Demand and U.S. Economic Growth* (Washington: Brookings Institution, 1965), 39–41, and H. A. J. Green, 'Embodied progress, investment and growth', *American Economic Review*, LVI, March 1966,

What I have shown so far is that a stock of capital valued correctly (and I show in Chapter 6 that there is only one 'correct' way to measure the aggregate stock of capital) is exactly the same thing as Solow's 'effective' capital, i.e. a stock of capital in which technological improvements are embedded in the commodities making up the stock. These two stock concepts will then exhibit the same rate of change in steady-state equilibrium and Solow's attempt to show that capital accumulation plays a more important role in economic growth than in the case of disembodied technology founders. I say 'correct' in this sense: I merely show that, given an equilibrium rate of return to commodity capital, it is possible to aggregate over the many vintages of commodity capital in a consistent fashion. I can then show that the neoclassical measurements of disembodied and embodied technological progress are the same. When I show in Chapter 5 that the neoclassical method is wrong in the case of disembodied technological progress, then it follows (and really requires no further proof) that it must be wrong in the embodied case. My demonstration that the neoclassical measure is wrong will *never* rest on consistent aggregated concepts like the stock of capital, but it is important to realize that the demonstration holds true when consistent aggregate concepts must of necessity be used.

However, so great are the possibilities for confusion in the area of disembodied versus embodied technological progress, 'effective' capital, etc., that I have deemed it necessary to work out the required analysis in Chapter 6.

In this chapter, I have set out some steady-state values of gross and net commodity-capital formation, depreciation, and gross and net commodity-capital stocks. To summarize the results, I set forth in Table 4.1 the value for the ith pieces of commodity capital in time-period t for gross and net commodity-capital formation, depreciation, and the gross and net commodity-capital stocks, under the different depreciation assumptions. By assumption $V_i(t)$ is taken as constant through time and the steady-state assumption involves that, at time t, all cells in Table 4.1 will be growing at the rate, g, at which gross capital formation in the ith commodity is taking place.

138–51. Brown, *Theory and Measurement of Technological Change*, notes that the internal weighting scheme between various vintages in Solow's 'effective' stock (i.e. the rate of factor substitutions among vintages) is the same as between the various vintages of capital goods in the net stock of commodity capital (i.e. the various vintage equilibrium relative prices will exactly reflect the various vintage relative rates of factor substitution). He concludes, contrary to Hickman and Green, however – and correctly, in my view – that the effective stock of capital and the net stock of commodity capital must be growing at the same rate. See also R. G. D. Allen, *Macroeconomic Theory* (London: Macmillan, 1967), 285, and C. E. Ferguson, *The Neoclassical Theory of Production and Distribution*, (Cambridge: Cambridge University Press, 1969), Ch. 13.

TABLE 4.1. *The value of commodity capital*

(Part *a*)

	Gross capital formation	Net capital formation	Depreciation
No depreciation	$I_i(t)\dfrac{V_i(t)}{R}$	$I_i(t)\dfrac{V_i(t)}{R}$	nil
Depreciation by evaporation	$I_i(t)\dfrac{V_i(t)}{R}$	$I_i(t)V_i(t)\left[\dfrac{g\Gamma+gR+\Gamma^2}{R(gH)(\Gamma+R)}\right]$	$\Gamma\dfrac{I_i(t)}{g+\Gamma}\dfrac{V_i(t)}{\Gamma+R}$
Depreciation by sudden death	$I_i(t)\dfrac{V_i(t)}{R}$	$\dfrac{I_iT(t)V_i(t)}{R}$ $\times\left[1-(e^R-1)\left\{\dfrac{e^{-RT}}{g-R}\dfrac{e^{-gT}}{g-R}\right\}\right]$	$I_iT(t)\dfrac{V_i(t)}{R}(e^R-1)$ $\times\left(\dfrac{e^{-RT}}{g-R}\dfrac{e^{-gT}}{g-R}\right)$
Depreciation by obsolescence	$I_i(t)\dfrac{V_i(t)}{R}$	$I_i(t)V_i(t)\left[\dfrac{g\delta+gR+\delta^2}{R(g+\delta)(\delta+R)}\right]$	$\delta\dfrac{I_i(t)V_i(t)}{R+\delta}\dfrac{1}{\delta+g}$

Notation: $I_i(t)$ = number of pieces of ith commodity capital born in year t; $V_i(t)$ = expected flow of gross returns accruing to each ith piece of commodity capital in year t, always assumed constant; R = the equilibrium net rate of return; Γ = the rate of 'depreciation by evaporation'; T = the life of commodity capital under the assumption of 'depreciation by sudden death'; δ = the rate of 'depreciation by obsolescence'; g = the rate of growth of commodity-capital formation.

(Part *b*)

	Gross stock	Net stock
No depreciation	$I_i(t)\dfrac{V_i(t)}{R}\dfrac{1}{g}$	$I_i(t)\dfrac{V_i(t)}{R}\dfrac{1}{g}$
Depreciation by evaporation	$I_i(t)\dfrac{V_i(t)}{(\Gamma+R)}\dfrac{1}{(g+\Gamma)}$	$I_i(t)\dfrac{V_i(t)}{(\Gamma+R)}\dfrac{1}{(g+\Gamma)}$
Depreciation by sudden death	$\dfrac{I_iT(t)V_i(t)}{R}[1-e^{-RT}]\left[\dfrac{1}{g}-\dfrac{e^{-gT}}{g}\right]$	$I_iT(t)\dfrac{V_i(t)}{R}\left[\left(\dfrac{1}{g}-\dfrac{e^{-gT}}{g}\right)-\left(\dfrac{e^{-RT}}{g-R}-\dfrac{e^{-gT}}{g-R}\right)\right]$
Depreciation by obsolescence	$I_i(t)\dfrac{V_i(t)}{R+\delta}\dfrac{1}{g}$	$I_i(t)\dfrac{V_i(t)}{R+\delta}\dfrac{1}{\delta+g}$

Notation: see (Part *a*).

4.6 Some additional measurement problems

So far in this chapter, I have not discussed explicitly the *aggregate* stock of capital for a steady-state economy. Consider the case of 'depreciation of obsolescence'. There would be an equilibrium net stock of commodity capital for every kind of commodity capital. That is, for each type of n commodities there would be m prices, ranging from the newest to the oldest still earning positive rentals. The stock of capital would then be composed of $m \times n$ vintages and types of commodities. There would be $m \times n$ prices. It would be unrealistic to expect any actual measurement of such an aggregate stock of commodity capital to be free of index number problems. The vintage structure of each type of commodity could remain unchanged, but because of different equilibrium rates of technological progress in the n capital-goods industries with a constant rate of profit,[1] the relative prices of the various types, along with their respective quantities, would be changing. As a consequence, no unambiguous measure of the physical aggregate stock of capital over time would be possible. And if rates of profit were changing as well, the index number ambiguity would be increased. Surely, however, index-number problems are well known.

I wish to turn to problems of Wicksell effects, both real and price, and the effect of 'switching' of techniques on the measurement of commodity capital. I shall deal first with Wicksell price effects.

In an economy where the calculations I have been considering are made for each kind of the ith commodity capital good, an unambiguous estimate of the aggregate stock of capital can be prepared – unambiguous, that is, apart from the well-known index-number problems. Two essential assumptions have been made so far. One is that the characteristics of the capital goods never change over time (or between economies). This assumption will be examined in Chapter 6, though what I am about to say is also important for the discussion there. Second, I have been assuming that, for the economy under consideration, the rate of growth and the net rate of return to capital remain unchanged. Such an assumption is appropriate to steady-state analysis. In such a case, in an economy of one consumption good and many capital goods, changes in the relative prices (with the consumption good as the numéraire) can only occur because of different rates of technological progress among the various sectors. However, if I was comparing two economies in their respective steady states, growing at the same rate but experiencing different net rates of return, could I compare the aggregate stocks of capital – each perfectly unambiguous in its own context? The discussion in Chapter 2 provides the answer. A comparison can be made, but what sense is to be made of the answers? As was shown, there need exist no monotonic relationship among the value of capital (whether expressed in terms of the consumption good or in terms of 'compounded' labour, Mrs Robinson's 'real capital'),

[1] In Chapter 5, I point out that technological progress can be occurring at different rates in n capital-goods industries and still be neutral in each sector and for the overall economy.

the value of net output (again valued in terms of the consumption good or labour) and the net rate of return. It remains possible to construct Champernowne's 'chain index' of the value of capital.[1] Consider a 'switch point' as discussed in Chapter 2 (equivalent to Champernowne's equally-competitive equipments). At a 'switch point', the maximum wage rate less the 'switch' wage rate, capitalized at the 'switch' net rate of return provides an estimate of the value, in terms of the consumption good,[2] of the stock of commodity capital per unit of labour. At the 'switch point' these capital estimates may be compared for two techniques and thus for any two consecutive techniques. A 'chain index' of capital values could thus be constructed.

It should be made clear that this is precisely what social accountants do when they construct capital stock estimates in so-called constant prices. First, the 'constant prices', while they are customarily capital-good prices, could just as well be consumption-good or labour prices. Second, a comparison of commodity-capital stocks between economies or between two points of time for a given economy involves valuing both countries' stocks or both times' stocks in terms of the prices ruling in one economy or at one time, and implicitly uses the 'switch' relationships. Consider Diagram 4.1, which is similar to Diagram 2.7. In a steady-state two-economy comparison, in economy A the wage-rate and net-rate-of-return combination $(\overline{W}, R)_A$ holds and in economy B $(\overline{W}, R)_B$ holds. In economy A, there will be associated with $(\overline{W}, R)_A$ a particular set of relative prices $(P_K/P_C)_A$; in B, there will be associated with $(\overline{W}, R)_B$ a set $(P_K/P_C)_B$. As Diagram 4.1 has been drawn, a 'switch point' intervenes; but that is not necessary. The relationship between the values, of the two commodity-capital stocks per unit of labour at the 'switch point' is known. It is

$$\frac{\dfrac{\overline{W}_{\max B}-\overline{W}_S}{R_S}}{\dfrac{\overline{W}_{\max A}-\overline{W}_S}{R_S}} = \frac{\displaystyle\sum_{i=1}^{n}\left(\frac{P_{K_i}}{P_C}\right)_S\left(\frac{K_i}{L}\right)_B}{\displaystyle\sum_{i=1}^{n}\left(\frac{P_{K_i}}{P_C}\right)_S\left(\frac{K_i}{L}\right)_A}$$

[1] D. C. Champernowne, 'The production function and the theory of capital: a comment' *Review of Economic Studies*, XXI (2), 1953–4, 112–35. Where food is understood to mean the consumption good, Champernowne's definition of a chain index of capital is (p. 116): 'The ratio of the quantities of capital in any two equipments which are both competitive at the same rate of interest (and food-wage-rate) is equal to the ratio of their costs calculated at that rate of interest (and food-wage-rate).'

[2] The value of capital per unit of labour at a 'switch point' is

$$\frac{\overline{W}_{\max}-\overline{W}_S}{R_S} = \sum_{i=1}^{n}\frac{P_{K_i}/P_C K_i}{L}$$

In terms of 'real capital', it is equal to

$$\frac{\overline{W}_{\max}-\overline{W}}{\overline{W}R} = \frac{\overline{W}_{\max}/\overline{W}-1}{R} = \sum_{1}^{n}\frac{P_{K_i}/\overline{W}P_C K_i}{L}$$

I can then write

$$\frac{\sum\limits_{i=1}^{n}\left(\frac{P_{K_i}}{P_C}\right)_A\left(\frac{K_i}{L}\right)_B}{\sum\limits_{i=1}^{n}\left(\frac{P_{K_i}}{P_C}\right)_A\left(\frac{K_i}{L}\right)_A} \equiv \frac{\sum\limits_{i=1}^{n}\left(\frac{P_{K_i}}{P_C}\right)_S\left(\frac{K_i}{L}\right)_A}{\sum\limits_{i=1}^{n}\left(\frac{P_{K_i}}{P_C}\right)_A\left(\frac{K_i}{L}\right)_A} \cdot \frac{\sum\limits_{i=1}^{n}\left(\frac{P_{K_i}}{P_C}\right)_S\left(\frac{K_i}{L}\right)_B}{\sum\limits_{i=1}^{n}\left(\frac{P_{K_i}}{P_C}\right)_B\left(\frac{K_i}{L}\right)_B} \cdot \frac{\sum\limits_{i=1}^{n}\left(\frac{P_{K_i}}{P_C}\right)_B\left(\frac{K_i}{L}\right)_B}{\sum\limits_{i=1}^{n}\left(\frac{P_{K_i}}{P_C}\right)_A\left(\frac{K_i}{L}\right)_B}$$

The term on the left is merely a Laspeyres quantity index, with the relative prices prevailing in economy A as weights. The denominator of the right-hand side is the correlative Paasche price index. The middle term in the numerator on the right-hand side is the 'switch' ratio, the commodity-

Diagram 4.1

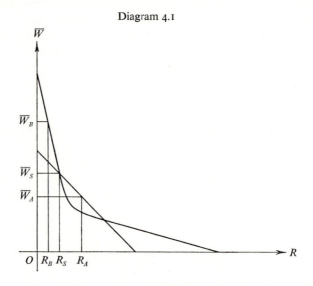

capital stocks in A and B valued at the 'switch' relative prices. The term to its left is nothing more than an expression for the Wicksell price effect in A as the rate of return is imagined to be changed from R_A to R_S. The term to its right is the comparable Wicksell price effect in B. Thus the total change in relative prices between the two economies where different rates of return hold is made up of two Wicksell price effects, each pertaining to one technique. For instance, Diagram 4.1 shows neither a positive nor a negative Wicksell effect in A. If we ignore the usual index-number ambiguities associated with 'chain indexes', the product of the left-hand and the right-hand sides of the numerator will equal the denominator and the ratio of the quantities at the 'switch point' will equal the ratio of the commodity capital stocks in 'constant prices'. The more 'switches', the more links in the 'chain'. Just as no monotonic relationship can be expected between ratios of the stocks at successive 'switch points' representing lower (higher)

Diagram 4.2

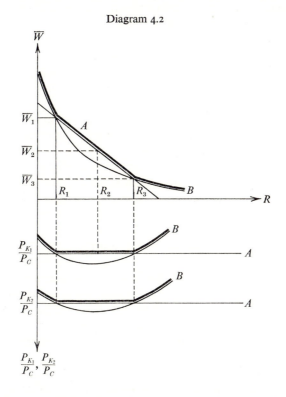

net rates of return, so no such relationship can be expected between the ratios in constant prices.[1] Even if a monotonic relationship were discovered, how could it be interpreted?[2]

To ensure that this point is completely understood, consider Diagram 4.2, which is a slight alteration to Diagram 2.7. Value technique B's stock of capital at technique A's prices, which hold when R_2 is the ruling rate of

[1] L. L. Pasinetti, 'Switches of technique and the "rate of return" in capital theory', *Economic Journal*, LXXIX, September 1969, 524 n. 1.

[2] Thus, Ferguson, after reviewing the switching controversy and arguing that what is relevant is econometric results, fails to say how such results would be interpreted. If the neoclassical postulate is, in fact, a testable hypothesis, then what determines the rate of return? See Ferguson, *Neoclassical Theory*. Hicks too has likened the 're-switching' problem to negative income effects swamping the 'Law' of Demand. See Hicks, *Capital and Growth*, 154.

profit. Clearly, at that R, A is a more profitable technique than B. The relative prices which hold at R_2 for technique A will be unchanged should either of the rates of profit R_1 and R_3 hold (since, as the linear factor price line in Diagram 4.2 implies, the factor-intensities are equal in all sectors for technique A). It can be seen from the Diagram that technique B's stock of capital, valued in the relative prices which hold for technique A, will be greater than that of technique A. Suppose now that there are three economies A, B_1 and B_2, each with the same labour force. Economy A uses technique A at the rate of profit R_2, B_1 uses technique B at a rate of profit less than R_1 and B_2 uses technique B at a rate of profit greater than R_3. A social accountant, comparing stocks of capital, *in the constant prices of economy A*, would find the stock of capital larger in B_1, where a lower rate of profit prevailed (in conformity with the standard parable) but he would also find the stock of capital larger in B_2, with a higher rate of profit (in contradiction to the standard parable).

It must be emphasized that construction of Champernowne chain indexes at 'switch points', which is what, as I have shown, social accountants strive to do, is an exercise in the comparison of *equilibrium* conditions. In the real world, of course, capital stocks can never be compared under such ideal conditions.

I turn now to real Wicksell effects. I deal with the case of a steady state of technological advance in a two-sector economy, for which the assumption of 'depreciation by obsolescence' holds. There is a given amount of homogeneous labour. The equilibrium price of a new machine equals the present value of its expected flow of quasi-rents (which under the 'depreciation by obsolescence' assumption is confidently expected to approach zero asymptotically) over its 'durability' period and also equals the compounded cost of producing it over its 'gestation' period. The life-cycle profile of the price of a piece of commodity capital, subject to a finite gestation period and to a finite durability period, determined by the rate of technological progress in which it cannot share ('depreciation by obsolescence'), is exhibited in Diagram 4.3. The stock of capital in 'use' in the capital-good sector will thus not only be a vector of various vintages of commodity capital on their way to eventual scrapping.

A *growing* inventory of machines in various stages of completion is being turned out as well. The pattern of inputs over the gestation period will consist of labour attached to different vintages of existing commodity capital. The net output of unfinished machines in the capital-good industry must be the value of the physical change in the inventories of such commodities. The value of an unfinished machine will equal its cost of production, compounded at the going net rate of return to capital since the beginning of its gestation. Thus, aside from completed vintage machines which are used in production, there is now the stock of unfinished machines also functioning as a commodity-capital input. The problem now emerges of distinguishing what is meant by the unit cost of production of the capital-good industry's output, since output is now in fact a composite of goods. As an unfinished machine progresses through its gestation period, its value must be rising over each period *at a minimum rate* equal to the

Diagram 4.3

Equilibrium price

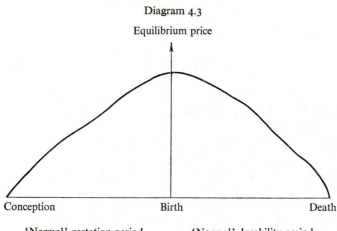

Conception   Birth   Death

'Normal' gestation period   'Normal' durability period

going net rate of return to commodity capital. It will, in general, of course, in the continuous-input point-output case, be rising at a faster rate, but the commodity capital involved in each augmentation over each period must be earning the going rate of return.[1] For the price of a finished machine to be an equilibrium price, the value of the quasi-rents – discounted at the going net rate of return over its durability period – expected to accrue to it, the current unit cost, and the cost of its production (including capital consumption) compounded at the going net rate of return, must all be the same.

The equilibrium price of a new machine at time t_0 then equals

(i) $\quad P_{K_0} = \displaystyle\int_0^t (Q_t - \overline{W}_t L_t) e^{-Rt} \, dt$

(ii) $\quad P_{K_0} = \displaystyle\int_{-t}^0 (\overline{W}_t L_t + R \sum_{v=1}^n P_{K, v_t} K_{v_t}) e^{Rt} \, dt$

(iii) $\quad P_{K_0} = \overline{W}_0 L_0 + R \sum_{v=1}^n P_{K, v_0} K_{v_0} + \delta \sum_{v=1}^n P_{K, v_0} K_{v_0}$

[1] If the value of the physical change in inventories of unfinished machines is assessed at equilibrium market prices for such goods-in-process, the commodity capital used in such accumulation is earning its equilibrium gross rate of return.

or: (i) the present value of the gross returns expected to accrue to it; (ii) the cost of the labour and various vintages of machines necessary for its production, compounded over its gestation period; and (iii) the unit cost of its production, which must include the returns which are to be earned by inventories of machines in various stages of completion. The equilibrium price an old machine of vintage v_t must equal

$$P_{K_v} = \int_v^{t\lambda} (Q_t - \overline{W}_t L_t) e^{-Rt} \, dt$$

i.e. the present value of the gross returns still expected to accrue to it. This equals

$$P_{K_v} = P_{K_0} - \int_0^v (Q_t - \overline{W}_t L_t) e^{-Rt} \, dt = \int_{-v}^0 (Q_t - \overline{W}_t L_t) e^{Rt} \, dt$$

i.e. the present value when new (equal to its cost when new), less the value of the gross returns which have accrued to it, compounded at the going net rate of return.

If there is only one technique in the production of capital goods, there will be, in general, only one set of wage rates and net rates of return which will permit the existence of such an equilibrium price. For the equilibrium wage rate and net rate of return to capital, the present value and compound cost of a new machine would be equal. For higher (lower) wage rates and lower (higher) net rates of return, there is no *a priori* reason to argue that the present values and compounded costs will be higher or lower, nor is there any reason to believe that the present values will equal the compounded costs. Different techniques, both of using and of producing the machine, would have to be adopted before the present value and compounded cost were restored to equality at the different wage rates and net rates of return to capital.

I now turn briefly to the consumption-good industry. The coefficients of technology of the consumption-good industry will be different from those of the capital-good industry, but machines last the same length of time in both. Because of differences in the coefficients, higher wage rates and lower net rates of return will involve different prices of machines in terms of consumption goods.[1]

Higher wages and lower rates of interest would probably lead to a discrepancy between the compounded cost of production and present value of machines and, hence, a disequilibrium situation. Either a new technique must be introduced or the wage rate and the net rate of return must return to equilibrium levels. There may well be a case in which no discrepancy would exist[2] and the price of capital goods in terms of con-

---

[1] See Chapter 2.
[2] This is highly unlikely. See J. Robinson, 'Economic growth and capital accumulation: a comment', *Economic Record*, XXXIII, April 1957, 106 n. 5.

sumption goods would be higher, lower, or just the same. The latter case makes no sense in this context. Considering two different economies with different wage rates and rates of return to capital, in the case where the value of the equilibrium stock of machines is higher in terms of consumption goods, then, as was shown in Chapter 2, a positive *price* Wicksell effect is recorded; where it is lower, there is a negative *price* Wicksell effect. If I was considering a *single* economy, which at some time experienced a rise in the nominal rate of saving which caused the rate of return to be lower (and I continue the highly unlikely assumption that the compounded costs of production and present values of machines remain unchanged, so that techniques are unchanged), then, omitting stability problems,[1] the rate of saving expressed in terms of consumption goods in *constant prices* would remain unchanged. In terms of current consumption-good prices, the rate of saving (accumulation) could conceivably be higher or lower. This is, I believe, what Swan meant when he argued that 'The Wicksell effect is nothing but an inventory revaluation.'[2] But in the alternative steady state sense used by Mrs Robinson, the rate of saving expressed in terms of consumption goods in constant prices must be different in the different economies.[3] Again, in the case of Mrs Robinson's 'real-capital'/labour ratio, when one is scanning over alternative one-technique steady states at lower rates of interest, the 'real-capital'/labour ratio must fall.[4]

As already indicated, it is, however, highly unlikely that the required equilibrium relationship between the compounded costs of production and present values of the new capital goods would be maintained across the steady states at different net rates of return. Wicksell argued that lower rates of return, brought about by greater savings (accumulation at full employment) would be associated with a longer 'length of production' (increased mechanization, deepening of capital, etc.), but to a lesser degree than if the capital accumulation had not been '...accompanied by an increase in wages which partly swallows it up'.[5] It is not clear that this analysis applies to a comparison of equilibrium positions or accumulation over time within a single economy. The existence of vintage pieces of capital in both industries (and unfinished machines in the capital-good industry) would appear to permit the industries to be treated as producing

---

[1] See Chapter 2.

[2] T. Swan, 'Economic growth and capital accumulation; Appendix: Notes on Capital, II, The Wicksell Effect', *Economic Record*, XXXII, November 1956, 355.

[3] Robinson, 'Economic growth and capital accumulation', 106. 'I was treating of comparisons between equilibrium positions, yet I talked about Wicksell and other "effects", which suggests a movement in time.'

[4] See Diagram 2.5 (p. 25) for an illustration of the required relationship between the price of capital goods in terms of consumption goods and wage rates.

[5] K. Wicksell, *Value, Capital and Rent* trans. S. H. Frohein (London: Allen and Unwin, 1954), 137. See also Uhr, *Economic Doctrines of Wicksell*, Ch. VI.

joint products. The consumption-good sector can be treated as producing consumption goods and machines which have 'aged' one year. The same would be true of the capital-good sector.[1] I could go further and turn the analysis into a commodity input/output rather than an industry input/output approach.[2] For my purposes, however, I believe that it is not necessary to so complicate the analysis. As I vary the net rate of return exogenously to sweep out alternate steady states with many techniques available,[3] then the findings of Cohen,[4] Sraffa,[5] etc., may well entail that at lower and lower interest rates, methods of *producing* capital goods are adopted which lead to lower (rather than higher) capital stocks in terms of consumption goods and 'real capital'.

In the discussion on 'switching' in Chapter 2, while different methods of producing the commodity capital were taken into account, no explicit mention was made of the fact that such changes would undoubtedly involve changes in the time taken to produce such capital goods. Once one takes into account the fact that capital goods take time to produce, one has taken into account the existence of many capital goods – the commodities in the various unfinished states on their way to completion. A 'switch' in technique, then, as lower rates of return are considered, might involve the production of commodities which took longer to produce. The 'real-capital'/labour ratio would rise. Equally, however, a 'switch' might involve the production of commodities with shorter gestation periods and the 'real-capital'/labour ratio would fall. In the first case the higher wage rates which would, by themselves, lead to a shortening of the time taken to produce commodities, would be more than offset by the effect of the lower rates of return. Of the two ways of producing commodities, the longer would be more profitable and the 'real-capital'/labour ratio would rise. In the second case, however, the shortening would not be offset. Of the two ways of producing the capital good, the one taking a shorter time would be more profitable and the 'real-capital'/labour ratio would fall. By 'longer' and 'shorter' is meant the weighted mean time for which

[1] See Meade, *Neo-Classical Theory*, 2nd ed., Appendix II, 123–4; Sraffa, *Production of Commodities*.

[2] See R. Stone *et al.*, *Input–Output Relationships*, 1954–66, Paper no. 3 of A Programme for Growth (London: Chapman and Hall for DAE, University of Cambridge, 1963), particularly Chapter II, dealing with industries and commodities. See also United Nations, *A System of National Accounts*, Ch. 3, The System as a Basis for Input–Output Analysis.

[3] I treat, that is, the net rate of return as a parameter '...whose exogenous variation sweeps out alternative steady states'. See R. M. Solow, 'The interest rate and transition between techniques', ed. C. H. Feinstein, *Socialism, Capitalism, and Economic Growth: Essays Presented to Maurice Dobb* (Cambridge: Cambridge University Press 1967), 30.

[4] Robinson, *Accumulation of Capital*, 2nd ed., 109: A curiosum attributed to R. Cohen

[5] Sraffa, *Production of Commodities*, Part III.

labour is invested over the gestation of a commodity. Clearly the value of such a stream of labour, valued at ruling wage rates and compounded at ruling rates of interest, can rise or fall as the ratio of the wage rate to the rate of return is altered. For further variations in the wage-rate/rate-of-return ratio, it is entirely possible that the original method of production, which was abandoned for a 'shorter' one, will itself return to profitable use. This 'reswitching' can not only occur with respect to the production of one particular capital good, but can be true for the economic system as a whole, as was shown in Chapter 2.[1]

It is clear that, once unfinished commodities, which reflect the fact that commodities take time to produce, are brought into the argument, then such inventories of commodities can be treated in the same way as finished capital goods. Rates of return must be earned on them as well, and such returns are part of the unit prices at which finished commodities are being sold. There is no need either to concern ourselves about when the original labour was invested, or to look at the capital-good sector as, for instance, a host of subsectors, each supplying the other with a different kind of commodity capital one period older. Of course, failure to break the capital-good sector up in that way involves the problem of joint production, but I have already pointed out that a method for handling such problems is known. Once I treat unfinished goods as capital goods, the analysis in Chapter 2 follows. It requires no further elaboration.

Inventories of goods-in-process thus fit in. They are 'uncompleted capital goods'. Inventories of final goods or raw materials, though they can easily be included in the analysis of Chapter 5, do not really fit in, being ruled out by the assumption of steady-state equilibrium with no uncertainty.

[1] L. Pasinetti, 'Changes in the rate of profit and switches in techniques', Paradoxes in Capital Theory: A Symposium, *Quarterly Journal of Economics*, LXXV, November 1966. Robinson and Naqvi have summarized as follows: 'In a forward switch, where the more mechanized technique becomes eligible at a lower rate of profit, there is a *positive real Wicksell effect;* a backward switch is a *negative real Wicksell effect*. A higher value of capital in terms of net output for a given technique associated with a lower rate of profit is a *positive price Wicksell effect*. A value of capital for a given technique invariant to the rate of profit (as in the labour theory of value case) is a *neutral price Wicksell effect*. A lower value of capital associated with a lower rate of profit is a *negative price Wicksell effect*... Then we can say that a backward switch arises from the less mechanized technique having a price effect which is substantially more negative (or less positive) compared with that of the more mechanized technique, to bring about a negative real effect. This terminology, perhaps, was not well chosen. There are no "effects" in this story, for nothing happens. We are merely carrying out comparisons of possible equilibrium positions.' J. Robinson and K. A. Naqvi, 'The badly behaved production function', *Quarterly Journal of Economics*, LXXXI, November 1967, 582.

4.7 Conclusion

In this chapter, I have discussed some of the major theoretical difficulties in measuring the stock of capital. There is one which I have not covered – the problem of 'quality change' – and I deal with that in Chapter 6. The 'reswitching' controversy, has however, surprisingly little relevance to what I want to say. In the next chapter I shall be comparing economic systems in steady-state growth at unchanging rates of return to capital. I shall not need to discuss an aggregate stock of capital at all. I shall deal with capital as a list of Physical Things, and I shall show that, even then, when technical progress is occurring, the traditional neoclassical analysis is wrong. The proponents of the 'switching' problem have correctly brushed the neoclassical cases of one and two commodities aside not only as being unrealistic but as incapable of generalization. I want to show that even in those worlds the neoclassical analysis is invalid. The 'switching' controversy has not denied the ability to construct estimates of the aggregate stock of capital under equilibrium conditions. It is merely that the aggregate would appear to be useless when it is derived. I shall also show that this is not quite right. I shall show that at times aggregation is useful, but that the aggregate cannot be used in the manner traditionally believed.

5

THE MEASUREMENT OF CHANGES IN
TECHNOLOGY AND CAPITAL*

5.1 Introduction

In Chapter 2, I dealt with some of the difficulties which are associated with the traditional concept of capital as a factor of production. It will be remembered that if one stays in a one commodity world, however unrealistic one may say that assumption is, or if one stays in a two commodity world – one consumption and one capital good, – the neoclassical analysis remains relatively unscathed by certain attacks on it. This is not meant to imply that the remaining assumptions underlying the analysis – savings automatically invested in a world postulated to be always in full employment equilibrium – are defensible. Most of the neoclassical literature dealing with the measurement of technical progress, which I reviewed in Chapter 3, assumes that the validity of the simple analysis, not particularly comforting in its own right, carries over into a world of technical change. This chapter shows that such a view is incorrect. What I want to do in this chapter, is to show that even under a set of assumptions where neoclassical analysis is most at home, its central proposition, that a distinction can be drawn and measured between commodity-capital accumulation and technical change, is without logical and theoretical foundation.

The central proposition of this study may now be stated. In a world of one or many commodities, when technical progress is occurring and the correct theoretical treatment of it is followed, the conception of commodities as inputs in terms of Physical Things is no longer possible. This is the basic fallacy in the neoclassical analysis. In moving from the static to the dynamic world of technical change, the traditional treatment neglects the fact that commodity *inputs* are capable of being produced with ever increasing efficiency. In the world of technical change, the fact that commodities (Physical Things, which are produced by the economic system) are

---

* Part of this chapter appears in a much shortened version as 'Professor Read and the measurement of total factor productivity', *Canadian Journal of Economics*, I, May 1968, 359–67. See also Read, 'Measure of total factor productivity'.

not primary inputs like labour and natural agents, becomes clear. The neglect of this fundamental point invalidates the neoclassical analysis.

Economists are accustomed to writing a technical relationship as $F(x_1, x_2, ..., x_n) = 0$, where x_1 to x_i are outputs and x_j to x_n are inputs. The parameters of the function F specify, it is said, the technical relationship. The nature of the outputs and inputs is precisely described in physical terms, e.g. so many loaves of bread per hour, a man hour of a baker with three years' experience, a machine hour of bread-making machine type XYZ, and so forth. Not all the physical characteristics are economically important. Some are significant in determining the prices which would be paid for the outputs and inputs. Some are not. The age of the machine may well affect its price, while its colour would be neither here nor there – unless the baker had a violent aversion to flaming red. Having described the machine in terms of its exact physical characteristics, one need not be concerned with the way in which it is made, in a world of statics when no technical change is occurring in machine-making. When one asks how much of the machine to use, one is concerned with its price, and only then will its conditions of production become extremely important. Yet economists have always appreciated the fact that capital goods are man- (and natural agent-) made. We might show the machine, then, as representing, standing for, or embodying 'original factors of production' – *if only we could*. All attempts to do this either (i) assume what is to be determined, or (ii) founder on the famous problem of trying to find out how much machine was required to produce so much machine was required to produce so much machine and so on – the problem of the infinite historical regress. Thus, one finds in the literature the assumption that machines are produced only by men, or that the time processes of production are known and are convergent. Moreover, such characteristics of the machine cannot be represented as a single quantity without the use of the rate of return to capital, which obviates the use of such a quantity for the theoretical determination of the rate of return. Furthermore, in the static context of the short run, the number of machines and their physical characteristics can be taken as data and no further prying into the nature of the capital goods is necessary.

In the dynamic context of technical change, a dramatic alteration in our thinking is required. As Harrod warns us, and as his quoted remarks in Chapter 3 illustrate, dynamics deals not with levels but with rates of change. Thus I need not ask: What are the primary inputs of production embodied in machines? I need ask rather: What is the rate of change of the primary inputs embodied in the growing number of machines or in general, commodity-capital goods? If I can find such a rate (or rates) of change then, in the dynamic environment of technical change, I can always reduce the growing amounts of commodity capital inputs to their primary input counterparts. In that case, it will be obviously illegitimate to treat the growing commodity capital flows and stocks as Physical Things, i.e. as inputs in their own right. Deeper questions about dynamic economic systems may then come to the fore.

Stationary and progressive economies may be contrasted by defining a stationary economy as one in which output or real net income per unit of labour input remains unchanged, and a progressive economy as one in which output or real net income per unit of labour input is growing. In an early work, Meade outlined three basic reasons why an economy would be progressive. They were (i) inventions, (ii) increasing returns to scale, and (iii) 'the use of a greater proportion of the other factors of production to labour, a phenomenon of a state in which either the population is diminishing or capital is being accumulated at a greater rate than the population is increasing'.[1]

In his later works on the subject, Meade states: 'An economy can grow for three reasons: first, because net savings are being made out of current income so that the stock of capital instruments of production is growing; second, because the working population is growing; and third, because technical progress allows more and more output to be produced by a given amount of resources as time passes.'[2]

By assumption, Meade excluded the influence on output of increasing returns to scale. When the working population is constant and no new ways of doing things are emerging, economic growth, as defined by Meade, can only occur if the ratio of scarce natural resources and man-made instruments to human effort increases. Such a situation entails, because of a falling rate of interest, a continual shift of the system from one path of steady-equilibrium expansion to another. As indicated in Chapter 2, in static conditions, higher commodity-capital/labour ratios may or may not be associated with higher ratios of real-wage rates to net rates of return. Certainly there were no compelling reasons to suggest that higher ratios of 'real capital' to labour would prevail. It was also pointed out in Chapter 3 that falling net rates of return require either perfect malleability of capital goods or perfect foresight. However, the case of greatest interest is that of an economy which is progressive due to technological advance, for it is in this context that problems associated with the treatment of commodity capital as an input arise.

If one conceives of the primary inputs in the process of economic production of man-made instruments and human effort, one surely falls

[1] J. E. Meade, *The Rate of Interest in a Progressive State* (London: Macmillan, 1933), 1-2.
[2] Meade, *Neo-Classical Theory of Economic Growth*, 1. These three reasons are repeated again in his *Growing Economy*, 23.

short of deeper analysis. Man-made instruments, heuristically speaking, represent, and have correctly been said to represent, in traditional economic theory, 'embodied' human effort in some sense, and deeper analysis of the process of economic production must 'reduce' man-made instruments to something like such terms.

5.2   The measurement of the rate of technical advance

Assume for simplicity that the economy we are describing is an equilibrium one-commodity economy, with no depreciation and with a homogeneous labour force. Then our simple social accounting identity for the economy would appear, following the notation of Chapter 2, as

$$Q \equiv \overline{WL} + RK \tag{5.1}$$

Taking derivatives with respect to time and rearranging terms, I have

$$q - [\alpha l + \beta k] \equiv \alpha \overline{w} + \beta r \equiv t \tag{5.2}$$

where, as indicated in Chapter 2, the symbol q means $\dfrac{1}{Q}\dfrac{dQ}{dt}$, etc. As I indicated in Chapter 3, this is the format in which most measures of technological change have been cast. The question is: How should k and r be assessed? In terms of commodity (prices) or real capital (prices)? How should measures of technological change be constructed?

Suppose I turn for the moment to a world which includes 'land' and where the social accounts are

$$Q \equiv \overline{WL} + RP_N N \tag{5.1a}$$

where N represents a stock of natural agents (e.g. land), P_N the price of a natural agent (an acre of land), and R the ruling rate of return. Then RP_N represents the rental (per acre per year) earned by the natural agents. When neutral technical change is occurring, W and RP_N would be rising at the same rate. If R is constant, W and P_N would be rising at the same rate as the technology is advancing. Thus

$$q \equiv \alpha \overline{w} + \beta(r + p_N) \equiv t$$

Consider now a world whose social accounts are

$$Q \equiv \overline{WL} + RP_K K + RP_N N \tag{5.1b}$$

where K is a stock of commodity capital made up of the same commodity as Q, so that $P_K \equiv 1$. Suppose neutral technical change is occurring and L, K and N are constant. The rate of saving is zero. The wage rate, the rental on natural agents and the rental (i.e. RP_K) on commodity capital will be rising at a rate equal to the rate of technical change. A contradiction is now seen. The rate of return is constant and the price of commodity capital must be rising along with the price of natural agents. But the price of a commodity as an input cannot differ from the price of the same commodity as an output. A rise in the price of the commodity as an output is, however, a monetary phenomenon which I have excluded by assumption. The commodity is the numéraire and therefore always $P_K \equiv 1$. How then can the value of the stock of commodities be rising along with the value of the stock of natural agents? If the rate of return were rising along with $\overline{W}$, then the price of natural agents would be constant. Now another contradiction arises. Even though there can be no change in commodity capital per unit of labour and land, borrowings and lendings on consumption account can take place. Should the rate of return begin to rise, the borrowing and lending activity will cause the price of natural agents to rise and the rate of return to remain constant. The price of the stock of commodity capital must also rise – which, as I have shown, leads to a contradiction. Under the assumptions of the model, a concept of technical change, with commodity inputs produced by the system *treated as if they were identical to nonproducible inputs like labour and natural agents*, is a logically impossible construct.

When commodity capital per unit of labour and land can be increased, with neutral technical change going on at a *constant* rate of saving, the rise in the physical stock of commodity capital takes the place of the rise in the price of the stock and is logically equivalent to the rise in the price of the stock of natural agents. The logical impossibility of treating commodity capital as a non-producible input is blurred over in the traditional analysis by the presence of accumulation in the one-commodity context. The accumulation is clearly, however, a consequence of the technical change, not a contribution to the growth of output *in addition* to the technical change. It is logically impossible, then, to distinguish between technical change and commodity-capital accumulation in the one commodity context.

If technical change is examined in the two-commodity context, the blur is removed and the contradiction involved in the neoclassical analysis is more clearly revealed. I show this later in this chapter.

Technical change also takes the form of *improved* outputs and inputs. I examine this case in Chapter 6: it is complex but not fundamentally different from the case of technical change with accumulation of commodities whose physical characteristics remain unchanged. The complexity arises because there is a need to distinguish between changes in price and changes in quantity when 'new, improved, better' capital and consumption goods are introduced. Once the intricacies are seen through, this case falls neatly into its place in the general scheme of the analysis advanced in this chapter.

I shall now examine the nature of technical change more rigorously.

5.3 A one-commodity model

I begin with the one-commodity model developed by Meade,[1] together with all his assumptions, and then consider his two treatments of technological advance. For the moment I shall ignore the assessment of commodity capital used up (i.e. depreciation) in the process of economic production. Described differently, Meade's steady-state-equilibrium-growth model depicts an economy in Mrs Robinson's golden age (not necessarily consumption-maximizing golden age) or an economy operating along Harrod's not necessarily welfare-optimum steady growth path. Reproducing Meade's model in terms of my social accounting identity, in which the measurement procedure picks up only equilibrium values, and, assuming that the labour input is constant, I have, from the left-hand side viewpoint of identity 5.2:

$$q - \beta k = t_{NNC} \qquad (5.3)$$

and from the right-hand side of identity 5.2:

$$\alpha \bar{w} + \beta r = t_{NNC} \qquad (5.4)$$

where t_{NNC} stands for the growth rate of neoclassical technological progress.

If I follow Meade's steady-state assumptions,[2] namely that the growth rate of the stock of commodity capital is equal to the growth rate of

---

[1] Meade, *Neo-Classical Theory of Economic Growth*, Ch. 4. I choose Meade because he states the neoclassical case with great lucidity and frankness.

[2] Meade begins with a linear homogeneous production function with unitary elasticity of substitution between labour and commodity capital, subject to technological advance posited neutral in the Hicks sense; that is, it does not alter the relative marginal physical products of the inputs, for given combinations of the inputs. The assumption that, in perfect competition, inputs are paid their marginal products and that average propensities to save out of factor incomes are constant, generates a steady-state configuration, such that the rate of growth of the commodity capital will be equal to the rate of growth of output. That is, given

$$Q = Q(L, K; T), \quad \dot{Q} = Q_K \dot{K} + dQ^T$$

where Q_K is the marginal physical product of capital and dQ^T is the incremental output arising from an advance in technology. Then

$$Q_K = \frac{Q e_K}{K}$$

where e_K is the constant partial production elasticity of the capital input. Thus,

$$\frac{\dot{Q}}{Q} = e_K \frac{\dot{K}}{K} + \frac{dQ^T}{Q}$$

output ($q = k$), and that the net rate of return to capital remains unchanged ($r = 0$), then the identities collapse to

$$q(1 - \beta) = t_{NNC} \qquad (5.5)$$

or

$$\alpha q = t_{NNC}$$

and

$$\alpha \overline{w} = t_{NNC}$$

The measures of the growth rate of technological progress which result, t_{NNC}, I call neoclassical. The important characteristic of them is that commodity inputs are assessed as commodity outputs. No account is taken of the obvious fact that the economy, as the state of technology advances, is able to reproduce each commodity input more efficiently than before.

This is the essential point made by Professor Read in the paper I mentioned in the preface. Precisely the same point was made by Pasinetti when he stated that traditional methods of measuring technological change 'have neglected an important characteristic of capital – that it is reproducible and that its process of production is also subject to technical change'.[1] The neoclassical measures of technological progress seek, as was pointed out in Chapter 3, to distinguish between accumulation of commodity capital and technological progress. I show that, when commodity capital is assessed as commodity capital, the distinction is a shallow and illegitimate one. When commodity capital is assessed as 'real capital' a more useful and deeper distinction can be drawn.

I shall replace the commodity-capital input in Meade's model by its

Hence, the rate of technological change à la Meade,

$$\frac{dQ^T}{Q} \equiv t_{NNC} = \frac{dQ}{Q} - e_K \frac{dK}{K}$$

is equivalent to that represented in identity (5.2). Assume further that $\Delta K = sQ$, so that

$$K(t) = s \int_0^t Q(t)\,dt = sQ_0 \int_0^t e^{qt}\,dt = sQ_0 \frac{e^{qt}}{q}\bigg]_0^t = -\frac{sQ_0}{q}[1 - e^{qt}]$$

such that

$$\dot{K}(t) = \frac{sQ_0}{q} - e^{qt}q \quad \text{and} \quad \frac{\dot{K}(t)}{K(t)} = q$$

Hence, the output/capital ratio is a constant, determined from the steady-state properties of the model. See Chapter 2, p. 19, n. 2.

[1] L. L. Pasinetti, 'On concepts and measures of changes in productivity', *The Review of Economics and Statistics*, XLI, August 1959, 270–82. Unfortunately, Pasinetti's approach leads to the result that technical change would be evidenced even when none was in fact occurring, and was correspondingly criticized by Solow. See R. M. Solow, 'Comment', *ibid.* and L. L. Pasinetti, 'Reply', *ibid.* This point arises again in Chapter 8 below.

'real capital' counterpart. Mrs Robinson says, to repeat the definition given in Chapter 2:

> We can divide the value in terms of commodities of the stock of capital in any economy by the wage per man-hour in terms of commodities ruling in that economy and so obtain the quantity of capital in terms of labour time.[1]

and, in setting up her two sector model of technological progress:

> The physical cost of an outfit of equipment for the consumption-good sector consists in a certain amount of labour-time and basic-plant-time; when a given rate of profit is ruling uniformly throughout an economy there is a determinate pattern of normal prices (governed by costs of production including profit at the ruling rate on the capital involved) which can be expressed in terms of labour-time. By the *real cost* of a piece of consumption–sector equipment we mean its price when new in terms of labour-time, at the ruling rate of profit.[2]

It is clear from these remarks that the real cost of the stock of commodity capital at any time for an economy in golden-age equilibrium is not just the 'original' labour cost 'embodied' in the capital goods but is such 'original' labour time compounded over the 'period of production' at the going net rate of return to commodity capital.[3] Within the context of Meade's model, which I have adopted as a reference point, the kind of technological advance occurring ensures that, in equilibrium, the 'period of production' and the net rate of return to commodity capital remain unchanged. Hence it is possible to arrive at an assessment of commodity capital in 'real capital' terms by dividing the stock of commodity capital expressed in terms of commodities, by the wage rate, expressed in terms of commodities, such that, as I show in Chapter 2

$$J \equiv \frac{K}{W/P} \tag{5.6}$$

and
$$j \equiv k+p-w \equiv k-(w-p) \tag{5.7}$$

The conditions of the model entail that[4]

$$q = w-p$$

or
$$j = k-q \tag{5.8}$$

[1] Robinson, *Accumulation of Capital*, 121.
[2] J. Robinson, 'A model of technical progress', *Essays in the theory of Economic Growth* (London: Macmillan, 1962), p. 89.
[3] In Chapter 2 above, I quote Samuelson as suggesting that Mrs Robinson's 'real capital' was a labour theory of value construct. This, as the above analysis shows, is clearly incorrect.
[4] That the rate of growth of the commodity-wage rate is equal to the rate of growth of output per unit of labour input follows from the assumption of constancy in the partial production elasticities of labour; *viz.*, $WL/PQ \equiv \alpha$, a constant, entails $w+l = p+q$, or $w-p = q-l$.

Hence, substituting the values for j from (5.8) for k in (5.3), I obtain

$$t_R = q - \beta(k - q) \qquad (5.9)$$

or
$$t_R = q$$

which, as Meade points out, is equivalent to the rate of technological progress (i.e. the rate of growth of output per labour input) as defined by Harrod and Robinson.[1]

Before evaluating the Harrod measure of the rate of technological advance, I would point out that it is extremely important for what follows to note that it can also be derived much more rigorously. Moreover, and I submit that this is fundamental, it can be derived *without* any reference to prices. Harrodian measures of the rate of technological change can be derived without expressing the stock of capital in terms of consumption goods. As will be shown, I *need* never refer to an aggregate commodity-capital input though I may find it useful to do so. What will be critically important in what follows is the fact that commodity-capital production is characterized by interdependence of the Leontief–Sraffa type. *The essential point about commodity capital as an input in the process of economic production is that it is reproducible.*[2] The meanings which various authors have attributed to technological advance clearly imply that, if technological advance has occurred over any given period, the current flow of an economy's output must be producible with fewer inputs than would have been necessary in an earlier period. A measure is sought which assesses the increased efficiency of the primary inputs possessed by the economy. We should attempt to eliminate from the calculations any increased intermediate inputs which the economy, because of technological advance, had been able to associate with the primary inputs to produce the greater flow of output. In attempting to assess the increased efficiency of the primary inputs of the economy, due to technological progress, it would clearly be a mistake to fail to account for the enhanced efficiency of such primary inputs in their ability to reproduce the growing amount of intermediate inputs. We should seek a measure of technological progress which accounts for the increased efficiency of those inputs in the economic system which are primary to it, that is, for the inputs which are non-reproducible (non-

---

[1] Meade, *Neo-classical Theory of Economic Growth*, Ch. 6, An Alternative treatment of technological progress.

[2] The assertion that labour is also reproducible is adequately dealt with by Kaldor in his 'The controversy on the theory of capital', *Essays on Value and Distribution* (London: Duckworth, 1960). As Kuenne argues: 'If capital goods are augmentable factors of production, they must consist in final analysis of nonaugmentable factors, the latter being defined as goods either fixed in amount or following laws of variation in quantity essentially non-economic in character.' R. E. Kuenne, *The Theory of General Economic Equilibrium* (Princeton: Princeton University Press, 1963), 229.

augmentable). Within the context of the assumptions of this book, in measuring technological advance, I shall be concerned with only those inputs which are primary (that is, non-reproducible) to the economic system. Again, the important question, to which this study attempts to provide an answer, is: Is there a non-labour primary input in the process of economic production?

It follows from what has been said that a more rigorous way of assessing the Harrod measure of the rate of technological advance should be possible. The neoclassical measure asks: Given the rate of technological progress, what is the rate of change of the primary and intermediate inputs required to maintain the rate of growth of output? The Harrod measure asks, *in addition*: Given the rate of technological progress, what is the rate of change of the *primary and intermediate inputs* required to maintain the rate of growth of the *intermediate inputs*? It follows that a measure of the rate of Harrod technological progress is obtained by simultaneous solution of these two questions. Thus I should write

$$q - \beta(k - t_R) \equiv t_R$$

or,
$$(1 - \beta)q \equiv (1 - \beta)t_R$$

or,
$$q \equiv t_R$$

The transformation being wrought is simple but fundamental. Instead of writing, along with Meade, $Q = Q(L, K; T)$ I write instead

$$Q = Q(L, K/T_R; T_R)$$

As I have indicated, economists in the past have made great efforts to describe and measure K/T_R, i.e. capital, rigorously in terms of 'original factors'. Such effort has been largely in vain, the reason being, I am convinced, that the question has always been put in the static context. If the production function as rewritten is differentiated, then, given the steady-state assumptions,
$$q - \beta(k - t_R) \equiv t_R$$

and
$$q \equiv t_R$$

In the dynamic context, we can then rigorously capture a concept which escapes us at the static level.

The same measure of the rate of technological advance results through this simultaneous solution for it as that which resulted when a measure of the growth rate of 'real capital', as defined by Mrs Robinson, was substituted for the rate of change of commodity capital in identity (5.9). It follows that an unambiguous (within the confines of the present model) assessment of Joan Robinson's 'real capital' becomes operational. This can be immediately seen by substituting the derived measure of the rate of Harrod technological progress in identity (5.10) back into the commodity capital input forms in (5.9), to derive the growth rate of real capital. That is,

$$j = k - q = 0 \qquad (5.11)$$

as we have already seen from identity (5.10).

This result is, of course, not surprising, since the Harrod measure of the rate of technological advance and of the growth rate of 'real-capital' input are simultaneously derived. As I shall show, this result is perfectly general, no matter how many sectors or how many heterogeneous commodity-capital inputs the system is postulated to possess. Individual-sector Harrod measures of the rate of technological progress, and individual-sector 'approximations' to the growth rate of 'real-capital' inputs in their respective production processes, may be derived. This is the real meaning and achievement of Read's suggested variant for the measurement of 'total factor productivity'. As Read was working towards his Harrod measure of the rate of technological change, he simultaneously hit upon a way of quantifying and making operational changes in 'real capital'.[1]

Within the confines of the first simple model in which it has been presented, the Harrod alternative to the neoclassical measure of the rate of technological advance would not appear to have great advantages. If it is assumed that the ratio of the working to the non-working population is constant, it follows that the Harrod measure of the rate of technological change yields not only a measure of the allowable non-inflationary increase in money wage rates,[2] but also a measure of the growth rate of real-wage rates which permits capitalists to enjoy an equi-proportionate rise in their real incomes. While the neoclassical measure and the assessment of the capital input as commodity-capital input would seem to be useful for drawing out the distinction between 'shifts of and movements along production functions', it must also be remembered that the changes in technique under examination are changes in intermediate/primary input ratios. The Harrod measure permits a much more fundamental distinction between improvements in the efficiency with which primary inputs are utilized in the process of economic production and changes in primary input combinations in response to changing relative prices of primary

---

[1] In fairness, what I have called the Harrod measure of the rate of technological advance should be christened the Harrod–Robinson–Read measure, since Read first developed his measurement method in 1951. I have not been able to find it explicitly drawn out in earlier literature. It is, of course, implicit, appearing, as the rate of increase in output per unit of labour input when technological progress is neutral, in Harrod's early Essay and in his *Towards a Dynamic Economics*, and in Mrs Robinson's definition of neutral progress as well.

[2] This was Read's major concern. See Read, 'Measure of total factor productivity'. It is the capital theoretic aspects of his measure which intrigue me.

inputs. All these claims or assertions may be viewed sceptically because they flow from the extremely simple assumptions of the model, in which the Harrod measure of technological progress and the measure of 'real capital' are developed. They suffice, however, to show that an attempt to 'go in behind' the façade of commodity capital in the process of economic production may yield some interesting results. At this stage of the analysis, however, I shall point out how the neoclassical conception of technological progress and the 'capital input' perform less satisfactorily than do the Harrod counterparts, as more complex questions are put to them.

5.4   The conventional nature of commodity capital

Professor Johnson has argued that the concept of labour as a factor of production is no longer appropriate in the formulation of contemporary economic theory.[1] This suggestion implies that, for certain purposes, the list of items making up the Who's Who of the stock of commodity capital is largely conventional and should be increased by adding human capital. I return to Meade's model and now assume that there are two such economies, alike in every respect save that, at some time in the past, just as they both attained their respective steady paths, one entered with a larger stock of commodity capital than the other. Since that time, the rates of improvements in techniques have been the same and the labour input in both economies is constant. Different levels of wage rates, of outputs and rates of return to capital prevail, such that the measured partial elasticities of productions are not the same in each economy. Then, the social accounting identities in neoclassical terms for the two economies will appear as

$$\text{Economy 1} \quad t_{NNC_1} \equiv q_1 - \beta_1 k_1$$
$$\equiv \alpha_1 q_1 \tag{5.12}$$
$$\text{Economy 2} \quad t_{NNC_2} \equiv \alpha_2 q_2$$

By assumption, the same rate of improvements in techniques prevails in both economies. Hence $q_1 = q_2$. However, also by assumption, the partial elasticities of production with respect to labour are different. It follows that

$$t_{NNC_1} \neq t_{NNC_2}$$

This seems to be a meaningless result. From the assumptions of the model, however, it follows that $j_1 = j_2$ and that therefore $t_{R_1} = t_{R_2}$.

This result is more meaningful. I shall now investigate these results a little further. First, is the model I have set out a possible one? Meade's

[1] H. G. Johnson, 'Towards a general theory of capital accumulation', *The Canadian Quandary* (Toronto: McGraw-Hill, 1963).

assumption of unity elasticity of substitution implies that the partial elasticities of production of the labour and commodity-capital inputs remain unchanged. In the two economies being compared, however, the partial elasticities of production in one are different from those holding in the other. The two economies have steady states, alike in terms of the rate at which new unbiased techniques are coming forward, but different in terms of *levels* of output, real-wage rates, net rates of return to capital and – unless through sheer chance – different, under the assumptions of the model, with respect to the partial elasticities of production revealed by the equilibrium social accounts. The particular partial elasticities of production of any economy in steady-state equilibrium as depicted by Meade will be solely an historical accident. If one such economy exists, an infinite number of other such economies may be said to exist, all with the same unbiased growth rate in techniques of production. For each of these economies, a different rate of technological advance would be revealed by their respective equilibrium social accounts when the capital input was assessed in commodity-capital terms. With the capital input assessed in 'real-capital' terms, all the rates of technological advance revealed are identical.[1] I return to Professor Johnson. By suggesting that much of the real-wages bill in any economy really represents part of the gross returns to 'commodity capital' so defined as to include human capital, he is, from the viewpoint of this essay, merely playing the social accountant's game of deciding what does and what does not constitute the Who's Who of goods making up the stock of commodity capital. For the analysis of the characteristics of economies in steady states, this represents no advance in our understanding of what is the capital input in the economic process.[2]

[1] I have always been somewhat surprised that no one has spotted this brittle conventionality of the neoclassical measure before. The reason is, I think, that the steady-state assumption is too often used for purposes other than the one for which it is designed, i.e. comparative study of dynamic equilibria.

[2] Professor Johnson's emphasis on human-capital accumulation is a salutary reminder that new and more complex machines cannot be expected to earn a steady rate of profit unless they are manned by better trained and educated men. The whole of national income can be regarded as returns to capital, commodity and human. The human-capital component of the stock of capital will, in the standard analysis, be treated in exactly the same way as commodity capital. Thus, I may write, for the standard analysis,

$$Q = Q(K_H, K_C; T),$$

where K_H represents the stock of human capital and K_C the stock of commodity capital. Then

$$q - [\beta_H k_H + \beta_C k_C] = t_{NNC},$$

and, since in the steady state $\beta_H + \beta_C = 1$ and $k_H = k_C = q$, t_{NNC} is zero. This meaningless result is the extreme case of comparing steady-state economies in which the partial elasticity of production of labour is less and less, eventually approaching zero. The alternative advocated here is

$$Q = Q(K_H/T_R, K_C/T_R; T_R),$$

As a final word on this first point, the particular partial elasticities of production which the equilibrium social accounts will reveal for the two economies will also be a function, as Mrs Robinson has shown, of the particular spectrum of techniques open to entrepreneurs in the two economies and the different propensities to save out of net returns to capital holding in the two economies. Again, it would appear to be incorrect for such *static* happen-stances to affect measured current rates of technological advance.

I have shown that the neoclassical assessment of the rate of technological advance in the context of simple Meade-type models is conventional and changes when the most trivial alternations in conventions, or classifications, are adopted. All assessments of what is the capital input in the economic process must, of course, be conventional. Clearly, however, the need is for an assessment which is invariant to trivial reclassifications and changes in conventions and which, therefore, holds out the promise of more powerful analysis.

I wish to reiterate the importance of this finding. If by a steady rate of technological advance we mean that, whatever comparative-statics pattern of rising real-wage rates and constant net rates of return to commodity capital may hold, new equilibrium techniques are being adopted over a standard time period at an unchanging rate, and if we also assume that the number (and composition) of labour inputs is growing at a steady rate equal to zero, then I should argue that, in different equilibrium positions (when the net rates of return to commodity capital, the ratio of commodity capital to commodity output, or the composition of labour differ from one equilibrium position to another), the growth rate of output and the rate of technological advance must be the *same* for all these equilibrium steady states. Yet this is precisely what does not hold in general for the neoclassical case.

For my paraphrase of Meade's model to be exact, I assume a unitary elasticity of substitution. In such a case, if entrepreneurs (for example) should disturb one steady-state equilibrium by attempting to carry out accumulation at a higher-than-equilibrium rate, then, the commodity-wage rate rises, the net rate of return to capital falls, and the commodity-capital/labour ratio rises. Given the assumption about the elasticity of

which yields $\quad q - [\beta_H(k_H - t_R) + \beta_O(k_O - t_R)] = t_R,$

or $\quad\quad\quad q[1 - (\beta_H + \beta_O)] = t_R[1 - (\beta_H + \beta_O)],$

or $\quad\quad\quad\quad q = t_R,$

as in the text. Thus, and this is significant, even though by definition there is no labour input in this limiting case, the Harrod–Robinson rate of technical change is positive and it remains possible to distinguish a zero rate of change of 'real capital' and the existence of a primary input more fundamental than the stock of commodity capital, human or otherwise.

102

substitution, the proportionate rise in the commodity-capital/labour ratio is equal to the proportionate rise in the ratio of the real-wage rate to the net rate of return to capital. There is, of course, not the slightest reason to expect technology to be described by a Cobb–Douglas production function. Thus in Meade's case, when the economy settles down to a new equilibrium steady state, the equilibrium partial elasticities of production may well, in the now steady state, differ from the old. So, given the rate of growth of the labour force, if the rate of growth of output were unchanged, then Meade would *have* to find that the steady-state rate of technological advance was higher or lower in the new steady state, depending upon whether the observed equilibrium partial elasticity of output with respect to labour had increased or decreased. Similarly, given the rate of growth of the labour force, *if* the recorded rate of technological advance were unchanged, then the recorded rate of growth of output would *have* to be higher or lower, depending upon whether the observed equilibrium partial elasticity of output with respect to labour had decreased or increased. These results are obviously contrary to what must be meant by a steady rate of technological advance. They are, as well, surely contrary to one's theoretical senses. Such conventionally brittle results are not obtained when commodity capital is replaced by its 'real capital' counterpart in the two equilibrium positions.

In one equilibrium steady state, I have

$$q_1 \equiv \beta_1 k_1 + t_{NNC_1}$$

In any other equilibrium state where the observed equilibrium partial elasticities of production, while still adding to one (to retain the constant-returns-to-scale argument), are different, for whatever reason,[1] I would have

$$q_2 \equiv \beta_2 k_2 + t_{NNC_2}$$

If $q_1 = q_2$, then $k_1 = k_2$ and I would have

$$\beta_1 k_1 + t_{NNC_1} = \beta_2 k_2 + t_{NNC_2}$$

or

$$(\beta_1 - \beta_2)k \equiv t_{NNC_2} - t_{NNC_1}$$

from whence I get

$$k = \frac{t_{NNC_2} - t_{NNC_1}}{\beta_1 - \beta_2}$$

Since, by assumption, the growth rate of the commodity-capital/labour ratio is unchanged, if the partial elasticity of output with respect to labour were higher, so that $\beta_2 < \beta_1$, t_{NNC_2} would have to be greater than t_{NNC_1}

---

[1] Using Meade's assumption of unitary elasticity of substitution, the reason would have to be a once-over burst of non-neutral advance in Meade's sense. Dropping the assumption about substitution, the changed elasticities could arise because of a change in the role of saving or a burst of neutral advance in Meade's sense.

by a proportionate amount required to prevent k from changing. Conversely, if it were the case that $t_{NNC_2} = t_{NNC_1}$, I would have

$$q_1 - \beta_1 k_1 \equiv q_2 - \beta_2 k_2$$

As I have shown $\qquad\qquad \alpha_1 q_1 \equiv \alpha_2 q_2$

This implies that where $\alpha_2 \lessgtr \alpha_1$, then $q_2 \lessgtr q_1$, as I have said. As I have argued, I find this a meaningless economic result for, given comparative steady-state systems in which the rates of technological change are the same, it is meaningless to admit the possibility of different equilibrium rates of growth of output and commodity capital and therefore different rates of growth of output and commodity capital per unit of labour input.

If two economies, with the same (constant) labour force and the same steady-state proportionate rate of growth of output, have different capital-partial-elasticities of production, then, in the traditional analysis, commodity-capital accumulation is said to play a relatively more (or less) important role than technical change in the growth of output. Where the capital elasticity is larger, the rate of technical advance is smaller and the failure of the rate of return to sink in the economy with the lower rate of technical advance is due to the greater responsiveness of output to capital accumulation.[1] In the special context of the one-commodity assumption, the response of the rate of return in neoclassical analysis is properly a static problem. In the framework of measurement advanced here, *if* no technical change is in fact taking place, then, again remembering the special context, the static neoclassical analysis is unimpaired. The Harrod–Robinson measures of technical change would be zero and traditional static analysis would hold. When technical change is occurring, however, there is *by definition* no meaning to a *given* responsiveness of output to capital accumulation. It is, as I have shown, the identical rates of technical change which permit the two economies to accumulate at the same rate without affecting the level of their respective rates of profit, because the commodity-capital inputs themselves are produced under conditions of ever-increasing efficiency. It is the neglect of this last point which undermines and invalidates the static concern of the responsiveness of output to *produced* means of production in the dynamic context of technical change.

Suppose, in the examination of the two growing economies, no knowledge of the 'production functions' existed. The shares of capital could be different (approaching unity in the limiting case) in each economy, while

---

[1] In the limiting case discussed in footnote 2 on p. 101, the neoclassical rate of technical change falls to zero, labour as an input has vanished (by assumption). Given constant returns to scale, output expands proportionately with capital and the rate of profit (equal to the output/commodity-capital ratio) remains constant 'along the von Neumann ray'. I am indebted to Dr L. L. Pasinetti for this observation.

the partial elasticities could be (i) as outlined in the various Cobb–Douglas cases, (ii) non-existent as in the Leontief case, and/or (iii) potentially changeable, as in the constant or variable elasticities of substitution production function cases. In all cases, the Harrod–Robinson measures of neutral technical change would properly be the same for both economies. In case (ii), the neoclassical measures would be different if shares were different, with no differences in the responsiveness of output with respect to capital to fall back on. In cases (iii), the neoclassical story becomes even more complex, as in each economy the different rates of technical change must be biased in a direction which depends critically on the static elasticity of substitution.[1] These last cases reveal the mounting complexity and complications to which neoclassical analysis is prey. One wonders why it continues to be used when the Harrod–Robinson explanation is so simple and straightforward. It reminds one of the increasingly complicated explanations about the solar system which were necessary to ensure consistency with the basic, traditional and, moreover, common sensical hypothesis that the Sun revolved around the Earth, when the correct hypothesis, which enormously simplified the superstructure of analysis, was so readily at hand.

To my mind, the implications of the results so far are that, first, neoclassical measures of the rate of technological progress, contributions to growth or what-have-you, are without theoretical foundation.[2] This is a strongly negative and critical statement which this study substantiates. Secondly, the simultaneous assessment of the Harrod rate of technological advance and 'real capital' permits more precise measurement of the possible non-inflationary rate of advance in money-wage rates and deeper insight into the way in which the fruits of advance are being distributed. Third, just as in the two hypothetical economies, the level of real-wage rates, net rates of return to capital, output, etc., can be different, and the level or 'amount' of 'real capital' can be different in the economies at the same point of time. In these remarks the respective levels have not been of significance. Under the assumptions of the model, it is the fact that the rates of growth of the two 'real-capital' inputs are identical which is of importance.

I would conclude this section by reviewing my two conclusions. First, even in the extremely simple economy adopted from Meade, the brittle

---

[1] For an example of the complicated taxonomies which arise, see Ferguson, *Neoclassical Theory*, Ch. 12.

[2] I have performed such exercises myself. See Lithwick, Post and Rymes, 'Postwar relations'. In Section II of that paper, total factor productivity calculations *à la* Kendrick were performed for the Canadian manufacturing sector. In a technical appendix to the paper, I outlined the reservations I had at the time. I now feel such calculations to be without any theoretical value whatever.

conventionality of the definition of neutral technological advance he favours (what I have called the neoclassical measure) is revealed. All. standard measures of technical change which have been adjusted to include more in the definition of capital (education, health, research and development capital, etc.) will show lower rates of technical change. These must be arbitrary. Second, and more importantly, I have shown that assessments of the Harrod rate of technological advance and the rate of growth of the 'real-capital' input can be simultaneously derived.

5.5 Depreciation

As I have shown in Chapter 4, various assumptions about the depreciation of stocks of commodity capital can be made.

(i) It can be assumed that pieces of commodity capital never wear out. This assumes away the problem of depreciation and is unhelpful.

(ii) In Meade's simple model, he assumed 'depreciation by evaporation'.[1] As I have shown in Chapter 4, such an assumption means that depreciation in any period can be taken as equal to the rate of 'depreciation by evaporation' multiplied by the stock of commodities, and that no distinction between gross and net stocks can be drawn. Thus, for such an economy, the equilibrium social-accounting identity would appear as

$$Q \equiv \overline{W}L + RK + \Gamma K \qquad (5.13)$$

where Q is now the number of commodities making up gross output and Γ is the rate of 'depreciation by evaporation'.

I perform the customary manipulations upon the identity to derive

$$q - [\beta k + \gamma(\delta + k)] \equiv [\alpha \overline{w} + \beta r] \qquad (5.14)$$

where δ is the rate of change in the rate of 'depreciation by evaporation'. The left-hand side of identity (5.14) given the assumptions, boils down to

$$t_{GNC} = \alpha q \qquad (5.15)$$

I call this the neoclassical *gross* rate of technological progress. It is shown in Chapter 4 that identity (5.13) may be rewritten as

$$Q - \Gamma K \equiv \overline{W}L + RK$$

After the customary manipulation, this becomes

$$t_{NNC} = \frac{\overline{W}L}{Q - \Gamma K} q_n$$

In steady-state equilibrium $q = k$, therefore $q_n = q$. But $Q - \Gamma K < Q$. Hence, what may be called the neoclassical *net* rate of technological

[1] Meade, *Neoclassical Theory of Economic Growth*, 7.

progress will be greater than the *gross* rate. Since the rate of 'depreciation by evaporation' is a *constant* part of the description of technology, what does it mean to argue in the neoclassical sense that, for different steady states, with the same growth rates of the labour input and technological progress, but with different rates of 'depreciation by evaporation' undergone by the respective stocks of commodity capital, the net rates of technological progress will be different?[1] This is, of course, exactly the same brittle result seen earlier, when narrower or broader definitions of the capital input were considered. It follows from my previous discussion that for all these steady states, when the proportionate rate of growth of commodity capital is being simultaneously transformed into the proportionate rate of growth of 'real capital' the gross and net rates of technological change will all be the same.

Again, I would reiterate that we are comparing rates of change for different steady states. A once-over change in the rate of 'depreciation by evaporation' will lead to new *levels* of commodity-capital stocks, commodity-wage rates and, perhaps, different partial elasticities of production with respect to labour, stocks of commodity capital in use, and commodity capital being used (whether such elasticities are conceived of in gross or net terms). Given the assumptions, there is no theoretical foundation at all for the assertion that the recorded rates of gross and net technological, change should be different from one steady state to another, as they are in the neoclassical case. I would again argue that the neoclassical measures are conventionally brittle in this respect and that the brittleness arises from the incorrect way in which the capital input is conceived in the neoclassical argument.

(iii) The assumption of 'depreciation by evaporation' can be replaced by assuming that commodity capital (i.e. each commodity) lasts a finite time and then collapses – the assumption of 'depreciation by sudden death'. This assumption is highly unrealistic but analysis based on it can be used as a preliminary insight to the analysis based on the more realistic assumption of 'depreciation by obsolescence'. As I indicated in Chapter 4, depreciation is, primarily, in this case, a value phenomenon, with the ratio of depreciation to the net stock of capital being a function of the rate of growth of capital, the physical life of commodity capital and the rate of return. I also indicated that, although each commodity-capital good had an expected life that depended upon its age, they all, old and new alike,

---

[1] See Lithwick, Post and Rymes, 'Postwar relations', for a demonstration of how the neoclassical rate of technological progress varies when the 'netness' of output is changed. Domar spotted this at the sectoral level but seemed to think it was an aggregation problem of some kind. See E. D. Domar, 'On the measurement of technological change', *Economic Journal*, LXXI, December 1961, 709–29.

shared equally in any technical change. Thus, the price of each commodity capital good, *when new*, was the same. The net stock of commodity capital would be made up of various ages of capital goods, each age having a different price. The equilibrium social accounts will appear as

$$Q = \overline{W}L + R\sum_{i=1}^{T} P_i K_i + \Gamma^* \sum_{i=1}^{T} P_i K_i \qquad (5.16)$$

where P_i is the equilibrium price of a commodity-capital good with $T-i$ periods to live. Then $\Sigma P_i K_i$ is the equilibrium value of the net stock of capital. As was shown in Chapter 4,[1] the ratio of depreciation to the net stock of capital, Γ^*, is equal to

$$\frac{1-e^R}{1 - \dfrac{(e^{gT}-1)}{gT} \dfrac{(R-g)T}{1-e^{-(R-g)T}}}$$

If the social accounts are manipulated in the standard fashion, I would then have (again assuming the labour input constant)

$$q - \sum_{i=1}^{T} \beta_i k_i \equiv t_{GNC} \qquad (5.17)$$

where β_i equals the gross returns accruing to the commodity capital with $T-i$ periods to live expressed as a fraction of the total output, Q, and k_i is the rate of growth of the stock of commodity capital having $T-i$ periods to live. In steady-state equilibrium, all ages are growing at the same constant rate, so $k_i = k$ for all commodity capital and the analysis for the case of depreciation by evaporation repeats itself. Again the neoclassical *net* rate of technical change, t_{NNC}, would differ meaninglessly from the gross rate in identity (5.17). The gross neoclassical rate of technical change would be

$$\left(1 - \sum_{i=1}^{T} \beta_i\right) q \equiv t_{GNC} \qquad (5.18)$$

The correct measure of the rate of technical change would again be given by

$$q - \left[\sum_{i=1}^{T} \beta_i(k_i - t_R)\right] \equiv t_R \qquad (5.19)$$

Again, under the steady-state assumptions I have

$$q \equiv t_R \qquad (5.20)$$

It is important to realize that the measures of technical change can be derived independently of prices. Since each commodity capital good, old and new alike, shares in the technical change, the standard format can be employed. That is, I can write

$$Q = Q(L, K_1, K_2, ..., K_i, ..., K_T; T)$$

[1] See Chapter 4, identity (4.28).

Since it is a one-commodity model, this can, if necessary, be aggregated to be

$$Q = Q(L, K; T)$$

where K now represents the *gross* stock of commodity capital. As I have shown, the standard measures of technical change would then be

$$q - \sum_{i=1}^{T} \beta_i k_i \equiv t_{GNC}$$

or

$$q - \beta k \equiv t_{GNC} \quad (\beta \equiv \sum_{i=1}^{T} \beta_i)$$

in steady-state equilibrium. Where no reference is being paid to prices the βs must be the gross partial elasticities of production of the various ages of the commodity capital.[1]

[1] Using the production function $Q = Q(L, K_1, K_2, ..., K_T; T)$, I can write, since dL is assumed to be zero,
$$dQ = Q_{K_1} dK_1 + ... + Q_{K_T} dK_T + dQ^T$$
where Q_{K_i} is the marginal gross physical product of commodity capital with $T - i$ periods to live. Then

$$\frac{dQ}{Q} = Q_{K_1} \frac{K_1}{Q} \frac{dK_1}{K_1} + ... + Q_{K_T} \frac{K_T}{Q} \frac{dK_T}{K_T} + \frac{dQ^T}{Q}$$

$$= \beta_1 k_1 + ... + \beta_T k_T + \frac{dQ^T}{Q}$$

Since, all pieces of commodity capital are the same regardless of their age,
$$Q_{K_1} = Q_{K_2} = ... = Q_{K_T} = Q_K$$
and, in steady-state equilibrium $k_1 = k_2 = ... = k_T = k$, I can write
$$q = Q_K / Q(K_1 + K_2 + ... + K_T) k$$
or,
$$q = \frac{Q_K K_i}{Q} [e^{-gi} + ... + 1 + ... + e^{g(T-i)}] k$$
so that
$$\beta = \sum_{i=1}^{T} \beta_i = \frac{Q_K K_i}{Q} [e^{-gi} + ... + 1 + ... + e^{g(T-i)}] k$$
If the social accounts are used, will $\dfrac{(R + \Gamma_i) P_i K_i}{Q} = \beta_i = \dfrac{Q_{K_i} K_i}{Q}$; that is, will
$(R + \Gamma_i) P_i = Q_{K_i}$? From Chapter 4, I know that
$$\Gamma_i = \frac{V_i e^{-R(T-i)}}{P_i} = \frac{R V_i e^{-R(T-i)}}{V_i(1 - e^{-R(T-i)})} = \frac{R e^{-R(T-i)}}{1 - e^{-R(T-i)}}$$
and therefore
$$(R + \Gamma_i) P_i = V_i$$
It is also the case, from Chapter 4, that
$$Q_{K_i} = \frac{R P_i}{1 - e^{-R(T-i)}} = V_i$$

Thus, whether the analysis is conducted wholly in terms of Physical Things or in terms of the equilibrium social accounts which are in terms of values, the result is exactly the same.

Again, from
$$Q = Q(L, K_1/T_R, K_2/T_R, \ldots, K_T/T_R; T_R)$$

I can write as the correct measure of the rate of technical change,

$$q - \sum_{i=1}^{T} \beta_1(k_i - t_R) = t_R$$

or,
$$q = t_R$$

as was shown before. All the previous criticisms of the neoclassical measures apply.

(iv) The most realistic assumption about depreciation is to assume that commodity capital falls in value over time because older pieces have been unable to share in technical changes. This assumption is 'depreciation by obsolescence', discussed in Chapter 4. With this assumption, commodity capital of different vintages cannot be treated as being identical: newer vintages are more productive and require less cooperative labour than older vintages. Commodity capital is not then perfectly malleable and cannot costlessly be squeezed into the shape that the latest techniques require.

If pieces of commodity capital were costlessly malleable, then some assumption such as 'depreciation by evaporation' (with terminal scrapping) or 'sudden death' would be necessary to provide finite lives for capital goods. Most realistically, it is the emergence of new pieces of commodity capital which can be associated more readily than older pieces with techniques of production that give improved output per unit of labour input, that eventually brings about the disappearance of the older pieces. Within the context of the simple model employed so far, the assumption of unchanging new commodity-capital price means, in terms of costs of production, that the total stock of commodity capital will be rising at its same rate of output. It is sometimes argued that, in terms of productive capacity, however, the stock is rising more rapidly. In Chapters 4 and 6, it is pointed out that this is Solow's 'effective capital' and can be envisaged as the pieces of commodity capital, growing in number, being assessed not in terms of *constant* commodity-capital prices but in terms of rising capacity 'prices'. This suggests that there are three ways of looking at the capital input: in terms of capacity to contribute to production, as commodity capital, or in the terms advanced here. As I show in Chapter 6, however, there is no legitimate distinction – within the context of long period equilibrium – between the first two concepts of the capital input.

The assumption of 'depreciation by obsolescence' is obviously more realistic than any of the others. True, commodity capital is to some extent malleable and transferable among activities (the phenomena of major alterations, repairs and renting) and some commodity capital is designed for general multi-activity purposes. I should think, however, that, by and large, the productive life of a piece of commodity capital is determined largely by economic events which, in the context of the model under discussion, are the steady improvements in techniques with which it is difficult to associate old pieces of commodity capital. The assumption of 'depreciation by obsolescence' raises the very difficult problem relating to the quality change of commodity inputs. This problem is investigated in Chapter 6 and its effects on the analysis used in the rest of this chapter examined. Since I find that there is no distinction between Solow's effective capital and the commodity-capital concept, then the finding is, of course, that the analysis of this chapter dealing with commodity capital stands. The rate of technical progress is equal to the rate of growth of output per unit of labour input. With limited transferability, the rate of obsolescence will be lower and pieces of commodity capital will have longer economic lives. As is shown in Chapter 6, the ratio of the *value* of depreciation to the value of either the gross or the net stock will vary as the rate of obsolescence varies. This will cause different ratios between the nominal net returns to commodity capital and the value of depreciation to be thrown up by the different equilibrium social accounts, each set of social accounts being relevant to one constant rate of obsolescence. Since each set of social accounts will reflect the results of the *same* rates of growth of the labour input and the same rate of emergence of new techniques, neoclassical net measures of the rate of technological advance will correspondingly vary with the different equilibrium rates of obsolescence. Again, the Harrod measure of the rate of technological change and the rate of growth of 'real capital' will remain unchanged. Once again, the brittle conventionality of the neoclassical measures is revealed.

Given the assumption of 'depreciation by obsolescence', the equilibrium social accounts will appear as

$$Q \equiv \overline{W}L + R\sum_{v=1}^{n} P_v K_v + \delta \sum_{v=1}^{n} P_v K_v \qquad (5.21)$$

where P_v is the price of the commodity capital, K_v, of vintage v and δ is the rate of 'depreciation by obsolescence'. The analysis for the assumption of 'depreciation by sudden death' can now be carried over to this case. There is a major difference, though – and that arises in the construction of the production function – to be dealt with in Chapter 6. The equilibrium accounts can be manipulated in the customary way to yield

$$q - \sum_{v=1}^{n} \beta_v k_v \equiv t_{NC}$$

and
$$q - \sum_{v=1}^{n} \beta_v(k_v - t_R) \equiv t_R$$

All the previous criticisms of the neoclassical construct apply.

111

For assumptions of steady state and 'depreciation by evaporation', the meaning of the recorded value of depreciation thrown up by the equilibrium set of accounts is clear. It is a measure of the consumption which must be foregone in order to replace those parts of the stock of commodity capital which are evaporating and which must be replaced if the stock is to continue its equilibrium growth. Owing to technological advance, however, the amount of 'real capital' required to replace each piece of commodity capital so evaporating will not be as great as that originally required to produce it, but will be equivalent to that amount of 'real capital' which is required for the production of a 'new' piece of commodity during the time period when the 'old' piece 'evaporates'. Thus, the rate of growth of 'real capital' requiring replacement will be less than the rate of growth of commodity capital requiring replacement.

When 'depreciation by sudden death' or 'by obsolescence' is assumed, the value of depreciation at any time period will exceed the value of replacement. Consider the case of 'depreciation by sudden death'. The argument must be that non-consumption of the amount given by the value of depreciation is necessary to maintain the productive capacity of the growing equilibrium commodity-capital stock, since each existent piece, during the current time-period, has drawn one time-period nearer to eventual death. In the case of 'depreciation by obsolescence', the value of depreciation must be that non-consumption which is necessary to maintain the productive capacity of growing commodity capital, in face of the fact that each older and inferior piece of commodity capital has been brought one time-period nearer its disappearance by the emergence, during the current time period, of a batch of newer and superior pieces of commodity capital. Once again the *amount* of 'real capital' will be less than the amount of commodity capital. Clearly, in growing economies subject to technological advance, the rate of increase in the 'real-capital' input required to reproduce each piece of commodity capital being depreciated will be less than the rate of increase in commodity capital so required.

5.6   A two-commodity two-sector model

I have shown that the neoclassical measures of the rate of technological change, even in the context of steady-state one-commodity one-sector models, are extremely brittle. The Harrod measure, together with its simultaneously derived counterpart, the rate of growth of the 'real-capital' input, would not seem to be subject to such a drawback and would appear more meaningful as well. Its real value emerges, however, when we move to two and multi-sector cases. Yet the analysis is really completely contained in the one-commodity one-sector case, though, as I said at the beginning of this chapter, the one-commodity one-sector case blurs the logical impossibility of distinguishing between technical change and commodity-capital accumulation. I shall argue that in a two-commodity two-sector steady-state configuration, in which relative prices are constant, the rate of meaningfully conceived technological progress must be equal in both sectors. I shall also argue that, if relative prices diverge at a steady state, differences in the rates of technological progress between sectors must be an exact predictor of the divergence of relative prices. Putting the argument the other way round, I ask this question: If, in the context of a two-commodity two-sector model, the outcome of events is such that relative prices display such and such a movement, then what valuation is the economic system in fact placing on the primary inputs? That is, what valuations of the labour and capital inputs, using the traditional dichotomy, are meaningfully consistent with the outcome of events? General-equilibrium analysis teaches us that relative prices are a function of preferences, resources and technology. In the simple two-sector cases to be discussed, I assume that demand is given, by assuming that a constant fraction of nominal national income is saved. I assume, therefore, that demand conditions are known. I continue to assume that the labour input is constant. In static analysis, the stock of capital is assumed constant. It is, so to speak, given from outside the framework of analysis. In dynamics, of course, the stock of commodity capital is to be determined inside the system and the non-labour primary input, to be determined like labour *outside* the system, must clearly be something different from commodity capital. I know then the state of preference and resources. The remaining determinant of relative prices is technology and I seek a description of changes in technology which determines, 'predicts', or is defined by change in relative prices.

Consider the equilibrium accounts for the two-commodity two-sector steady-state system.

$$P_C C \equiv WL_C + RP_K K_C + \Gamma P_K K_C$$

$$P_K I \equiv WL_K + RP_K K_K + \Gamma P_K K_K \tag{5.22}$$

Given the analysis in the preceding section of this chapter, I shall henceforth ignore the phenomenon of depreciation. Of course, all of the brittleness of the neoclassical measures on this point, observed in the one-commodity one-sector case, carry over into the two-commodity two-sector case. The customary manipulation of identities (5.22) yields

$$c - \beta_C k_C \equiv [\alpha_C w + \beta_C (r + p_K)] - p_C$$

$$i - \beta_C k_K \equiv [\alpha_K w + \beta_K (r + p_K)] - p_K \tag{5.23}$$

Under certain steady-state assumptions, I have

$$t_{ONC} \equiv \alpha_C C$$

$$t_{KNC} \equiv \alpha_K i \qquad (5.24)$$

The steady-state assumption is that technological progress is taking place in such a way that output per unit of labour input is rising at the *same* rate in both sectors, *physical* commodity-capital/output ratios are remaining unchanged in both sectors and a constant net rate of return to capital holds over both sectors.[1]

While the growth rates of output per unit of labour input in both sectors are the same, there is no reason for the recorded partial elasticities of production with respect to labour in the two sectors to be the same. Save for a fluke, the two neoclassical measures of the rate of technological change, exhibited in identities (4.23), will differ between the two sectors. Such measures could not be used, *without adjustment*, for the prediction of the course of relative prices.[2] Applying the device outlined in the one-sector case to derive Harrod measures of the rates of technological progress, I have for the two-sector case:

$$c - [\beta_C(k_C - t_{KR})] \equiv t_{CR}$$

$$i - [\beta_K(k_K - t_{KR})] \equiv t_{KR} \qquad (5.25)$$

To obtain a measure of the rate of increase in 'real capital' being used in the production of consumption goods, I transform the growth rate of the stock of commodity capital used in the production of the consumption good by the growth rate of technological progress in the production of the investment good. I do the same in the investment-good sector. Simultaneously, I derive measures of the rate of technological progress in both sectors which, as I shall show, provide an exact prediction of the course of relative prices. When the two relationships are solved for the two measures of the rate of technological change, I have:[3]

$$t_{CR} \equiv t_{CNC} + \frac{\beta_C}{1 - \beta_K} t_{KNC}$$

$$t_{KR} \equiv \frac{t_{KNC}}{1 - \beta_K} \qquad (5.26)$$

---

[1] The assumptions imply that the distribution of the labour force between the two sectors also remains unchanged: technological progress is neutral in Mrs Robinson's sense.

[2] See P. A. Diamond, 'Disembodied technical change in a two-sector model', *Review of Economic Studies*, XXXII, April 1965, 161–8. Diamond makes the adjustments but while doing so apparently does not appreciate the implications for the neoclassical concepts of capital and technological progress.

[3] From identities (5.25), I have

$$t_{CR} - \beta_C t_{KR} \equiv c - [\beta_C k_C] = t_{ONC}$$

$$(1 - \beta_K) t_{KR} \equiv i - [\beta_K k_K] = t_{KNC}$$

Drawing upon the assumptions outlined in (5.24), I have

$$t_{C_R} \equiv \alpha_C c + \beta_C i$$

$$t_{K_R} \equiv i$$

or

$$t_{C_R} \equiv c$$

$$t_{K_R} \equiv i$$

Hence, with the Harrod measures of the rate of technological progress simultaneously determined as being equal in the two sectors, it would be possible to predict *exactly* that relative prices will remain constant.

The equilibrium social accounts can be rewritten as:

$$1 = \overline{W} A_C + \frac{R P_K}{P_C} B_C$$

$$\frac{P_K}{P_C} = \overline{W} A_K + \frac{R P_K}{P_C} B_K \qquad (5.27)$$

The coefficients (A_C, B_C, A_K, B_K) represent an equilibrium technology. Behavioural assumptions may be introduced to determine R, and hence $\overline{W}$ and P_K/P_C, as I have shown in Chapter 2, as

$$\overline{W} = \frac{1 - R B_K / A_C}{1 - R[B_K - (A_K/A_C) B_C]}$$

$$\frac{P_K}{P_C} = \frac{A_K / A_C}{1 - R[B_K - (A_K/A_C) B_C]} \qquad (5.28)$$

With the kind of technological change being posited in the above model, the capital coefficients (B_C, B_K) are constant and the labour coefficients (A_C, A_K) are declining at equal rates. The ratio of A_C/A_K, the price of commodity capital in terms of the consumption good, will therefore remain unchanged and the consumption-good wage rate will be rising at the rate at which A_C is declining.

Suppose there were one consumption good but n capital goods in the model.

The equilibrium relationships would then appear as

$$P_C C = W L_C + R \sum_{i=1}^{n} P_i K_{iC}$$

$$P_j I_j \equiv W L_j + R \sum_{i=1}^{n} P_i K_{ij} \quad (j = 1, ..., n) \qquad (5.29)$$

or since

$$\Delta = \begin{bmatrix} 1 & -\beta_C \\ 0 & 1 - \beta_K \end{bmatrix} = 1 - \beta_K$$

I have (5.24). If $\Delta \leqslant 0$, then real-wage rates would be negative or zero.

I will have n consumption-good prices of commodity capital, the consumption-good wage rate and the net rate of return. These relationships may be expressed, in the now customary way, as:

$$c - \sum_{i=1}^{n} \beta_{iC} k_{iC} \equiv [\alpha_C w + \sum_{i=1}^{n} \beta_{iC}(r + P_{KiC})] - p_C$$

$$i_j - \sum_{i=1}^{n} \beta_{ij} k_{ij} \equiv [\alpha_j w + \sum_{i=1}^{n} \beta_{ij}(r + P_{Kij})] - p_{Kj} \quad (j = 1, \ldots, n) \quad (5.30)$$

Employing the left-hand side and the steady-state assumptions outlined above for the two-sector case, I would have:

$$t_{C_{NC}} \equiv \alpha_C c$$

$$t_{j_{NC}} \equiv \alpha_j i_j \quad (j = 1, \ldots, n) \tag{5.31}$$

In each sector, the growth rate of output per unit of labour input will be the same. Again, since there is, in general, no reason to expect

$$\alpha_C c = \alpha_j i_j \quad (j = 1, \ldots, n)$$

I may conclude safely that

$$t_{C_{NC}} \neq t_{j_{NC}} \quad (j = 1, \ldots, n)$$

Under the assumptions outlined, the relative prices of the capital goods expressed in terms of the consumption-good numéraire will remain constant. Again, then, the neoclassical measures of technological progress at the sector level will fail to predict the course of relative prices correctly. If, however, Read's device is employed, I shall have:

$$t_{C_R} = c - \sum_{i=1}^{n} \beta_{iC}(k_{iC} - t_{i_R})$$

$$t_{j_R} = i_j - \sum_{i=1}^{n} \beta_{ij}(k_{ij} - t_{i_R}) \quad (i, j = 1, \ldots, n)$$

or,

$$t_{C_R} - \sum_{i=1}^{n} \beta_{iC} t_{i_R} = t_{C_{NC}}$$

$$t_{j_R} - \sum_{i=1}^{n} \beta_{ij} t_{i_R} = t_{j_{NC}} \tag{5.32}$$

or, in terms of an open Leontief model, where the output of the consumption-good industry is not an input into any of the capital-good industries, i.e. labour is not an augmentable reproducible input in the economic process,

$$t_R = [I - \beta]^{-1} t_{NC} \tag{5.33}$$

where t_R is an $n \times 1$ column vector of rates of Harrod technological progress and t_{NC} is an $n \times 1$ column vector of rates of neoclassical technological progress.[1] Because of the assumptions, Harrod gross (and net) rates of technological progress in the consumption-good sector and the n capital-good sectors would all be the same and would, therefore, be perfect predictors of the course of all n relative prices. Again, the neo-classical measures of the rate of technological change would, except by sheer chance, differ from sector to sector.

If I compare different steady states, alike in terms of the rate of growth of labour and/or the rate at which the efficiency of labour was being improved, but different because (say) of a once-over change in the behavioural assumptions determining the net rate of return to commodity capital, or (say) a once-over bias in the manner in which improvements in efficiency were distributed amongst the labour inputs, then my analysis would show the same rate of technological change in all sectors in both states. It would also show, after an intervening divergence in the movements of relative prices, constancy in relative prices in both states. The neoclassical measures of the gross rate of technological change would differ from one steady state to another, a result which demonstrates their brittle conventionality and essential meaninglessness. Since all the Harrod gross (or net) rates of technological progress in the steady-state case will be equal to the rate of growth of output per unit of labour input, it follows that, for any given n-capital-good steady state, whatever the sectoral distribution of labour, the rate at which the efficiency of such labour is improving is everywhere the same. Such technological advance is neutral in Harrodian terms.[2] This is surely a more meaningful definition of neutrality in technological advance than one drawn up in terms of the increased relative efficiencies of both labour and intermediate inputs (i.e. all forms of commodity capital) since, if the rate at which the economic systems were transforming labour into output were the same throughout all sectors, it should be expected that the relative prices of the different components of output would remain unchanged.

As the two-industry and n-capital-good-industry steady-state analysis shows, however, one cannot solve for the Harrodian neutral rate of

[1] The matrix β is defined as:

$$
\begin{matrix}
0 & \beta_{1c} & \beta_{2c} & \cdots & \beta_{nc} \\
0 & \beta_{11} & \beta_{21} & \cdots & \beta_{n1} \\
0 & \beta_{12} & \beta_{22} & \cdots & \beta_{n2} \\
\vdots & & & & \\
0 & \beta_{1n} & \beta_{2n} & \cdots & \beta_{nn}
\end{matrix}
$$

[2] In defining neutral advance, Harrod says: '...the productivity of labour embodied in machines is raised in equal measure with that of those engaged on minding machines; it implies an equal rise of productivity on the part of all labour however far back or forward it may be between the inception and the final stage in production.' Harrod, *Towards a Dynamic Economics*, 23. See also A. P. Lerner, 'On some recent developments in capital theory', *American Economic Review*, LV, May 1965, 284–95.

technological progress in any sector taken just by itself. Rather, *such a result is determined by solving simultaneously for all the sectoral rates of technological progress.* To solve for the Harrod rate of technological progress in the consumption-good sector it is necessary to take into account the rate of technological progress in each and all of the n capital-good sectors. That is, in assessing the rate of increase in the efficiency with which the consumption-good sector is transforming primary inputs into the consumption good, it is necessary to take into account the simultaneous increases in efficiency with which all sectors, *either directly or indirectly,* are supplying the consumption-good sector with commodity-capital inputs. It is to be noted, again, that this simultaneous solution for the rate of Harrodian neutral technological advance sector by sector involves the simultaneous solution for the rate of increase in 'real capital' at use sector by sector.[1] Here then we have the identity between Harrodian and Robinsonian concepts of neutral technological advance.

The industrial interdependence of the concept of technological change which I am advancing is a critical feature. Yet Harrod has given the impression that his concept of technological change is a partial equilibrium concept.[2] In criticizing Hicks' definition of neutrality, Harrod says: '...the neutrality of the invention depends on circumstances quite unrelated to the intrinsic character of the invention itself. My definition determines the matter solely by reference to the invention itself.'[3] And again: 'His [i.e. Hicks'] depends partly on the outside circumstances, mine on the intrinsic character of the invention only.'[4] Yet what Harrod means by this is clear from his statements to the effect that he uses a goods standard[5] and that: 'The neutrality of an invention would be determined on my definition by reference to what happens to the capital coefficient, if the rate of interest is constant.'[6] Thus, if the net rate of return to capital is unchanged and in each and every industry the capital/output ratios, *expressed in terms of consumption goods,* remain constant, the technological progress I call Harrodian will be neutral in each industry and for the economy as whole.

In the two-sector model examined, the system decomposes in such a way that the Harrod rates of technological progress for the n-capital-good sectors may be assessed without reference to the consumption-good industry. As Sraffa would say, the consumption sector is non-basic, i.e. technological progress in it does not change the efficiency with which

---

[1] For any sector j, the rate of increase in the ith real capital will be equal to $k_{ij} - t_{i_R}$.

[2] See Asimakopulos and Weldon, 'A synoptic view', 57 n. 15, where it is stated: '...it is not correct, as Harrod claims (*Towards a Dynamic Economics*, 27), that his rules depend "on the intrinsic character of the invention only".'

[3] Harrod, *Towards a Dynamic Economics*, 24–5.

[4] *Ibid.* 27.   [5] *Ibid.* 34.   [6] *Ibid.* 27.

the rest of the sectors operate, whereas technological change in any of the sectors to which the consumption-good sector is directly *or indirectly* related will change the efficiency with which the consumption sector operates.[1]

In the *n*-capital-good-industries case, I may well have a sector producing (say) circulating capital in the form of materials, without using in either stock or flow form the output of any of the other $n-1$ sectors.[2] It would be possible to assess the Harrod rate of technological advance for this sector independently of the rest of the industries but, of course, its assessment is necessary for the assessment of the rates of technological change of the industries connected *directly or indirectly* with it. In the two-industry case, of course, the rate of technological change for the capital-good industry may be derived independently.

It might also be argued that technological advance permits the economy to augment or reproduce labour more effectively. Earlier I have argued against this. The Harrod measures show the rate of increase in output per unit of labour in the production of the consumption good and the rate of increase in output per unit of labour (compounded at the equilibrium rate of return over the equilibrium periods of production) given up in the production of future consumption goods (i.e. the labour which would have to be given up in the potential reproduction of the existing flow of services emanating from commodity capital). It is difficult to see what more fundamental concept of primary inputs beyond human effort and 'waiting' could be imagined. Such a concept is, however, required if higher rates of technological progress, showing the ability of the system more effectively to augment or reproduce labour given up, are to be recorded. Moreover, and this is the critical point, such a treatment would contribute no theoretical novelty. That is, I would merely say that there exists a sector

---

[1] 'If an invention were to reduce by half the quantity of each of the means of production which are required to produce a unit of a "luxury" commodity of this [non-basic] type, the commodity itself would be halved in price, but there would be no further consequences; the price-relations of the other products and the rate of profits would remain unaffected. But if such a change occurred in the production of a commodity of the opposite type, which *does* enter the means of production, all prices would be affected and the rate of profits would be changed.' P. Sraffa, *Production of Commodities by Means of Commodities*, 7–8.

[2] Even in the case of a sector producing circulating capital (which is being immediately used up upon production) without calling upon the output of any of the other *n*-capital-good sectors, 'real capital', as well as labour in the traditional sense, still appears as a primary input in the production of circulating capital since, for such a sector, our equilibrium accounts will appear, suitably transformed, as

$$t_{mR} \equiv m - \beta_m(m_S - t_{mR})$$

since m_S will represent the rate of change in the stock of material (in different stages of being worked up) commodity capital found over any time length of production in this sector. Since $m = m_S$, it really is just the same as the one-commodity one-sector case.

producing labour services for use in other sectors. The commodity input into the production of labour service would then be the consumption good. The consumption-good sector would thereby become the $n+1$th capital-good sector. I would have a completely closed system if workers did not 'save' and there was no consumption out of returns to capital. If, however, workers did 'save' and there was consumption out of returns to capital, part of the output of the consumption-good sector would be used for consumption purposes. I would then have a labour sector, a consumption-good sector and $n+1$ capital-good sectors, and the analysis developed so far would be essentially repeated.

The model with one consumption-good sector and n capital-good sectors has been used here to dramatize in yet another way the difference between neoclassical and Harrod conceptions of the rate of technological progress. I argue that the neoclassical conceptions are partial-equilibrium measures, which, when developed for any one sector, hold within the compound of *ceteris paribus*, the technology in use in all other sectors supplying the sector under review with the various forms of commodity capital. The Harrod conception is the correct dynamic general-equilibrium measure. As I have shown

$$t_R = [I-\beta]^{-1} t_{NC} \tag{5.33}$$

The same equations may be used, of course, to solve for the $n+1$ neoclassical measures of the various rates of technological change. Like all partial-equilibrium measures, all that such measures would entail would be the setting of the off-diagonal entries in β at zero levels. The fact that in the general-equilibrium case the off-diagonal entries are not zero (and cannot, in general, be zero in any theoretically acceptable general-equilibrium model) surely demonstrates powerfully the superiority of the Harrod case. In one-sector models it is *logically* inconsistent to set the 'off-diagonal entries' equal to zero. Yet this is what the neoclassical concept in fact does. In two- or n-sector models, it is not *logically* inconsistent to set the off-diagonal entries equal to zero in dealing with any one sector[1] (providing it does not produce some of its own commodity input), but it is logically inconsistent to do so if one is simultaneously attempting to assess the rate of technological change in other sectors as well.

The general format for the measurement of the Harrod rates of technological change in models with one consumption-good sector and n capital-good sectors can be used to obtain neoclassical measures as well. It is immediately clear, however, that when the neoclassical measures are used by inserting zeros off-diagonally in the matrix β, the ability of the economic

[1] One cannot then, of course, ask any questions of the resulting measure which can properly be asked only within a general-equilibrium context.

system to reproduce and augment the flow and stock of intermediate inputs is being neglected. The significance of this is that the neoclassical concept of commodity capital as a primary input in the process of economic production is incorrect.

While the partial-equilibrium nature of the neoclassical concepts is misleading,[1] the basic fault is the treatment of commodity-capital inputs as if they were non-reproducible or non-basic.

I now turn to the possibility of diverging relative prices. Here I must move with care. If I assume that full-employment conditions continue to prevail, then in my view there are three central phenomena with which I may be concerned. First, preferences either may demonstrate non-neutrality or indeed may change. Second, the emerging new technology may be biased. Third, the rates of neutral technical change may be different amongst the sectors. I wish to direct my attention only to the third phenomenon.

Earlier, I argued that meaningful sectoral measures of the rates of technical change should be able to predict the course of relative prices. The price of the capital good in terms of the consumption good will be rising (falling) at a rate which is exactly equal to the difference between the Harrod rates of technical change in the two sectors. If overall Harrod–Robinson neutrality is imposed on the two-sector system, and improvements in the techniques used in each sector are such that the rate of growth of output per unit of labour input (in terms of capital goods) in the capital-good sector is greater than (less than) the rate of growth of output per unit of labour input (in terms of consumption goods) in the consumption-good sector, then, in equilibrium growth, in order to preserve similarity in nominal wage rates and net rates of return to capital (and equiproportionately different 'own product' wage rates and net rates of return to capital), it would be necessary for the capital/output ratio in physical units in the consumption-good sector to rise (fall) and for the price of capital goods in terms of consumption goods to fall (rise) in such a way that the capital/output ratio expressed in terms of consumption goods in the consumption-good sector would remain constant. The two neoclassical measures of the rate of technological change would be

$$t_{C_{NC}} \equiv \alpha_C c + \beta_C (c - k_C) \tag{5.34}$$

$$t_{R_{NC}} \equiv \alpha_K i$$

[1] '...the so-called method of *partial equilibrium* consists of nothing more than a liberal sprinkling of zeros into the equations of general equilibrium. In the hands of a master practitioner, the method will yield useful results; if not handled with caution and delicacy, it can easily yield nonsensical conclusions.' Samuelson, *Foundations of Economic Analysis*, 27.

The two Harrod measures of the rate of technological change would be

$$t_{C_R} \equiv \alpha_C c + \beta_C(c-k_C) + \beta_C i \qquad (5.35)$$

$$t_{K_R} \equiv i$$

Which set of measures of the rates of technological change will exactly predict the course of relative prices? If identities (5.28) are differentiated, with A_K, A_C and B_C allowed to vary, I obtain:

$$p_K - p_C \equiv \alpha_C[c-i] + \beta_C(c-k_C) \qquad (5.36)$$

From identities (5.35) I have:

$$t_{C_R} - t_{K_R} \equiv \alpha_C[c-i] + \beta_C(c-k_C). \qquad (5.37)$$

The two Harrod measures of the rate of technological change will exactly predict the cause of the consumption-good price of the capital good. From identities (5.34), I have:

$$t_{C_{NC}} - t_{K_{NC}} \equiv \alpha_C(c-l_C) + \beta_C(c-k_C) - \alpha_K(i-l_K). \qquad (5.38)$$

There is no reason for (5.38) to predict even the *direction* of the change in relative prices.[1] In this case, the divergence in relative prices is caused by the improvements in technique, which are revealed as different rates of increase in output per unit of labour input in the two sectors. While the 'real-capital'/labour ratio in each sector remains unchanged, the rate of increase in output per unit of combined labour and 'real-capital' inputs in the two sectors is different.[2] It is this latter state of affairs which must be ascertained by meaningful measures of the rate of technological change. If the rate of technological change is greater in the capital-good sector than in the consumption-good sector then we should expect the capital/output ratio in the consumption-good sector to rise, because it is in this fashion that the economic system substitutes indirect for direct primary inputs in the production of consumption goods, since the indirect inputs are enjoying a relatively greater improvement in efficiency. The fall in the consumption-good price of the capital good reflects precisely the phenomenon that the economic system can reproduce and augment its commodity-

---

[1] Identity (5.38) will be the same as (5.36) and (5.37) only in the fluke case that $\alpha_K = \alpha_C$. But in that case the two sectors are the same, the model collapses back to the one-commodity one-sector case and the price of the capital good in terms of the consumption good is identically one.

[2] The rates of change in 'real capital' in the two sectors are:

$$k_C - t_{K_R} \equiv k_C - i \equiv 0$$

$$k_K - t_{K_R} \equiv k_K - i \equiv 0$$

and, since, for overall neutrality in the Harrod–Robinson sense to hold, the sectoral distribution of the labour inputs are constant, 'real-capital'/labour ratios in the sectors remain unchanged.

capital input relatively more efficiently than it can produce the final-good output. The efficiency with which the production of future consumption is being enhanced is greater than that of the production of present consumption.

In a model with one consumption-good sector and n capital-good sectors, subject to overall Harrod–Robinson neutrality in technical change, but with different Harrod rates of technical change holding in each sector, the 'own capital/output' ratios in physical terms in each capital-good sector will remain constant (i.e. $i_i = k_{ii}$) while the 'other capital/output' ratios will vary. Furthermore, for any sector, it is possible that

$$i_i - k_{ji} > i_i - k_{ki} > 0,$$

which entails that the indirect primary inputs embodied in K_{ji} are increasing in efficiency less rapidly than those embodied in K_{ki}, and that they are both increasing in efficiency less rapidly than the direct primary inputs employed in the production of K_i. It is important to emphasize again that the increases in efficiency, the rate of Harrod technological change, of the indirect primary inputs embodied in (say) K_j cannot be assessed without assessing simultaneously the rates of Harrod technological change in all the sectors supplying the jth sector with commodity inputs. Moreover, this is the only theoretically defensible way in which the capital input being used in the various sectors may be assessed.

Here it is important to note that, when Harrod and Robinson speak of technological change being neutral in terms of equal proportionate rates of increase in output per unit of labour input across all industries (for a given industrial distribution of the labour input), all outputs are measured in terms of the consumption-good numéraire. Thus, it is not inconsistent to have different rates of Harrod technological progress, when commodity capital is replaced by 'real capital', amongst industries all of which are still neutral in Harrod's sense. Harrod's criticism[1] of the labour standard of value (that is, a wage-rate numéraire) relates to output, not input, measures.[2]

5.7 Sundry observations

The major points have now been made. I wish to conclude this chapter by reference to the measurement of accumulation. It will be noted that

[1] Harrod, *Towards a Dynamic Economics*, 29 ff.
[2] Consider the one-commodity model again. With Harrod-neutral technological change, 'real capital' would be constant, i.e. $k - t_R = 0$. The real wage would be rising at the rate q and capital formation expressed in wage units would therefore be constant – that is, since $\overline{w} = q$, $i (= k = q) - \overline{w} = 0$. It would be unhelpful to measure output in terms of inputs – which is what Harrod argues. But no one is suggesting this be done. The critical thing is, as this study points out, that in dynamics it is distinctly unhelpful to conceive of *inputs* in terms of outputs.

nowhere have I argued that commodity capital as an *output* should be reassessed in 'real-capital' form. Questions have come up, however, about the rate of accumulation expressed in natural units or in terms of the consumption good.

In the two-sector case, suppose that technical improvements were taking place naturally in the consumer-good sector, but that none were taking place in the capital-good sector. I should then have, for the neoclassical version

$$t_{C_{NO}} = \alpha_C c + \beta_C(c - k_C)$$

$$t_{K_{NO}} = 0 \qquad\qquad (5.39)$$

and for the Harrod version

$$t_{C_R} = \alpha_C c + \beta_C(c - k_C) \qquad (5.40)$$

$$t_{K_R} = 0$$

In this case, and in this case only, the neoclassical and Harrod measures of the rate of technological progress are coincidentally the same. It is obviously that special case in which the efficiency of the economic system in reproducing and augmenting the growing stock of commodity capital is not being enhanced. It is the only case where the neoclassical treatment of capital as a non-basic is correct.

Some controversy about this case has appeared in the literature. If the labour input is growing at the same rate in both sectors, the Harrod technological progress is neutral and accumulation of commodity capital at a rate equal to the rate of growth of the labour input is taking place. If the labour input in both sectors is constant, then, as Kennedy[1] and Asimakopulos[2] have pointed out, no net accumulation in terms of commodity capital (i.e. machines) will be taking place. What is happening in the model is that the consumption-good price of commodity capital and the consumption-good real-wage rate will be rising at the same rate as output per unit of labour input and output per unit of commodity-capital input in the consumption-good sector.

In the capital-good sector, the marginal physical products of labour and commodity capital are constant if output is measured in terms of additional commodity capital. In the consumption-good sector, the marginal physical products of labour and commodity capital are rising at the same rate as improvements in technology are taking place in that sector. If, in the capital-good sector, *output* is measured in terms of consumption goods, then the marginal physical products of labour and commodity capital will be rising

---

[1] C. Kennedy, 'The character of improvements and of technical progress', *Economic Journal*, LXXII, December 1962, 899–911.

[2] A. Asimakopulos, 'The definition of neutral inventions', *Economic Journal*, LXXIII, December 1963, 675–80.

at the same rate as they are in the consumption-good sector.[1] If, in both sectors, the commodity-capital input is valued in terms of consumption goods and output is valued in terms of consumption goods, the marginal physical product of 'capital' will be constant. If commodity capital is measured in terms of 'real capital' in both sectors, then in the consumption-good sector the marginal physical product of 'capital' will be rising at the rate of technological progress in that sector; in the capital-good sector, if output is measured in terms of commodity capital, the marginal physical product of 'capital' will be constant, and if it is measured in terms of consumption goods, the marginal physical product of 'real capital' will be rising at the rate of technological progress in the consumption-good sector.

If commodity capital is measured in terms of its own units, no net accumulation will be taking place; if it is measured in terms of consumption goods, the rate of net accumulation will be equal to the rate of technological progress in the consumption-good sector.

If commodity capital is measured in terms of its own units, the neoclassical and Harrod rates of technical progress will be coincidentally the same and the industrial differences in them will exactly predict the course of the price of commodity capital in terms of the consumption good. If the commodity capital is measured in terms of 'real capital', the same analysis holds. If commodity capital is measured in terms of consumption goods, the marginal physical product of 'capital' (i.e. the net rate of return to 'capital') is constant in both sectors and the capital/output relationships in both sectors are constant. Thus, the rate of technological progress, overall and in both sectors, is neutral (though differing between sectors), and is the same whether assessed in Hicks–Meade or Harrod–Robinson terms. As I pointed out, however, it is a special case. The concepts remain fundamentally different.

In the two-sector case, suppose that no improvements in technology were taking place in the consumption-good sector but that such improvements were taking place neutrally in the capital-good sector.[2] I should then have for the neoclassical version:

$$t_{C_{NO}} \equiv \alpha_C c + \beta_C(c - k_C) \tag{5.41}$$

$$t_{K_{NO}} \equiv \alpha_K i$$

and for the Harrod version:

$$t_{C_R} \equiv \alpha_C c + \beta_C(c - k_C) + \beta_C i \tag{5.42}$$

$$t_{K_R} \equiv i.$$

---

[1] Kennedy has called this derived technical progress in the capital good sector. Cf. C. Kennedy, 'Technical progress and investment', *Economic Journal*, LXXI, 1961, 292–9.

[2] What Kennedy would call technical progress proper in the capital-good sector. Cf. Kennedy, 'Technical progress'.

In this case, in the consumption-good sector the neoclassical rate of technical change must be *zero* (that is, I shall have $\alpha_C c = \beta_C (k_C - c)$), whereas the Harrod rate of technical change in the same sector will be:

$$t_{C_R} \equiv \beta_C^{\cdot} i < t_{K_R} = i$$

This case illustrates that, because of technological improvements in the capital-good sector, the consumption-good sector experiences a rise in its capital/output ratio in physical units, which reflects the substitution of indirect primary for direct primary inputs in the production of consumption goods. The substitution permits a positive rate of increase in output of consumption goods per unit of labour input employed in that sector, such that, when the growing commodity input in that sector is reduced to its growing 'real capital' counterpart, while the 'real-capital'/labour ratio is constant, the rate of increase in output per unit of combined labour and 'real-capital' input in the production of consumption goods is positive. That positive rate of increase, though less than in the capital-good sector, is what the Harrod measure of the rate of technical change shows. It is clear that the efficiency with which the economic system is producing consumption goods *is* improving. The traditional neoclassical argument would be that a movement along the consumption-good industry's production function has occurred, rather than a shift. If the production function is correctly drawn up, in terms of the relationship between output and direct and indirect primary inputs, it is clear that a 'shift' in such a 'production function' has occurred in the consumption-good sector.

Again, if the labour input in both sectors is constant, it follows that, if commodity capital is measured in its own units, the rate of accumulation will be equal to the Harrod rate of technical change in the capital-good sector. Conversely, if commodity capital is measured in terms of consumption goods, there will be no net accumulation. *In this case*, if commodity capital is measured in terms of consumption goods *as an input* in both sectors, then, if the measurement is carried out along neoclassical lines, a positive rate of technical change will be observed in the consumption-good sector and the rate of technical change in each sector measured along neoclassical lines will equal the rate of technical change measured along the Harrod lines.[1] This fact is of crucial importance. It provides the link between the concept of 'real capital' as an input in the process of

---

[1] This is easily seen. The price of commodity capital in terms of consumption goods is falling at a rate equal to the Harrod rate of technological advance in the capital-good sector. Hence, when the commodity-capital input in both sectors is expressed in terms of consumption goods, the commodity capital is in fact being transformed in exactly the method outlined above for the determination of Harrod rates of technological change.

economic production and the concept of capital as a consumption fund, advocated by Hicks.[1]

In the general case, which I have discussed above, improvements in techniques are occurring in both (in *n* capital-good) sectors. As Asimakopulos states

Unequal technical progress in the two sectors is to be expected, and the relative values of the two types of goods will not necessarily change in proportion to the difference in technical improvement. For those inventions, which are on balance Harrod neutral, the constancy of the capital–output ratio will in part be due to the revaluation of existing capital and in part to new net accumulation. The two definitions [Hicks–Meade vs. Harrod–Robinson] will not be equivalent in these situations even if the production functions are of the Cobb–Douglas type.[2]

Asimakopulos is correct in asserting that the two (neoclassical vs. Harrod) concepts of the rate of neutral technological advance will differ in the general case – but the difference is fundamental. As I have shown, the course of relative prices is predicted exactly by the difference in the Harrod rates of technical change. It is not the form of the production function which is relevant. Rather it is the assumption of neutrality which is necessary to preserve Harrodian, dynamic equilibrium.

A 'production function' drawn up in terms of 'real capital' is more complex than the neoclassical version in terms of commodity capital, when technological progress occurs.[3] Yet clearly the notion of 'real capital' is the notion of capital Harrod wishes to employ as an input.[4]

5.8 The measurement of technical change in terms of prices

So far in this chapter, I have shown that the measurement of technical change is customarily conceived of and drawn up in terms of rates of growth of outputs and inputs. The two competing measures described were in terms of commodity capital and 'real capital' respectively. In terms of neoclassical analysis, one differentiates between movements along a production function and shifts in it. In terms of Harrod–Robinson analysis, one distinguishes movements among 'real-capital-ratio' curves.

[1] Hicks, *Theory of Wages*, 345, and *Capital and Growth*, Chapter xxiv, The Production Function. See Chapter 8 below.
[2] A. Asimakopulos, 'Definition of neutral inventions', 679–80.
[3] C. Kennedy, 'Harrod on "Neutrality"', *Economic Journal*, LXXII, March 1962, 249–50.
[4] Harrod says: 'If we define a unit of capital as so much waiting in respect of a unit of non-capital factors of production, then it should be supposed that the quantity of capital is growing at the same rate as the non-capital factors of production.' R. F. Harrod, 'The neutrality of improvements', *Economic Journal*, LXXI, June 1961, 303. As I have shown, this is precisely what the use of 'real capital' as a primary input, would entail under the assumptions set out.

Technological change can also be conceived of and measured in terms of the prices of inputs and outputs; the corresponding neoclassical measure is in terms of the rate at which Samuelson's[1] factor price frontier '*tilts* out' while the corresponding Harrod–Robinson measure is in terms of the rate at which the factor-price frontier '*shifts* out'. For simplicity, these cases are illustrated in Diagram 5.1, using the case of one-sector one-technique neutral technological progress.

Diagram 5.1 reveals both a close relationship and a fundamental difference between the competing measures of technological progress. It also conveys the essential lack of symmetry in the neoclassical version. The neoclassical version speaks of constancy in the commodity-capital/output ratio, a falling labour/output ratio and a rising wage/rental ratio. The Harrod–Robinson version speaks of falling 'real-capital'/output and labour/output ratios and a constant wage/'real-capital' price ratio. The neoclassical asymmetry appears as a lack of constancy in the ratio of primary inputs and also in their relative prices. The Harrod–Robinson alternative, however, conveys, as one would expect under conditions of neutral technological change, constancy in the ratio of the primary inputs and their changing prices.

I return to my identities. Ignoring depreciation, it will be recalled that, in the one-sector case, from

$$PQ = WL + RPK$$

I could obtain, with my customary manipulation,

$$q - \beta k = [\alpha w + \beta(r+p)] - p$$

I shall now concentrate the analysis on the right-hand side. The neoclassical measure of the rate at which the factor-price frontier is being 'tilted out' asymmetrically is

$$\alpha(w-p) + \beta(r+p-p) = t_{rk} \tag{5.43}$$

The term, $r+p-p$, is the growth rate of the rate of return to commodity capital, r, plus the growth rate of the nominal price of commodity capital, p, minus the growth rate of the price of output, p. In the one-commodity model the two p's would *appear* to be identical and in the neoclassical version they are. Here, exactly, is the error. Clearly, the identity between the two p's is coincidental. One refers to an output and one refers (or should refer) to an input.[2] Again, I argue that, if technological progress is to take on any meaning at all, clearly, as rates of change, the former (the rate of growth of the input price), should be greater than the latter (the

---

[1] Samuelson, *Foundations of Economic Analysis*.
[2] This is the logical impossibility of distinguishing between technical change and commodity capital formation, with which this chapter opened.

Diagram 5.1. One-sector neutral technological progress

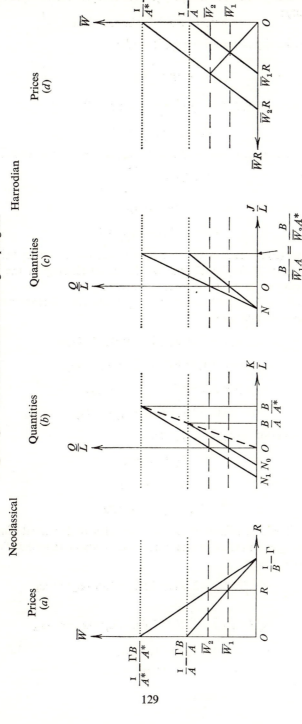

129

rate of growth of the output price). The Harrod version provides this result exactly:

$$\alpha(w-p)+\beta(r+p+t_R-p) \equiv t_R \qquad (5.44)$$

When this identity is solved for t_R, it reads:

$$w-p+\frac{\beta}{\alpha}r \equiv t_R \qquad (5.45)$$

When the neoclassical identity is solved for t_{NC}, it reads:

$$\alpha(w-p)+\beta(r) = t_{NC} \qquad (5.46)$$

If the one-sector case discussed above, when $r = 0$, is reproduced here, I have:

$$\alpha(w-p) \equiv t_{NC} \qquad (5.47)$$

$$w-p \equiv t_R$$

so that:
$$\alpha(w-p)+\beta(w-p) \equiv t_R \qquad (5.48)$$

which shows (*a*) the rate at which the 'neo-Keynesian' factor price line is being neutrally 'shifted out' and (*b*) the equal sharing in the fruits of technological progress by capitalists and workers.

I move directly to the two-sector case, where the Harrod measures of technological change are:

$$\alpha_C w+\beta_C(r+p_K+t_{K_R})-p_C \equiv t_{C_R}$$

$$\alpha_K w+\beta_K(r+p_K+t_{K_R})-p_K \equiv t_{K_R}$$

or
$$\alpha_C(w-p_C)+\beta_C(r+p_K-p_C+t_{K_R}) \equiv t_{C_R}$$

$$\alpha_K(w-p_K)+\beta_K(r+t_{K_R}) \equiv t_{K_R}$$

Thus, a solution to t_{C_R} and t_{K_R} yields

$$t_{C_R} \equiv w-p_C$$

and
$$t_{K_R} \equiv w-p_K$$

or
$$t_{C_R}-t_{K_R} \equiv p_K-p_C$$

The fundamental relationship between rates of technical change and rates of divergence in relative prices is seen once again. In terms of *n*-capital-good models, I have

$$\alpha_C(w-p_C)+\sum_{i=1}^{n}\beta_{iC}(r+p_{K_{iC}}-p_C+t_{K_{iR}}) = t_{C_R}$$

$$\alpha_{K_j}(w-p_{K_j})+\sum_{i=1}^{n}\beta_{ij}(r+p_{K_j}-p_{K_j}+t_{K_{jR}}) = t_{K_{jR}}$$

$$(j = 1, ..., n)$$

and essentially the same analysis as was provided above can be repeated.

Thus, in an important sense, the conception and measurement of technological progress in terms of prices represents the 'dual' of the conception and measurement in terms of quantities. In a truly dynamic model, there is no given amount of commodity capital. The presence of technological progress compels us to consider 'real capital' as the relevant capital input and its price, RP_K/W (or, more correctly, their dynamic counterparts), as the truly basic concepts of inputs and input prices.

5.9 Conclusion

In this chapter, I have shown that, under certain assumptions, it is possible to derive rigorously and simultaneously sectoral measures of the rate of change of 'real capital' and what I have called Harrod–Robinson sectoral measures of the rate of technical change. I have argued that the latter are logically consistent general-equilibrium measures of the phenomena of technical change which, by their demonstrated ability to predict exactly the course of relative prices, are explicitly transforming the commodity capital at use throughout the economic system into the Harrod–Robinson capital concept. I have demonstrated the superiority of this concept of capital, outlined the brittle conventionality of the commodity-capital input concept inherent in modern neoclassical economics and shown that the neoclassical concepts of technical change, based as they are on the commodity-capital input concept, suffer accordingly.

There is one remaining difficulty to set right. As I have repeatedly argued, technical change most realistically takes the form of improvements in labour, commodity-capital-goods and consumption-goods outputs. I have already shown that, when technical change takes the form of improvements in commodity-capital goods, the phenomenon of 'depreciation by obsolescence' arises and, if equilibrium social accounts are used, the incorrect neoclassical and the correct Harrod–Robinson measures of technical change can be derived. The equilibrium accounts introduce prices into the measurement of technical change and, even though I have shown that there is an essential dual relationship involved, it remains to be shown that, in the face of this type of technical change, the measures discussed in this chapter remain completely unaffected. To that task I now turn.

6

THE PROBLEM OF QUALITY CHANGE AND
ITS MEASUREMENT IN RELATION TO
CAPITAL AND TECHNICAL CHANGE

6.1 Introduction

Improvements in technology can be improvements in methods, in models or in men.[1] Improvements in methods are technical improvements, to the concept and measurement of which Chapter 5 was devoted. Improvements in men, if at some cost, represent investment in human capital, which is nothing more than another form of commodity capital and so are also covered by the analysis of Chapter 5. Improvements in men without cost are improvements in methods. Improvements in models represent a case which appears to offer some problems. Technical change can appear in the guise of the use of 'better', i.e. more efficient, capital goods, which are both part of the intermediate inputs used by an economy and part of the output which it produces. It can also emerge in the form of 'better' consumption goods, which appear only as outputs.[2]

In this chapter I deal with improvements in the models of capital goods. The treatment will, however, be general, in the sense that, if a satisfactory

---

[1] H. A. J. Green, 'Embodied progress, investment and growth', *American Economic Review*, LVI, March 1966, 138–51.

[2] The technical change which is classed as improvements in methods is, in terms of neoclassical production functions, output-expanding (cf. Meade, *Growing Economy*, 56–7) or product-augmenting (cf. T. C. Koopmans, 'Objectives, constraints, and outcomes in optimal growth models', *Econometrica*, XXXV, January 1967, 1–15). It is often expressed, as indicated in Chapter 3, as $Q = A e^{\alpha t} F(K, L)$. Costless improvement in men is called labour-augmenting, is written $Q = F(KL e^{l't})$, and is *misleadingly* often referred to as Harrodian technical change. Improvement in models of capital goods is called capital-augmenting, is written inaccurately as $Q = F(K e^{k't}, L)$ and is referred to as embodied technical progress, *with or without vintage effects*. On all this, see Meade, *The Growing Economy*, and E. S. Phelps, 'Axioms for factor-augmenting technical progress' in *Golden Rules of Economic Growth*. Improvements in the models of output could be written, again inaccurately, as $Q e^{q't} = F(K, L)$. The inaccuracy in these production-function expressions for improvements in models of capital goods and outputs arises because they fail to capture the fact that, when outputs are also inputs, anything which 'improves' outputs must simultaneously improve inputs, and vice versa.

method is discovered for dealing with improvements of capital goods then, since capital goods are both outputs and inputs for any economic system, that method should be valid for dealing with improvements in consumption goods as well. As I pointed out in Chapter 5, the problem is to derive a method to separate changes in prices from changes in quantities when 'new, improved, better' capital and consumption goods are introduced.

In Chapter 4 I noted that the phenomenon of 'depreciation by obsolescence' arises because the transferability of old capital goods from association with labour in old techniques of production to association with labour in new techniques of production involves rising short run costs. One can envisage, in a steady-state context, an optimum rate of renovation of existing capital goods. That optimum rate would determine the average life time of capital goods, given the rate of improvements in technology and the rate of growth of the labour force. If renovation costs are nil, and 'depreciation by sudden death and evaporation' are excluded by assumption, then capital goods last forever. If renovation costs are positive and sharply rising in the short run, the average lifetime of capital goods is reduced and the limiting case, with infinite renovation costs, sees the average lifetime of capital goods determined strictly, in steady-state equilibrium, by the rate of improvements in technology. In this chapter, I wish to devote more attention to the measurement of commodity and 'effective' capital when capital goods are subject to 'qualitative improvement', when, by definition, old capital goods can only at some cost be renovated to be as good as new.

6.2 Cases of output and input augmentation

In the analysis I shall make the same one- and two-commodity steady-state assumptions as I did in Chapter 5. If improvements are in methods and are neutrally and costlessly diffused over all men and machines, old and new, then men and machines are not subject to obsolescence, and the measurement of the stock of commodities and the concepts of the neoclassical and Harrod rates of technical change run along the lines laid out in the last parts of Chapters 4 and 5. In this case, I showed in Chapter 5 that the neoclassical and Harrod growth rates of technology were:

$$t_{NC} = q - \beta k = \alpha q = \alpha \bar{w} \tag{6.1}$$

and
$$t_R = q - \beta(k - t_R) = q = \bar{w} \tag{6.2}$$

If technological progress is manifested as improvements in men, costlessly diffused over all men, old and new, the measure of the rate of neoclassical labour-augmenting technological progress will be:

$$t_{NC} = q - [\alpha l' + \beta k] \tag{6.3}$$

where l' is the growth rate in efficiency of the labour force. From (6.3), it follows that $q = l'$, or, the neoclassical measure would appear to be equal to the Harrod rate of technical change.

What if technological change is manifested as improvements in machines, costlessly and neutrally diffused over all machines, old and new? Care must be taken with this case. In the case of improvements in technology which are manifested as improvements in methods, then in steady-state equilibrium the rate of growth of the stock of 'machines' is equal to the rate of growth of output. In the case where improvements in technology are manifested as improvements in men, the results depend on how we count men. In the third case, both commodity input and output must be evaluated with caution.

If I am to discuss growth rates of outputs and capital inputs, or compare outputs and inputs across economies, that is, if I am to continue to use the comparative dynamics of Chapters 2, 4 and 5, I must be able to compare outputs and inputs over time and across economies. I must, then, find a satisfactory method which permits me to say that *this* machine represents so much more (or less) 'machine' than does *that* machine, or that new corn represents so much more corn than the old variety.

Because this problem is dealt with in the neoclassical literature, in order to compare my results with those already available I shall be extremely neoclassical. The neoclassical theory must be very precise as to what is meant by capital, since the distinction between capital accumulation and technical change entails that capital accumulation can be accurately conceived and measured. I am also being neoclassical for the usual reason that I wish to investigate the neoclassical argument on its most favourable grounds. I shall consider a number of cases where capital goods (called machines) are improving in their 'quality' and where the rate of increase in such quality *can* be measured. I shall show that a number of puzzles arise, puzzles which can only be resolved when it is realized that the growth rates of standard (in a sense to be shown) machines and the growth rates of their improvement in quality *cannot* be separated. A valid method of measuring changes in improving machines is then discussed. It will be seen that there is only *one* way in which commodity capital can be measured. There is no meaningful distinction to be drawn between standard machines and 'efficient' machines. Solow's 'effective' capital is no different from the standard concept of the commodity-capital input and there is no distinction to be drawn between disembodied and embodied technical change. Once this is seen, the analysis of Chapter 5 can be said to be comprehensive.

I examine first the one-commodity model. I assume initially that the improvements in the commodity are diffused over all commodities, regardless of their age. There are no vintage effects. No other kinds of depreciation occur.[1] This case is trivial but serves as a useful introduction. The output (corn, say, measured in bushels) is growing at the rate q and is improving at the rate q'. The rate of technical change, in neoclassical terms, is

$$q+q'-[\beta(k+q')] \equiv t_{NC} \qquad (6.4)$$

or,

$$\alpha(q+q') \equiv t_{NC}$$

The Harrod–Robinson rate of technical change is

$$q+q' = t_R. \qquad (6.5)$$

All that happens is that the rate of technical change is raised by the rate of improvement of the one commodity.

I note also that, in steady-state neoclassical analysis, when capital is being 'improved', the 'contribution' of capital accumulation to growth, in *ex post* terms, is unchanged.[2]

If the social accounts were expressed in nominal terms rather than in terms of the commodity numéraire, I would have

$$PQ \equiv WL+RPK$$

in the rates of change neoclassical format,

$$q+q'-\beta(k+q') \equiv [\alpha(w-(p-q'))+\beta(r+(p-q')))]-(p-q') \equiv t_{NC} \quad (6.6)$$

and in the Harrod–Robinson format

$$q+q'-\beta(k+q'-t_R) \equiv [\alpha(w-(p-q'))+\beta(r+(p-q')+t_R)]-(p-q') \equiv t_R \qquad (6.7)$$

This formulation reveals explicitly what the rate of improvement, q', of commodities is. It is the rate at which the rate of price change of the commodities is 'biased' upward, because of the 'failure' of the qualitative improvement in the commodity to be included in the measurement of the

---

[1] Using the production function approach, I would write $Q e^{q't} = F(K e^{q't}, L)$ and, upon differentiation, derive identity (6.4). The improvement factor is inserted into both the output and input arguments of the production function and the inaccuracy mentioned in footnote 2, p. 132, removed.

[2] If, from $q+q'-[\beta(k+q')] \equiv t_{NC}$, I write $1 \equiv \beta(k+q')/(q+q')+t_{NC}/(q+q')$, then, as seen previously, this is $1 \equiv \beta+\alpha$, i.e. capital's 'contribution to growth' is β and the 'contribution' of the advance in knowledge is α. Thus, in a comparison of steady states where technical change is not and is 'embodied' in machines (both old and new), the contribution of capital to steady growth is unchanged. It may of course be the case that the βs will differ over such comparisons. See, for instance, R. C. O. Matthews, 'The new view of investment: Comment', *Quarterly Journal of Economics*, LXXVIII, February 1964, 164–76, reprinted in eds. J. Stiglitz and H. Uzawa, *Readings in the Modern Theory of Economic Growth* (Cambridge: M.I.T. Press, 1969). I have already shown, in Chapter 5, however, the uninteresting nature of such a result.

price change. This is an old argument, one which social accountants have been dealing with for many years now. The price of corn as corn is changing at the rate p but, if account is taken of the rate at which it is improving, the 'unbiased' price of corn is changing at the rate $(p-q')$.

What of the case where older capital goods do not share in the technical improvements? As indicated in Chapter 4, this is the case of 'depreciation by obsolescence'. In the previous case, the corn input and output were both improved varieties of corn. In this case, improved corn is produced from seed corn of varying varieties – as if the seed corn were made up of some of the many different varieties of corn which were part of the output of past periods. (The one-commodity simplification is beginning to be strained.) 'New improved' seed corn requires fewer units of labour than does old seed corn to produce the same flow of corn output. Each existing variety of seed corn will then have an equilibrium price, relative to 'new, improved' corn, such that it earns the prevailing rate of profit. Each equilibrium price will be a function, as was indicated in Chapter 4, of the real-wage rate and the rate at which it is expected to rise, the degree to which the ratio of seed corn to labour can be varied for each variety of seed corn, and the prevailing rate of profit. An aggregate stock of corn *can* be constructed with such prices and the prices will, of course, be different for any difference in the labour input, through its influence on the wage rate, in the rate of saving, through its inflence on the rate of profit and in the rate of technical change, through its influence on the rate at which real-wage rates are expected to rise over time.

There are two ways of approaching this case. First, the commodity capital produced in each time period can be said to 'embody' the technology of that period, so that with each period's capital goods there will be associated currently a flow of labour and output.[1] I can write

$$Q(v, t) = F_v(L(v, t), K(v, t)T_v)$$

where $K(v, t)$ is the commodity capital produced $(t-v)$ periods ago, 'augmented' by the technology in use then, still in use 'today' (T_v), and $Q(v, t)$ and $L(v, t)$ are the associated flows of output and labour input. The total output produced today, $Q(t)$, is equal to the sum of all the outputs associated with the various vintages of the commodity capitals,

$$\int_{-\infty}^{t} Q(v, t)\mathrm{d}v$$

An aggregate production function can be constructed showing aggregate

---

[1] For a complete discussion on neoclassical 'vintage' models, see Ferguson, *Neoclassical Theory of Production*, Ch. 13.

output as a function of the total labour input and an effective or augmented stock of commodity capital, or,[1]

$$Q(t) = F[L(t), J(t)], \quad J(t) = \int_{-\infty}^{t} K(v, t) T_v \, dv$$

How, exactly, would $J(t)$ be constructed? What is the meaning of commodity capital of different vintages added together with the 'technology' or 'productivity weights'? The only economically meaningful way of aggregating over all the 'vintages' of commodity-capital goods is by means of their prices – and the effective or augmented stock of capital is then nothing more than the net stock of commodity capital outlined in Chapter 4, when 'depreciation by obsolescence' was being discussed.[2]

Will the net stock of commodity capital and the 'effective' stock of capital by growing at the same rate? Yes! The fact that the 'effective' stock of capital and the net stock of commodity capital are the same shows once again that no aggregate capital concept is possible without the use of prices – i.e. without using an already determined rate of profit – and that no such aggregate can be used to determine the rate of profit. Furthermore, such aggregates will be subject to all the 'switching' difficulties noted in Chapters 2 and 4. I can, however, use prices to confirm the affirmative answer to the question about the growth rates of the 'two' capital concepts.

Can estimates of the net stock of commodity capital be prepared using, in fact, two sets of prices, one set 'adjusted' for the qualitative differences between capital goods and one unadjusted? Compare two machines, one new 'today' and one new 'tomorrow' and assume that the machines,

---

[1] Given the rate of return, the ratio of commodity capital vintage v to its associated labour, $K(v,t)T_v/L(v,t)$ is a function of the real-wage rate, $\overline{W}(t)$. Hence, I can write

$$Q(v, t) = F_v[L(v, t), L(v, t)H(\overline{W}(t))]$$

and employing the usual neoclassical assumption that F_v is homogeneous of degree one, I can write

$$Q(v, t) = L(v, t)F_v[\mathrm{I}, H(\overline{W}(t))]$$

Aggregating, assuming that F_v is the same for all v and noting that $H(\overline{W}(t))$ is independent of v, I can write

$$Q(t) = \int_{-\infty}^{t} Q(v, t) \, dv = F[\mathrm{I}, H(\overline{W}(t))] \int_{-\infty}^{t} L(v, t) \, dv$$

The total labour input, $L(t)$ is equal to $\int_{-\infty}^{t} L(v, t) \, dv$ so that

$$Q(t) = F[\mathrm{I}, H(\overline{W}(t))] L(t) = F[L(t), H(\overline{W}(t)) L(t)]$$

Note also that $L(t) = \mathrm{I}/H(\overline{W}(t)) \int_{-\infty}^{t} K(v, t) T_v \, dv$ so that

$$Q(t) = F[L(t), J(t)]$$

as above.

[2] It would thus appear that Solow's effective stock and net stock of commodity capital are identical, as Brown, Allen and Ferguson conclude and as was noted in Chapter 4. (See footnote 1, p. 75.)

when new, have the same nominal price (in line with my assumption that there is no monetary inflation). If better techniques have been 'embodied' in 'tomorrow's' machine, clearly the equal nominal prices are not appropriate weights with which to compare them. The prices which are appropriate are those which hold when the two 'vintages' are on the market together: just the prices I developed in Chapter 4 and just the prices used to weight the various vintages together into the net-stock concept. The comparison of different vintages of commodity capital *over time* requires the use of relative prices *over time* (i.e. price indexes) which exhibit the same relationship as do the relative prices over 'vintages' *during one period of time*. The crucial point is that no price comparisons over time would ever be drawn using the nominal prices. They would be adjusted for the qualitative differences in the capital goods over time, by means of the relative vintage prices. There are no price indexes unadjusted and adjusted for quality change: there is only one valid price index, only one set of relative prices with which to construct the net stock of capital.[1]

'Effective' capital and the net stock of commodity capital are not only the same concepts statically but they will be growing at exactly the same rate in steady-state equilibrium. Thus, there is no distinction between 'effective' and commodity capital and no measurement of technical change can possibly distinguish between disembodied and embodied variants. Solow's distinction between 'effective' and commodity capital and embodied and disembodied technical change is empty. In Chapter 4, I showed that one could only distinguish Solow's concepts from the standard neoclassical constructs if one could distinguish quality-adjusted and unadjusted price indexes. I have now provided the answer to that question. I deal more extensively with this point later in this chapter.

One immediate implication of the foregoing is that identities (6.4) to (6.6) need further examination. There is no distinction to be drawn between the rate of growth of output, q, and the rate of its 'improvement', q'. Nor is there any distinction to be drawn between the rate of change in its price, unadjusted for quality, p, and the rate of change in its price, adjusted for changes in its quality, $p-q'$. These identities collapse back to identities (6.1) and (6.2).

Most importantly, the analysis of Chapter 5, which showed the erroneous nature of the neoclassical concepts of technical change, stands unimpaired. The rate of growth of commodity capital is replaced by the rate of growth of the net stock of commodity capital. From Chapter 5, I can again write

$$Q \equiv \overline{W}L + R\sum_{v=1}^{n} P_v K_v + \delta \sum_{v=1}^{n} P_v K_v \qquad (6.8)$$

[1] The practical problems involved in constructing 'valid' price indexes are touched upon later in this chapter.

Remembering that in steady-state equilibrium the rate of 'depreciation by obsolescence', δ, and the net rate of return to capital, R, are constant, I can write

$$q - \sum_{v=1}^{n} \beta_v k_v + \sum_{v=1}^{n} \gamma_v k_v \equiv \alpha\overline{w} + \sum_{v=1}^{n} \beta_v p_v + \sum_{v=1}^{n} \gamma_v p_v \equiv t_{NC} \qquad (6.9)$$

where k_v is the rate of growth of the commodity capital of vintage v,[1] β_v (equal to RP_v/Q) is its correct weight, its weight in the net stock, P_v, multiplied by the prevailing rate of return multiplied by the capital (of vintage v)/output ratio, and similarly for γ_v. Identity (6.9) is the incorrect neoclassical version of technical change. The correct conception of technical change is

$$q - \sum_{v=1}^{n} (\beta_v + \gamma_v)(k_v - t_R) \equiv \alpha\overline{w} + \sum_{v=1}^{n} (\beta_v + \gamma_v)(p_v + t_R) \equiv t_R \qquad (6.10)$$

Thus, even though commodity capital will never again be reproduced in exactly the same form, the fact that the improved efficiency of the economic system is replacing it with 'better' forms must still be taken into account in any correct assessment of technical change.

The second way of approaching this case of vintage models of capital goods is to examine production relationships of the type portrayed by Sraffa,[2] though set out in the more usual standard input/output format, as shown in the accompanying table. For any process v which uses vintage v commodity capital, K_v, the social accounts are

$$P_v K(v, t) + \overline{W}(t)L(v, t) + RP_v K(v,t) \qquad (6.11)$$

$$\equiv Q(v, t) + P_{v-1} K(v-1, t)$$

where it is assumed that processes, as well as producing a part of the final output of the system, $Q(v, t)$, produce commodity capital one vintage older and, as well as having as inputs labour, $\overline{W}(t)L(v, t)$, and net returns to capital, $RP_v K(v, t)$, have inputs of commodity capital one vintage younger.[3] The older vintages are passed on to older processes and the younger vintages received from 'younger' processes.

[1] It might be thought the rate of growth of capital of vintage v would be zero (or even negative, if 'depreciation by evaporation' were added to the assumptions). However, as time goes by, each vintage component of the net stock is growing at the same rate as the aggregate net stock in steady-state equilibrium.

[2] Sraffa, *Production of Commodities*, Ch. x, 'Fixed capital'.

[3] It will be noted that in identity (6.11), the commodity capital output of the v process is written $P_{v-1}K(v-1, t)$. Strictly, this should be $P_{v-1}K(v, t)$ since a process, under the assumption of 'depreciation by evaporation' only, cannot pass along less commodity capital than was handed along to it *originally*, though it is currently receiving a larger amount of commodity capital owing to the general growth of the system. The reason for the difference is a notational one, since I want the $(v-1)$ process to be earning a rate of return on $K(v-1, t)$, the commodity capital appropriate to it.

	Vintages						Final output	Total output
	t	$\ldots$	v	$v-1$	$\ldots$	1		
Vintages $\quad v$	$SQ(v,t)$		$P_v K(v,t)$				$(1-S)Q(v,t)$	$Q(v,t)+P_{v-1}K(v-1,t)$
$v-1$	$SQ(v-1,t)$			$P_{v-1}K(v-1,t)$	$P_{v-2}K(v-2,t)$		$(1-S)Q(v-1,t)$	$Q(v-1,t)+P_{v-2}K(v-2,t)$
$\vdots$ $\quad 1$								
Labour			$\overline{W}(t)L(v,t)$	$\overline{W}(t)L(v-1,t)$				
Capital			$RP_v K(v,t)$	$RP_{v-1}K(v-1,t)$				
Total input			$Q(v,t)$ $+P_{v-1}K(v-1,t)$	$Q(v-1,t)$ $+P_{v-2}K(v-2,t)$				

From Chapter 4, I know that P_{v-1} equals $P_v e^{-\delta}$, where δ is the rate of 'depreciation by evaporation' and, consequently, identity (6.11) can be written as

$$\overline{W}(t) + RP_v K(v, t) + (1 - e^{\delta}) P_v K(v, t) \equiv Q(v, t) \qquad (6.12)$$

or approximately

$$\overline{W}(t) + RP_v K(v, t) + \delta P_v K(v, t) \equiv Q(v, t) \qquad (6.13)$$

or, the standard social accounts, which can be differentiated to derive neoclassical and Harrod–Robinson measures of technical advance.

In the form derived from identity (6.11), the Harrod–Robinson measures are, for process v,

$$\delta_v q(v, t) + \epsilon_v k(v - 1, t) - [\alpha_v l(v, t) + \beta_v [k(v, t) - t_{R_{v+1}}]$$

$$+ \gamma_v [k(v, t) - t_{R_{v+1}}]] \equiv [\alpha_v w(t) + \beta_v (r + p_v + t_{R_{v+1}})$$

$$+ \gamma_v (p_v + t_{R_{v+1}})] - \epsilon_v p_{v-1} \equiv t_{R_v} \qquad (6.14)$$

where, for example, $k(v, t)$ is the growth rate at time t of the inputs of commodity capital vintage v in the process v, etc., p_{v-1} is the rate of change of the price of commodity capital of vintage $(v - 1)$, etc., and t_{R_v} is the rate of technical change in the process v. The weights are, in addition to those already familiar, δ_v, the share of final output in the total output of the process, $Q(v, t)/[Q(v, t) + P_{v-1} K(v - 1, t)]$, etc.

As always, the Harrod–Robinson measures capture the interrelatedness of technical change. Each process is affected by the technical change of the process which precedes it and since each process contributes to the input of the process, t, using the latest techniques, each process also affects the process which precedes it.[1]

Under the assumptions of a steady state, one can aggregate over all the technical change measures to derive the one shown in identity (6.10). There is, strictly speaking, no need to aggregate the Harrod–Robinson measures, but it can be done if required. Thus, in Chapter 5, when measures of the rate of technical change for the consumption and capital sectors were worked out, there was no aggregate measure of the rate of technical change provided. As I shall now show, this can be done, if aggregate measures are wanted.

In the two-sector case, if technical change took only the form of 'new improved' capital goods, then, though they would have constant nominal

---

[1] From the input/output format, it can be seen that the final output of process v, $Q(v, t)$, can be divided into two parts: the first goes to meet the consumption needs of the system, $(1 - s) Q(v, t)$, where s is the rate of saving; the second goes to meet the needs of the latest process for new commodity capital, $sQ(v, t)$. Total new commodity capital, $\dot{K}(t, t)$, equals $\int_{-\infty}^{t} sQ(v, t) dv$ equals $sQ(t)$. The interrelatedness, indeed the indecomposability, of the 'vintage' system may thus be seen.

values (by my assumption of no monetary inflation), the consumption-good prices of capital goods would be falling *over time*.[1] In steady-state equilibrium, I would have, using the neoclassical variant, for each sector,[2]

$$c-(\beta_C+\gamma_C)k_C \equiv \alpha_C\bar{w}+(\beta_C+\gamma_C)(r+p) \equiv t_{C_{NC}}$$

$$i-(\beta_K+\gamma_K)k_K \equiv \alpha_K\bar{w}+(\beta_K+\gamma_K)(r+p)-p \equiv t_{K_{NC}} \qquad (6.15)$$

where k_C, for example, is the growth rate of the *net* stock of commodity capital in the consumption-good sector and β_C, for example, is the share of the net returns to commodity capital in the value of the output of the consumption-good sector. An aggregate measure of technical change, given the nominal[3] proportional rate of saving would be

$$(1-s)c+si-[(1-s)(\beta_C+\gamma_C)k_C+s(\beta_K+\gamma_K)k_K] \equiv [(1-s)\alpha_C+s\alpha_K]\bar{w}$$

$$+[(1-s)(\beta_C+\gamma_C)+s(\beta_K+\gamma_K)](r+p)-sp \equiv t_{NC} \quad (6.16)$$

Given the steady-state assumptions, the neoclassical measures would show no technical change in the consumption good sector. The aggregate measures would then yield

$$s[i-(\beta_K+\gamma_K)k_K] \equiv s\{[\alpha_K\bar{w}+(\beta_K+\gamma_K)(r+p)]-p\} \equiv t_{NC} \quad (6.17)$$

or,
$$s\alpha_K i \equiv s\alpha_K(\bar{w}-p)t_{NC}$$

and the neoclassical measures would become a function of the fraction of wage income in the capital-good sector in the *aggregate* product. The aggregate neoclassical measures also equal

$$(1-s)c+[s-\{(1-s)(\beta_C+\gamma_C)+s(\beta_K+\gamma_K)\}]i$$

$$\equiv [(1-s)\alpha_C+s\alpha_K]\bar{w}-[s-\{(1-s)(\beta_C+\gamma_C)+s(\beta_K+\gamma_K)\}]p \equiv t_{NC} \quad (6.18)$$

---

[1] By this I mean that the consumption-good price of 'tomorrow's' capital good *when new* would be *higher* when compared to the consumption-good price of 'today's' capital good *when new*, if they were on the market at the same time. If technical change were also occurring in the consumption-good sector, or if the consumption good was also being 'improved' over time, it might well be the case that the consumption-good price of capital goods would be constant, or even rising *over time*. See Chapter 5 for an analysis of the growth rate of relative prices in steady-state equilibrium.

[2] The neoclassical measures are gross measures, i.e. γ_C or γ_K is the share of 'depreciation by obsolescence' in the value of the two-sectors' output. I showed, in Chapter 5, that the neoclassical measures were critically sensitive to the 'netness' of the concepts, a stricture which applies *a fortiori* when the only 'valid' aggregate commodity-capital concept is the *net* stock of capital.

[3] In his 'Technical change and the measurement of capital and output', *Review of Economic Studies*, XXXII, October 1965, 289–90. P. A. Diamond has indicated that an s^* drawn up, not from the nominal accounts, but from a constant price set of accounts [i.e. $s^* \equiv p_0I_1/(C_1+p_0I_1)$] will lead to biases in measured rates of growth. Thus, $(1-s)c+si \neq (1-s^*)c+s^*i$. The constant price weights should, of course, never be used, as my use of the current price or nominal proportional rate of saving suggests.

If $c = i$ so that $p = 0$, then this collapses to

$$[(1-s)\alpha_C + s\alpha_K]c \equiv [(1-s)\alpha_C + s\alpha_K]\bar{w} \equiv t_{NC} \qquad (6.19)$$

By assumption, however, $i > c$ (i.e. the growth rate of commodity-capital accumulation exceeds the growth rate of the output of consumption goods) and t_{NC} must be some weighted average of c and i. For non-Golden-Rule cases, one of the weights, $s - \{(1-s)(\beta_C + \gamma_C) + s(\beta_K + \gamma_K)\} < 0$ (i.e. the share of net returns and depreciation in aggregate product), will be greater than the proportional rate of saving.[1]

For the Harrod–Robinson measures of technical change at the sectoral level, I shall have

$$c - (\beta_C + \gamma_C)(k_C - t_{K_R}) \equiv [\alpha_C \bar{w} + \beta_C(r + p + t_{K_R}) + \gamma_C(p + t_{K_R})] \equiv t_{C_R}$$

$$i - (\beta_K + \gamma_K)(k_K - t_{K_R}) \equiv [\alpha_K \bar{w} + \beta_K(r + p + t_{K_R}) + \gamma_K(p + t_{K_R})] - p \equiv t_{K_R}$$
$$(6.20)$$

and, at the aggregate level

$$(1-s)c + si - [(1-s)(\beta_C + \gamma_C)(k_C - t_R) + s(\beta_K + \gamma_K)(k_K - t_R)]$$
$$\equiv \{[(1-s)\alpha_C + s\alpha_K]\bar{w} + [(i-s)\beta_C + s\beta_K](r + p + t_R)\} - sp \equiv t_R \quad (6.21)$$

From the assumptions, I can rewrite the aggregate measure as

$$s\alpha_K i \equiv s\alpha_K(w - p) \equiv [(1-s)\alpha_C + s\alpha_K]t_R \qquad (6.22)$$

Thus, the aggregate measure of the Harrod–Robinson rate of technical progress is a function of the distribution of the labour force between the two sectors, since $s\alpha_K/[(1-s)\alpha_C + s\alpha_K]$ equals L_K/L.

If aggregate measures are desired, such Harrod–Robinson measures can be produced. I would myself prefer to remain at the disaggregated sectoral level of analysis.

6.3 Quality change

I indicated earlier that I would show how 'valid' price indexes, which capture the improvement over time in commodities, are constructed. The problem with which I am confronted is that when new models of capital goods are introduced, I have no easy way of comparing them with old models.

---

[1] Curiously, if $s = (1-s)(\beta_C + \gamma_C) + s(\beta_K + \gamma_K)$, i.e. the gross proportional rate of saving equals the share of the net return to capital, and 'depreciation by obsolescence' in aggregate product (the Golden Rule) holds, then, again, I have

$$(1-s)c \equiv [(1-s)\alpha_C + s\alpha_K]w \equiv t_{NC}$$

or the standard neoclassical result for the one-commodity case, even if $c \neq i$ and $p \neq 0$.

Recent theoretical and empirical work on the problem of the qualitative improvement in models of commodities deals essentially with new combinations of *old* characteristics of commodities.[1] Such a procedure, one which social accountants involved in the production of price and quality indexes have been both explicitly and implicitly following for years, cannot handle the problem of the truly new model, which embodies a new (or set of new) characteristic(s). When a truly new model is introduced, how does one compare it with the old?

If the old and new models co-exist in time and I assume that their relative prices are equilibrium prices, then the relative prices must be taken as representing how much 'more' the new is than the old.[2] This only tells us that we can use equilibrium prices to aggregate over a stock of heterogeneous items, on the assumption that such relative prices correctly represent the relative present values of the various items. If the old and new models do not co-exist, additional procedures must be entertained. The characteristics approach, in which the new model is merely a different combination of characteristics held by the old model (or family of old models), purports to tell us what would have been the equilibrium present value of the new model relative to that of the old model if the new model had, in fact, co-existed with the old. This value will, *in equilibrium*, be precisely the same as the cost of production of the new model if it had, in fact, been produced at the same time as the old.[3]

Now the same procedure must be used for the truly new model; that is, the model with which no old models co-exist and which entails at least one truly novel characteristic. Again, in equilibrium, one should be able to ask what the relative equilibrium prices of the new and old model would be if co-existence was assumed to hold. If one cannot compare the output characteristics of new and old models, one can compare the input characteristics and, *in equilibrium*, the same results should be derived.

[1] See, for example, Z. Griliches, 'Hedonic price indices for automobiles: an econometric analysis of quality change', *Government Price Statistics*, I; K. J. Lancaster, 'A new approach to consumer theory', *Journal of Political Economy*, LXXIV, April 1966, 133–56, and R. J. Gordon, 'Measurement bias in price indexes for capital goods', International Association for Research in Income and Wealth, Israel, 1969.

[2] This is the Champernowne 'chain index' argument elucidated in Chapter 4.

[3] G. Jaszi, 'An improved way of measuring quality change', *The Review of Economics and Statistics*, XLIV, August 1962, 332–5. See also A. Asimakopulos, *The Reliability of Selected Price Indexes for Measuring Price Trends* (Ottawa: Queen's Printer for Royal Commission on Banking and Finance, 1962), II (5). I shall ignore the problem that, if the old model (i.e. bundle of characteristics) were priced in terms of the new bundle of characteristics – i.e. as if the old model had been maintained so as to be, in fact, co-existent with the new – a set of relative values between old and new would be determined, which would not necessarily be the same set as that generated under the assumption that the new model was produced earlier so as to be co-existent with the old. This problem is merely a variant of the index number problem, which I am attempting to eliminate so that it will not fog an already intricate discussion.

To the extent that co-existence of old and new models prevails (or can be made to prevail), no problems arise. Little, if any, empirical knowledge exists about the relative importance of the case of non-coexistence between old and new models. Faced with such cases, however, a convention must be followed, and the appropriate one is that pursued by national economic accountants, whether using the Griliches or Jaszi approach, which are identical under equilibrium conditions.

An example will make this discussion clear. If two different machines exist simultaneously on a market in equilibrium, their relative prices will accurately reflect the marginal rate of substitution between them and provide us with a satisfactory weighting system to aggregate over the different machines. If model B comes on the market 'tomorrow' at a price, P_1^B, and model A goes off the market 'today' at a price, P_0^A, how do we compare the machines? If the physical characteristics of model B are such that 'today' they would have determined a price, P_0^B, then I can say the price relative between 'today' and 'tomorrow' is P_1^B/P_0^B and the comparability of the machines is established. Similarly, I can ask the question: What would it have cost to produce model B 'today' under 'today's' technical conditions and at 'today's' rate of profit and wage rates? Since each of the characteristics will have implied input costs, the estimated cost of producing model B 'today' would be P_0^B, the same price as determined by the characteristics approach.

The assumption of equilibrium is a difficult one to swallow.[1] No more is involved in accepting it, however, than in accepting the relative prices of coexisting machines, consumption goods or commodities of any kind, or the relative wage rates of different kinds of labour, as reflecting accurately their respective rates of substitution. Economic data of any kind are approximations and all measurements in any science are essentially conventional.

The point I seek to make can be made absolutely clear by noting that, under the one-commodity assumption, it is possible to envisage only two situations: one where output per unit of labour input is rising, in the sense that the number of commodities per unit of labour input is rising, with each of the commodities retaining one set of physical characteristics with which they may be identified; and one where output per unit of labour input is rising in the sense that, though the 'number' of commodities per unit of labour input is remaining unchanged, the 'quality' of each commodity is increasing, in so far as the set of physical characteristics which identifies each commodity at any one point of time is continuously changing. The words 'number' and 'quality' in the second case are in quotes because,

[1] See the comments by Tibor Barna on Hicks, 'The measurement of capital in relation' in eds. F. A. Lutz and D. C. Hague, *The Theory of Capital*, 303 ff.

as I have tried to show here, such words have no meaning. There is no economic meaning which could be attached to an index of the 'number' of commodities in the second case. No national economic accountant, proceeding to construct output and input quantity and price indexes in steady-state equilibrium, using either what may be called the output (Griliches) or input (Jaszi) characteristics approach, could come up with indexes in the second case which would differ in any way from those constructed for the first case. In short, no meaning can be attached to a price index unadjusted or adjusted for quality change – there is just one index which can be developed.[1]

These conclusions indicate that I derive the same rate of growth for Harrod technical change as was derived when it was assumed that technical change consisted of improvements in methods, neutrally and costlessly diffused over all men and machines, old and new. There is no difference, then, between output- and capital-augmenting technological change and they both simultaneously boil down to Harrod's case.

Jorgenson[2] has pointed out that Solow's 'effective' capital can be

[1] Much of the debate about the extent to which actual price indexes fail to reflect 'quality change' is confused. The only problem is how *well* the national economic accountants are actually performing their tasks. The conceptual basis behind the overlap case discussed is perfectly clear; the question is always how soon the overlap information is to be introduced, and that question simply boils down to the question of when it may be assumed that equilibrium or 'normal' conditions prevail. Thus, the Stigler Report (cf. Joint Economic Committees, *Government Price Statistics*, Washington: U.S. Government Printing Office, 1961) recommends that information arising from overlap cases be applied when the nominal price of the new commodity, given the customary history of prices, is falling relatively to the old. That recommendation is simply seen as an assertion that a return to equilibrium or 'normal' conditions occurs more rapidly than U.S. national economic accountants' behaviour in 'splicing' would suggest. Similarly it can be argued that, in the case where no overlap persists, the national economic accountant does not take account of a sufficient number of output or input characteristics in attempting hypothetical overlap information, but this merely means that national economic accountants do not take into account a sufficient number of characteristics in preparing price and/or quantity indexes in general. Thus the quarrel is merely about the extent to which the national economic accountant is following the correct procedure: there can be no question about the correctness of the procedure itself.

[2] D. Jorgenson, 'The embodiment hypothesis', *Journal of Political Economy*, LXXIV, February 1966, 1–17. Solow wanted to show that capital accumulation was more important for growth than his own earlier work had suggested. As Jorgenson shows, the effect on growth is the same whether the investment occurs in old or in new machines. An old machine costs 100 units of corn, a new machine costs 110 units. The ruling rate of return is 5 %, so that each old machine contributes 5 units of extra corn and each new machine contributes 5.5 units. Suppose now that savings of 1100 units of corn are devoted to accumulation. If old machines are produced, eleven are obtained and output rises by 55. If new machines are produced, ten are obtained and output rises by 55. An increase in the net stock of corn of 1100 units sees a rise in output of 55 units of corn either way. The fact that newer techniques are embodied in new machines does not mean that extra investment is correspondingly more productive and more important for growth.

obtained *simply* by assuming that the 'deflators' used to construct capital-stock estimates are 'biased' upward by their 'failure' to account adequately for the 'improvement in the quality' of the capital goods. What Jorgenson fails (I think) to realize is that there is in theory if not in practice no 'bias': i.e. there is one and only one price index. As a consequence, there can be no distinction between 'effective' and commodity capital.

If one cannot distinguish between 'effective' and commodity capital, then, as Jorgenson argues, one cannot distinguish between capital- and output-augmenting technical change. As this study argues, both these traditional concepts of technical change must be replaced by the Harrod–Robinson, or what is misleadingly called the labour-augmenting, concept of technical change.

If technical change is being embodied in only new commodity capital, all that really needs to be said is that capital goods are subject to 'depreciation by obsolescence'. Vintage effects aside, we learn nothing more about the concepts of technical change and capital as an input in the process of economic production.[1]

One final important point. If measures of commodity-capital accumulation, commodity-capital stock, consumption-good output, or output in general over time all suffer ambiguities *over time* because of the 'quality change' problem, all empirical constructs in economics which relate to growth are weakened. The measurement of technical change in Harrod–Robinson terms will, however, always require further adjustment to the capital-input data to reflect the reproducibility of capitalistic production. No matter how well or how badly the commodity-capital inputs are measured, the neoclassical measures of technical change will be fundamentally wrong.

---

[1] Consider a steady-state vintage-capital world where all prices are known and the net rate of return to capital is given. Suppose commodity capital is subject to 'depreciation by evaporation', Γ, *and* obsolescence, δ. The national economic accountant would then record the ratio of depreciation to the net stock of commodity capital as $\Gamma + \delta$. (See identities (4.15) and (4.51).) By comparing the prices of two pieces of commodity capital, the first one year 'younger' than the other, the national economic accountant could immediately determine the rate of 'depreciation by obsolescence'. (The ratio of (4.36) to (4.38) is $1 - e^{-\delta} \simeq \delta$.) From Chapter 4, p. 68, the national economic accountant could also learn that $\delta = \alpha t_R / 1 - \alpha$, where αt_R is Solow's rate of embodied technical progress. Thus, the difference between the total rate of depreciation and the ratio of prices, together with information on α, labour's partial elasticity of production, will determine αt_R – the rate of embodied technological progress. Thus, Hall is right when he says: '...if data on the prices of used machines and the interest rate are available, then the index of embodied technical change and the deterioration function can in fact be calculated from these data.' R. E. Hall, 'Technical change and capital from the point of view of the dual', *Review of Economic Studies*, xxxv, January 1968, 43. This is, of course, not a refutation of Jorgenson's position as I interpret it, since all forms of neoclassical capital-augmenting technological progress are indistinguishable and are to be replaced in analysis by the Harrodian concept.

6.4 Conclusion

In this chapter I have shown that careful scrutiny of what one means by 'improvements in machines', i.e. in general, changes in the quality of commodity capital, reveals that measures of technical change based on the distinction between commodity capital and 'effective' or augmented-commodity capital are empty. It is the argument of this book that all measures of technical change are contained in Harrod's concept. The distinction between embodied and disembodied technological change is just another way of depicting 'depreciation by obsolescence'.

7

ON THE CONCEPT OF NET OUTPUT

7.1 Introduction

In previous chapters, I have been critical of the standard neoclassical constructs. The adoption of such constructs by national economic accountants in their expression of national economic accounts in constant prices has led to the production of erroneous measures of output. This chapter examines this contention and shows the invalidity of many current measures of output and price change.

The relevance of the argument of this study to the dynamic theory of international trade is also very briefly shown. Essentially, this chapter is a generalization of my criticism of the capital input in neoclassical production functions subject to technological change to include *all* commodity-capital inputs. *It is one of the more practical aspects of what I have to say.*

7.2 Notation

In addition to the notation already introduced in Chapter 2, I will use one or two more symbols. I define I_N to mean commodity capital produced by the Nth capital-good sector. In this chapter, I_{MN} will denote commodity capital produced (sold) by the Mth capital-good sector and used (purchased) by the Nth capital-good sector and P_M will denote its price. In the first part of this chapter, dealing with an open economy, EX will denote a commodity export and IM a commodity import. The partial elasticity of production for imports in domestic production is denoted by δ. As before, all proportionate growth rates will be represented by small letters, i.e. $\dfrac{d(\ln IM)}{dt} \equiv im$. Other incidental notation is introduced where needed.

7.3 Some output concepts

In economic theory it is commonly assumed that, given a transformation function, inputs can without difficulty or ambiguity be treated as negative

149

outputs.[1] The analogous concept in national economic accounting is a productive activity's so-called 'value added', V, such that

$$V \equiv P_N I_N - \sum_{M=1}^{n} P_M I_{MN} \qquad (7.1)$$

where $P_N I_N$ is the nominal value of the gross output of the Nth industry (firm, activity, what you will) and $\sum_{M=1}^{n} P_M I_{MN}$ is the total value of the Nth industry's intermediate inputs flowing from the M industries (including N). This concept of value-added or income originating is one of the most fundamental concepts in national economic accounting. In current prices, it is unambiguous, except for well-known accounting conundrums.

When these measures of value added, at the activity, sector or economy-wide level (for an open economy), are produced in 'constant prices', they are, however, without economic meaning. Since it is almost impossible to examine any journal article or monograph dealing with growth and its industrial composition, production functions, productivity, etc. without encountering the use of such measures, their lack of theoretical meaning is a serious matter.

To avoid any semantic confusion, I explain exactly what are the different concepts of output used in national economic accounting. Census value-added means that the value of intermediate inputs includes only some intermediate inputs, such as materials and power used in (say) manufacturing operations. Gross domestic production originating in a sector means that *all* intermediate inputs are deducted. Net domestic product originating is the concept which includes capital consumption allowances (or depreciation) in intermediate inputs. In current prices, such measures of income originating are perfectly meaningful. Indeed, in the history of national economic accounting, it was by the use of such measures, when

---

[1] Indeed, ignoring externalities, I may write the transformation function for the ith firm as

$$T_i(..., X_{ij}, ...; X_{ji}, ...; ..., X_{is}, ...; ..., X_{si}, ...) = 0$$

$$(i = 1, ..., n)$$

where X_{ij} is the commodity output of the ith firm used by the jth firm, X_{ji} is the commodity output of the jth firm used by the ith firm, X_{is} is the output of the ith firm used by the sth household and X_{si} is the primary input service provided by the sth household to the ith firm. Similarly I may write the utility function for the sth household as

$$U_s = U_s(... X_{is}, ...; ... X_{si}, ...) \quad \text{where} \quad S = 1, ..., M$$

In the transformation function, I have intermediate inputs and outputs, final outputs and primary inputs, and in the utility function final outputs and primary inputs. Final outputs and primary inputs can be treated as positive and negative arguments of transformation and utility functions. Intermediate inputs can be treated *simultaneously* as positive and negative arguments of transformation functions.

summed over all industries, that income for a country as a whole was originally measured. Another concept of net output for a sector which is sometimes used is that of a sector's final output. A sector's gross output may be broken down into two parts: intermediate and final output. A sector's net or final output, then, will be its total (or gross) output less that part of its gross output which is required for the support of itself and all other sectors of the economy. By net output of a sector I shall mean the national economic accountant's concept of its gross output less intermediate *inputs* used by *that* sector. By final output of a sector, I shall mean its gross output less *its* intermediate *outputs* used by itself or *other* sectors. The concept of final output, at least for activities producing one commodity, is perfectly meaningful in a physical sense. It is the amount of the activity's output which is surplus, that is, beyond that part of the activity's output required as intermediate input, not only by itself but by other activities as well. An activity whose final output is negative is simply not a viable activity. For an activity engaged in the joint production of two or more commodities, the concept of final output is no longer an unambiguous physical concept but must be expressed in value terms.[1] A sector's gross output equals its gross input, so that gross output less intermediate input equals the value of the services of primary inputs. Summing over all sectors for a closed economy, the flow of intermediate output equals the flow of intermediate input and therefore the flow of final output equals the value of the services of primary inputs. This is, of course, a familiar national economic accounting identity. What happens to these summations and identities when they are expressed in constant prices?

I take it as given that index number problems are well known. A Laspeyres index of the gross output of a sector may differ from the corresponding Paasche index. I also take it as given that no time need be lost in attempting to construct some 'ideal' index. If I consider a sector producing two commodities whose proportions are not fixed by technology, an index number problem can arise, which is so severe that, over a period of time, in terms of one set of prices, the activity's total gross output is higher, while in terms of another set of prices the total gross output is lower. Nothing can be done about such index number problems. If they are sufficiently severe, there is no way in which the economist can assert that an industry's gross output is up or down. Analysis based on such comparisons must stop. This index number problem arises whether one is dealing with constant-price intermediate inputs, gross outputs or final

---

[1] An example was provided in Chapter 6 when, following Sraffa, I treated fixed commodity capital of different 'vintages' as outputs and inputs into each separate 'vintage' process, with each process simultaneously contributing to the total output.

outputs. It can arise from multi-product outputs of sectors or for the economy as a whole.

Constant-price net output indexes for an activity may be expressed in Laspeyres or Paasche forms, with correlative price indexes. I have, for a one-commodity gross-output sector:

$$\frac{P_{N_1}I_{N_1} - \sum_M P_{M_1}I_{MN_1}}{P_{N_0}I_{N_0} - \sum_M P_{M_0}I_{MN_0}} \equiv$$

(i)
$$\frac{P_{N_1}I_{N_0} - \sum_M P_{M_1}I_{MN_0}}{P_{N_0}I_{N_0} - \sum_M P_{M_0}I_{MN_0}} \frac{P_{N_1}I_{N_1} - \sum_M P_{M_1}I_{MN_1}}{P_{N_1}I_{N_0} - \sum_M P_{M_1}I_{MN_0}} \qquad (7.2)$$

or

(ii)
$$\frac{P_{N_1}I_{N_1} - \sum_M P_{M_1}I_{MN_1}}{P_{N_0}I_{N_1} - \sum_M P_{M_0}I_{MN_1}} \frac{P_{N_0}I_{N_1} - \sum_M P_{M_0}I_{MN_1}}{P_{N_0}I_{N_0} - \sum_M P_{M_0}I_{MN_0}}$$

A value index of net output is equal to a Laspeyres index of the 'price' of net output times a Paasche index of the 'quantity' of net output, *or* a Paasche index of the 'price' of net output times a Laspeyres index of the 'quantity' of net output. The sum of net outputs over all activities is equal to the sum of final outputs over all activities in current prices. The identity must, of course, hold true in constant prices.[1]

In terms of my standard notation, the growth rate of the value of the Nth sector's net output, v_N, is

$$\frac{1}{1-\epsilon}(i_N + p_N) - \frac{\epsilon}{1-\epsilon}[i_{MN} + p_M] \qquad (7.3)$$

where
$$\epsilon_M \equiv \frac{P_M I_{MN}}{P_N I_N} \quad \text{and} \quad \epsilon = \sum_{M=1}^{n} \epsilon_M \equiv \frac{\sum_{M=1}^{n} P_M I_{MN}}{P_N I_N}$$

The growth rate of the constant-price net output is

$$v - \left[\frac{1}{1-\epsilon}(p_N) - \frac{\epsilon}{1-\epsilon}(p_M)\right] = \frac{1}{1-\epsilon}(i_N) - \frac{\epsilon}{1-\epsilon}(i_{MN}) \qquad (7.4)$$

The accounts for the Nth sector, using the notation of Chapter 2, are

$$P_N I_N \equiv WL_N + \sum_{M=1}^{n}(R+\Gamma)P_M K_{MN} + \sum_{M=1}^{n} P_M I_{MN} \qquad (7.5)$$

[1] In Canada, for instance, Expenditures associated with Gross National Product (GNE) are deflated directly. With adjustments for the net international flow of interest and dividends, and indirect taxes less subsidies, a deflated measure of Expenditures associated with Gross Domestic Product at factor cost may be generated. This is identically equal, save for a new constant price residual error of estimate, to the sum of constant-price Gross Domestic Product at factor cost originating by sector.

With a constant rate of 'depreciation by evaporation' Γ, (again for arithmetic simplicity), I have

$$i_N - [\alpha l_N + (\beta + \gamma) k_{MN} + \epsilon i_{MN}] \equiv [\alpha w + (\beta + \gamma)[r + p_M] + \epsilon[p_M]] - p_N \quad (7.6)$$

where $\beta + \gamma = \sum_M (\beta_M + \gamma_M)$. These are merely the constant-price national accounts mentioned by Jorgenson and Griliches and discussed in Chapter 3 above. Identity (7.6) can be rearranged to yield

$$\frac{1}{1 - \epsilon}(i_N) - \frac{\epsilon}{1 - \epsilon}(i_{MN}) - \left[\frac{\alpha}{1 - \epsilon} l_N + \frac{(\beta + \gamma)}{(1 - \epsilon)} k_{MN}\right]$$

$$\equiv \left[\frac{\alpha}{1 - \epsilon} w + \frac{(\beta + \gamma)}{(1 - \epsilon)}(r + p_M)\right] - \left[\frac{1}{1 - \epsilon}(p_N) - \frac{\epsilon}{1 - \epsilon}(p_M)\right] \quad (7.7)$$

which clearly contains identity (7.4). Are these net output indicators valid? My criticism of them is a particular application of my criticisms directed against the neoclassical concept of technical change.

7.4   Aggregate constant-price net output

I begin consideration of what such indexes of net output mean by considering the case of an open economy. It has long been recognized that deflated final-output measures for an economy suffer from ambiguities when the prices of exports and imports exhibit different movements.[1] That is, suppose for an open economy I have the social accounts

$$Y \equiv P_C C + P_K I + \Gamma P_K K + P_{EX} EX \equiv WL + (R + \Gamma) P_K K + P_{IM} IM \quad (7.8)$$

Re-expressed in terms of my standard growth rate notation with a constant rate of 'depreciation by evaporation', I have,

$$\alpha^* c + \beta^* i + \gamma^* k + \delta^* ex - [\alpha l + (\beta + \gamma) k + \delta im]$$

$$\equiv \alpha w + (\beta + \gamma)(r + p_k) + \delta p_{IM} - [\alpha^* p_c + \beta^* p_K + \gamma^* p_K + \delta^* p_{EX}] \quad (7.9)$$

where $\alpha^* \equiv P_C C / Y$, $\beta^* \equiv P_K I / Y$ (the share of net investment in gross output), $\gamma^* \equiv \Gamma P_K K / Y$ and $\delta^* = P_{EX} EX / Y$. If the economy's trade is balanced (i.e. $\delta^* = \delta$), then the identity may be rewritten as

$$\alpha^* c + \beta^* i + \gamma^* k + \delta^* (ex - im) - [\alpha l + (\beta + \gamma)]$$

$$\equiv \alpha w + (\beta + \gamma)(r + p_K) - [\alpha^* p_C + (\beta^* + \gamma^*) p_K + \delta^* (p_{EX} - p_{IM})] \quad (7.10)$$

The term in the left-hand side of identity (7.10) is obviously the neoclassical measure of technical change of the economy, with the term

$$\alpha^* c + \beta^* i + \gamma^* k + \delta^* (ex - im)$$

[1] The many other problems involved in deflating final output directly are surveyed in B. J. Emery and T. K. Rymes, 'Price indexes in a social accounting framework', eds. A. Asimakopulos and J. Henripin, *C.P.S.A. Conferences on Statistics*, 1962 *and* 1963, *Papers* (Toronto: University of Toronto Press, 1964).

being the growth rate of national product and the term $\alpha l + (\beta + \gamma)k$ being the growth rate of national primary inputs. The term $(p_{EX} - p_{IM})$ is obviously the growth rate of the net barter terms of trade. Suppose the economy in question were not subject to technological change and that initially the net barter terms of trade were not changing. For such an economy in steady-state equilibrium, all growth rates of outputs and inputs would equal l (the growth rate of labour), all prices would show no growth rate and the rate of technological change will be zero. All is well.

Consider now an improvement in the net barter terms of trade, which arises because of technological change in the rest of the world. Assume first that all imports flow directly into final-demand categories, i.e. the households of our hypothetical economy purchase imports directly. If, for the economy being considered, domestic levels of output and prices remain unchanged, but import prices fall and the quantities of imports rise, then constant-price final expenditures on domestic product will, of course, show no change, even though it can be argued, because of the favourable development of the net barter terms of trade, that the real income of the residents of the economy has increased. A long literature has developed two points. First, there is a need for a terms of trade adjustment to constant-price final expenditures on domestic product if the resulting index is to be interpreted as measuring real income. There is no need for an adjustment if the constant price total is interpreted as a measure of domestic production.[1]

A more complicated and important question arises when trade is deemed to take place in capital goods and intermediate inputs. In both cases, the trade goods enter as inputs in the process of domestic production. Consider first the case when all imports are intermediate inputs. If such imports fall in price and foreign intermediate inputs are substituted for domestic intermediate inputs, the final output of the domestic economy will be increased. I again make assumptions with which traditional analysis is most at home. To clarify the discussion, I assume that the *final* output of the domestic economy is homogeneous and is a function of the homogeneous domestic labour force, the domestically-produced stock of capital and imports of intermediate inputs. I shall assume that the domestic labour force is constant and that the improvement in the terms of trade generates an increase in savings, which are invested in the domestic stock of commodity capital. Under such assumptions, if the economy were operating under perfectly competitive steady-state rules of behaviour, I would have

$$c - \delta im - [\beta + \gamma]k = 0 \tag{7.11}$$

---

[1] The latest piece of work in this literature of which I am aware is R. C. Geary, 'The general price level and the external trading gain', a paper presented at the International Association for Research in Income and Wealth, Ireland Conference, 20–6 August 1967 (mimeo).

that is, the growth rate of *final* output of the domestic economy is

$$\alpha^* c + (\beta^* + \gamma^*) k + \delta^* ex = c \tag{7.12}$$

by the assumption of a homogeneous final output, and is equal to

$$(\beta + \gamma) k + \delta im$$

The growth rate of the *net* output of the economy is

$$\frac{c}{1-\delta} - \frac{\delta}{1-\delta} im$$

which, since

$$m = \frac{\alpha + \delta}{\delta} c, \quad \text{equals} \quad \frac{(\beta + \gamma)}{1-\delta} c \quad \text{or} \quad c - \delta im = (\beta + \gamma) k$$

as shown. The growth rate of net output will be less than the growth rate of final output and the domestic economy will show no technical change in the neoclassical sense. The appearance of cheaper foreign-produced intermediate inputs acts, however, just like Harrod-neutral technological progress in the home economy. Substitutions of the cheaper intermediate inputs raises rates of return and frees resources in the home economy, in response to which domestic accumulation of commodity capital occurs and final output is increased. I continue to postulate that the full employment level of domestic activity is somehow maintained. The domestic stock of commodity capital will rise proportionately with final output.[1] However, the ratio of intermediate inputs imported to domestic final output would tend to rise, because of the substitution effect. But if this ratio were expressed in terms of domestic final output, it would show no change.

As I argued in Chapter 6, the basic mistake which is made in the deflated net output concept is the attempt to distinguish, when commodities are treated as both outputs and inputs, between shifts in and movements along production functions. By hypothesis, the imported intermediate inputs have cheapened because of improvements in techniques in the foreign country (or countries) and when the domestic economy substitutes foreign-produced intermediate inputs for those domestically produced, it is, in reality, combining its own primary inputs, unchanged in their economic efficiency, with foreign primary inputs, with their enhanced economic efficiency. The efficiency with which both domestic and foreign

---

[1] Actually, it would probably rise by slightly more. If inventories of commodities in the pipeline of production are considered, as they should be, as part of the domestic stock of capital, then the ratio of inventories of imported intermediate inputs to domestic final output would tend to rise, so that the ratio of the constant-price domestic stock of commodity capital to final output would rise. Expressed in terms of domestic final output, of course, the ratio would remain unchanged.

primary inputs are engaged in producing domestic final output has increased. Harrod–Robinson measures of technical change for the domestic economy would entail the abandonment of the concept of deflated *net* output. The technical change taking place simultaneously in both countries would have to be determined by solutions for both the countries. This is exactly the same as the case dealt with in Chapter 5, where technical change, in the neoclassical sense, was deemed to be occurring in the capital-good sector only.

The standard constant-price net-output measure for an economy reflects current-period quantities of gross outputs and intermediate inputs in terms of base-period prices. In the simple example considered, the gross output for the integrated economy is its final output, while its intermediate inputs are its imports. The changing relationship between the physical quantities making up final outputs and imports reflects the changing relative technologies of the home economy *vis à vis* foreign economies. To measure current-period outputs and inputs in base-period prices is to ask what would have been the income originating if the current-period outputs and inputs had been assembled under base-period conditions of techno-logy. This is, itself, a meaningless question, since under base-period conditions of technology, the optimum quantity of imported intermediate inputs was in fact being used. The rise in the ratio of imported intermediate inputs per unit of domestic final output reflects the improvements in technology abroad. To express net output in constant base-period prices is merely to create a fictitious measure of output with no meaning. It is important to note that by assuming that final output and imports are both homogeneous (though each different), no index-number problem in the traditional sense is involved.

The fallacious interpretation of price movements which can be caused by use of the concept of net output may also be illustrated by using the price side of (7.10), namely

$$\alpha w + (\beta + \gamma)(r + p_K) - [\alpha^* p_C + (\beta^* + \gamma^*) p_K + \delta^* (p_{EX} - p_{IM})] \quad (7.13)$$

By assumption, the growth rate of the commodity terms of trade is $p_{EX} - p_{IM}$. I assume that nominal final output rose by an amount sufficient to preserve the nominal price level of the homogeneous commodity being produced, and that the accumulation which occurred was sufficient to keep the nominal rate of return constant. Then identity (7.11) may be rewritten as

$$\alpha w - \delta^* (p_{EX} - p_{IM}) \equiv 0$$

$$w - \frac{\delta^*}{\alpha} (-p_{IM}) \equiv 0 \quad (7.14)$$

or, the nominal money-wage rate may rise at a rate equal to $\delta^*/\alpha(-p_{IM})$

without there being any inflation in the price level. This is, of course, just the rate at which domestic final output per unit of labour input is rising. The growth rate of the price of *net* output will be

$$\alpha^* p_C + (\beta^* \gamma^*) p_K + \delta^* (p_{EX} - p_{IM}) = \delta^* (-p_{IM}) \qquad (7.15)$$

which suggests that the domestic economy is experiencing inflation. It clearly is not. Central bankers who rely on such price measures will be misled.[1]

To summarize this section of the chapter, I have noted that deflated net output for an open economy is a construct which has two weaknesses. One is associated with an improvement in the real income of an economy due to an improvement in the terms of trade relating to trade in final-consumption goods. This is not a serious problem, since various conventions can be developed to measure the 'trading gain', which have as much and no more validity than all the other conventions involved in the construction of index numbers. The other, which in my view is a fatal weakness, is where trade takes place in intermediate inputs. In this case, the constant-price measure of an economy's so-called net output would diverge meaninglessly from the constant-price final-output measure. Since in most countries direct deflation of gross national product (or in Canada, what is known as constant dollar expenditures on gross national product) proceeds in the fashion described above and a large part of international trade takes place in intermediate inputs, I conclude that, as measures of domestic or national production, the net-output measures may be seriously misleading and are fundamentally erroneous. The basic fallacy is, of course, the neoclassical attempt to distinguish between shifts in production functions abroad and accumulation of imported intermediate inputs at home. If the measures of technical change advocated in Chapter 5 were applied in the case discussed, the home economy would show Harrod–Robinson technical change, though less than the rest of the world, and the commodity terms of trade would be exactly as predicted by the two Harrod–Robinson growth rates of technology.[2]

[1] In an earlier paper (Emery and Rymes, 'Price Indexes') I advocated the use of such price indexes. Even in that paper a cautionary note was sounded and I would now argue that, whereas such an aggregate price index is of some use for a closed economy (or one trading only in final consumables), it is of no use for an open economy.

[2] National accountants in the U.K. have long been suspicious of the deflated net output concept at the economy level, but their suspicions have been caused largely by the search for the correct treatment of deflated import duties. Two considerations have, I think, led to a neglect of the problem discussed: (i) international trade theory has, until recently, neglected the role of intermediate inputs; and (ii) much of the writing on terms of trade has taken place in countries where trade is not very important. The fundamental reason why the problem has been neglected is that, until recently, traditional theory has been concerned with the static theory of production. Only now are we beginning to put forward a dynamic theory of *Production of Commodities by Means of Commodities*.

7.5   Disaggregate constant-price net outputs

I indicated earlier that the concept and uses of constant-price net output at the disaggregated activity or sector level are becoming increasingly common. They are equally faulty. Consider the Laspeyres index of constant-price net output of the Nth sector:

$$\frac{P_{NO}I_{NI} - \sum_M P_{MO}I_{MNI}}{P_{NO}I_{NO} - \sum_M P_{MO}I_{MNO}}$$

It is recognized in the social accounting literature that this measure of net output can conceivably take on zero or even negative values.[1] This is customarily treated as an extreme index-number problem, where the sector substitutes intermediate inputs whose prices are falling relatively, up to the point where the constant-price intermediate inputs equal, or are greater than, the constant-price gross outputs. This is regarded as hypothetically possible and where it arises, the phenomenon is said to indicate a need to reweight the indexes. No suggestion is seriously made that the output concept is wrong.[2]

Two points must, however, be made. First, the phenomenon of a sector's constant-price net output moving differently from its constant-price final output is *not*, as I have shown, an index-number problem in the traditional sense. Second, while negative levels of such indexes are clearly absurd, the fact remains that *any* level of the net-output measures is meaningless. I shall elaborate on these points. First, however, I shall modify the concept of a sector's final output which was discussed above. I shall refer to that part of a sector's gross output which goes beyond itself as final output to itself. Thus, for any sector, its gross output may be broken down into three parts: (i) the intra-sector output (e.g. coal used to produce coal); (ii) intermediate output which flows outside the sector to meet the intermediate input needs of other sectors; and (iii) that part of its gross output which flows into the economy's final demand categories. That output which is final to the sector itself clearly consists of the sum of (ii) and (iii).

A sector, as in the whole-economy example of the preceding section, can produce one homogeneous output and use only one homogeneous intermediate input. If technical change in the direct or indirect production of

---

[1] A similar phenomenon is cropping up in the literature on the so-called theory of *effective* tariff protection.

[2] In P. David, 'Deflation of value added', *Review of Economics and Statistics*, XLIV, May 1962, 148–55, the ludicrous results that such indexes may from time to time produce are recognized. David, however, attributes such results to particularly complex index-number problems. He does not realize that the whole concept is erroneous. See also P. David, 'Measuring real net output: a proposed index', *Review of Economics and Statistics*, XLVIII, November 1966, 419–25.

the *intermediate input* is greater than the technical change *within* the industry itself, then, in general, we should expect a rise in the ratio of intermediate inputs to gross output in the sector. Production in the sector under review will become, in the traditional sense of substitution in response to changing relative prices, more intermediate-input-intensive. The gross output of the sector will rise, but less proportionately than its intermediate input. A constant-price measure of net output will rise less than the gross-output measure.

If I assume that the gross output of the sector is a function of its labour input, the stock of capital and intermediate input, and that, in response to a cheapening of the intermediate input, only this input is increased in its use,[1] then the growth rate of the sector's gross output will be positive, while the rate of increase in the sector's net output will be zero. The result follows directly from the argument that the growth rate of gross output will be equal to the growth rate of the intermediate input multiplied by its partial elasticity of production.

The rationale customarily used to support this result is that, while the movements of gross outputs and intermediate inputs reflect changing relative technologies, in base-period terms the value added by this sector to the economy's total net output has remained unchanged. The gross output of the primary inputs directly engaged in the sector under review has, however, increased *because* they act in collaboration with the increased efficiency of the primary inputs indirectly engaged in producing that gross output. The basic fault with the net-output measure is that it seeks to isolate technical change in the sector in which it arises. The traditional defence of the net-output concept is, in fact, that it distinguishes shifts from movements along production functions. The phenomenon of technical change is, however, a general-equilibrium problem, which does not permit the traditional distinction to be meaningfully made. Belief in the viability of the traditional distinction provides the backbone of modern neoclassical analysis. It also provides the rationale for accepting as meaningful the net measures of output being discussed. In cases where what is believed to be an index number problem in the classical sense generates nonsense measures of sector's net output, the meaninglessness of such measures becomes embarrassingly evident to all.

In Chapter 5, I have shown that, when technical change is taking place, the *correct* measure of such progress in the Nth sector is

$$i_N - [\alpha_N l_N + \sum_M (\beta_{MN} + \gamma_{MN})[k_{MN} - t_{R_M}] + \sum_M \delta_{MN}(i_{MN} - t_{R_M})] = t_{R_N} \quad (7.16)$$

[1] Additional accumulation and labour-force growth in the sector may occur. If such additions are taken account of (as in the open economy case above), I make the argument more rigorous in the general-equilibrium sense. However, I add nothing of substance to the particular argument being made.

Possible measures of net output could be derived from this if desired. It is clearly preferable to work with gross output as the relevant output concept for the industry in question. A supposed advantage of the traditional net-output concept is that aggregation over all sectors leads to a constant-price measure of the *final* output of a closed economy. (Aggregation over the sectors of an open economy still leaves the problem of imported intermediate inputs and differences between final and net output for the domestic economy.) Aggregation of final outputs to each sector over all sectors can be done by combining sectors in such a way that intra-sector outputs and inputs are sequentially eliminated as the process of aggregation proceeds. Such an aggregation procedure over final outputs to each sector yields the correct measure of total final output for both closed and open economies.[1] A search for a procedure by which measures of technical change and output can be aggregated over an inter-related set of sectors in a neo-classical manner is really, as I have shown, a denial of the general-equilibrium phenomenon being discussed. The Harrod–Robinson measures, while taking into account general equilibrium requirements, can nevertheless also be aggregated over sectors in the manner suggested.

In this section I have demonstrated the inadequacies of the traditional measure of net output. I have advocated the use of gross output as the relevant and meaningful measure of sector output and argued the case for the final-output concept as correct for aggregation purposes.

One further comment on the concept of net output may be useful. The utilization by a sector of more intermediate input, assuming that technology in the sector is well behaved in the traditional sense, will, it is said, increase the marginal physical product of inputs primary to the sector. A perfectly competitive sector, faced with given primary input prices, would seek to hire more primary inputs and raise gross outputs until equilibrium competitive output conditions held once more. The net-output concept would suggest that one should talk about a rise in the *net* marginal physical products of the primary inputs, together with a fall in their *net* price. These net marginal products and net prices cannot be read from either the technology or the market, in the general case of technology which permits substitution. Constant-price measures of outputs and inputs are constructs which are never found in the real world. If the world can be assumed to be so simple (e.g. the homogeneous outputs and inputs in my case) that the index-number problems plaguing such constructs can be removed, then the constructs ought to make sense. This the net-output construct does not do. In my judgment, the construct is one which should

---

[1] For a further discussion of such an aggregation procedure, see Emery and Rymes, 'Price Indexes'.

be abandoned – and with it almost every industry and economy constant-price net-output measure produced by statistical authorities around the world.

7.6 Conclusion

In this chapter, I have attempted to show that the traditional concept of net output, in which intermediate inputs are treated as negative outputs, when cast in constant-price terms yields measures of output which are without economic meaning. I have shown that such a formulation raises a number of awkward and intractable problems at the sector, and open economy, level. I have also shown that the correct measure of output is gross or final. I have indicated, by drawing upon the analysis provided in Chapter 5, that the basic fault of the net-output measure, in a world subject to technical change, is that it reflects the traditional attempt, with inputs assessed as commodity outputs, to distinguish between shifts in and movements along a production function. The case for the Harrod–Robinson concepts of technical change intrudes even into the 'real' world of national economic accounting. Pure theory has, in this case, an immediately practical use.

8

PROFESSOR HICKS AND CONCEPTS OF CAPITAL AND THE PRODUCTION FUNCTION*

8.1 Introduction

In this chapter, I examine, in both the static and the more important dynamic contexts, the concepts of capital and the production function developed recently by Professor J. R. Hicks. He has been studying two concepts of capital. The first, which conceives of capital as Physical Things, such as machines, blast furnaces, etc., he seems to abandon in the dynamic context of technical change. The second deals with capital in terms of a Consumption Fund. With the rejection of the first I agree and have argued that it should be replaced by a concept found in the writings of Harrod. I shall show that the concept finally accepted by Hicks suffers from a number of ambiguities and also is found in an unambiguous state within the Harrodian system.

I use Hicks' writings because, like Meade, he states the neoclassical case so clearly and, unlike Meade, appears most uncomfortable with its concepts.

I employ in this chapter the apparatus for comparing steady-state equilibria employed throughout this book.

8.2 Four recent writings by Hicks

Describing himself as one of those who seeks to find a rehabilitated 'Production Function' in some form or another, Professor Hicks introduced, in his contribution to the Corfu Conference, two concepts of capital: a forward-looking concept and a backward-looking concept.[1] The forward-looking concept was capital measured in terms of the product

---

* An emended version of a paper given to the Department of Economics Seminar at Queen's University, 3 February 1969. I am grateful to Professor Dan Usher for comments he made at that time. A later version was given to the Department of Economics Seminar of the University of Strathclyde on 4 December 1969. I am also extremely appreciative of comments by Sir John Hicks on an earlier draft.

[1] Hicks, 'The measurement of capital in relation'.

162

which capital can produce with a given amount of labour and given technical conditions. Hicks felt this to be unhelpful since in his view it led to the result that 'a larger capital so applied *must* then produce a larger product'.[1] As will be seen later, though, this is the concept which Hicks ends up by supporting. The backward-looking capital concept, measured in its own units (machines, blast furnaces, etc.), would appear to give a clear meaning to the Marginal Productivity of Capital. Addressing himself to the standard format $Q = X(L, K)$, Hicks says:

> ...let us take our stand at time t; and let us both prefix to t a process leading up to t, and also adjoin to t a process leading on from t (the technique appropriate to time t being preserved, in the way it should be, throughout each of these processes). Then K is a reflection of the backward-looking process, and Q is a reflection of the forward-looking process. If K had been larger, that would mean that more labour or saving had been applied in the former process; if Q is larger, that will mean that the flow of consumption goods is larger (as a whole) in the latter process. So that if capital has a positive marginal productivity, an increase in input, or a reduction in output, in the former process makes possible an increase in output (without reduction in input) in the latter process. The Marginal Productivity of Capital is the Marginal Productivity of Roundaboutness, after all.[2]

The important thing in this conclusion is the insistence that, in a static environment, the inputs and outputs in the production function be related in terms of the optimal techniques currently in use at time t.

One of the statisticians at the Corfu Conference, Tibor Barna, remarked on Hicks' paper that

> He [Barna] found it necessary to use two alternative concepts, which he believed to be similar to those of Professor Hicks. He had called the one capital in terms of resources and the other capital in terms of its own productive efficiency... – with technical progress, the resources embodied in capital yielded more and more final output. So, whenever we measured the stock of capital over time we were bound to get a difference between the two measures.... One could show that all the so-called indices of capital goods measured neither input nor output but something in between. *The usual statement was that it was a price-index ignoring 'quality change'. Quality change was very difficult to define and it was much easier to define and measure Professor Hicks' two indices.*[3]

Does this mean that the difference between Hicks' concepts arises from the qualitative improvement in capital goods? If so, Barna is wrong. His statement brings the problem of the qualitative improvement in capital goods to the fore and asks us, in fact, to distinguish between new capital goods which remain physically unchanged and new capital goods which

[1] *Ibid.*, 30.
[2] *Ibid.*, pp. 30–1. I have altered Hicks' notation to that used throughout this paper.
[3] *Ibid.*, 303. My emphasis.

change their form over time or over different economies. For the latter we may say that the own-productivity efficiency of the capital goods is changed or that improvements in technology have been embodied in them.[1] It would appear that this idea can be generalized to include labour- and output-augmenting, as well as capital-augmenting, variants.[2] As I have shown,[3] however, only one measure of capital is meaningful and can be empirically produced: there is no difference between capital and augmented or embodied or effective capital. There would appear then to be only one backward-looking concept of capital, with which we have to concern ourselves. Hicks is thus able to say:

We can speak of the *technology of time A*, in spite of the fact that (in a technically advancing economy) some of the capital goods existing at time A will be obsolete; they would not have been made in that form if A-knowledge had existed at the time of their original construction. The actual physical make-up of the A-capital is always a datum. When we are measuring it as output, it is the technology of *making* those capital goods which is relevant; their obsolescence does not enter into question. When we are measuring it as input, it is the use which can now be made of these actual goods which matters; it does not matter that better ways of making them, or superior substitutes for them, have been discovered.[4]

It can be concluded thus far that Hicks in his forward-looking concept conceives of capital in terms of consumption goods and in his backward-looking concept conceives of capital goods in terms of their own units.

In his long commentary on the second edition of *The Theory of Wages*, the two concepts become respectively the 'Fund' and the 'Physical Things' concepts. Hicks says

...whereas the Physical concept treats capital as consisting of actual capital goods, the Fund concept reduces it to equivalent consumption goods, the consumption goods that are foregone to get it. Not that we should think (as some of the cruder statements of the Old Classical Economists almost suggest) of the whole social capital being accumulated, over any period, however long, by abstinence from consumption; it is simply at the margin that capital is valued (on the Fund approach) by consumption foregone.[5]

Hicks' forward-looking, or Fund, concept would appear to be Fisherian. It deals with the marginal rate at which present consumption goods foregone can be transformed into future consumption goods. It is Solow's concern with the social rate of return to investment which interests Hicks here.[6] To move from the marginal physical product (expressed as the present value of future consumption goods) of a Physical Thing to the

[1] Solow, *Capital Theory*, 42.   [2] Meade, *Growing Economy*, 57.
[3] See Chapter 6.
[4] Hicks, 'The measurement of capital in relation', 25.
[5] Hicks, *Theory of Wages*, 343.
[6] Solow, *Capital Theory*. See also Usher, 'Traditional Capital Theory'.

marginal efficiency of consumption foregone requires the marginal rate at which consumption foregone can be transformed into today's Physical Things, i.e. the price of 'machines' in terms of consumption goods.[1]

In standard one-commodity presentations, the capital input, expressed in terms of the Fund and Physical Things concepts, will be identical. In two-commodity worlds, however, in terms of Physical Things we would have

$$C = C(L_C, K_C)$$

$$I = I(L_K, K_K)$$

whereas in terms of the Fund Concept the two production functions would appear as

$$C = C\left(L_C, \frac{P_K}{P_C} K_C\right)$$

$$I = I\left(L_K, \frac{P_K}{P_C} K_K\right)$$

where the capital inputs as Physical Things, K_C and K_K, are re-expressed in terms of the Consumption-Fund concept, by means of the price of commodity capital in terms of the consumption good.

Which way of representing technology is better? If a technical improvement occurs in the capital-good sector, the second set of production relationships would suggest that output in both sectors can be produced at a lower cost in terms of consumption goods foregone. Hicks says

The distinction which I have been drawing between the Physical concept of capital and the Fund concept is highly relevant to the question of inventions. What is really the main reason...why I do not care to use the Fund concept *when making static comparisons* is that it gives such odd results when we come to deal with changes in technology. Consider the effects of an invention which affects productivity in the investment goods trades only. So long as we are using the Physical concept, this is just like any other invention; it only affects a part of the Social Product (that devoted to Investment), but from that point of view it is exactly on a par with an invention which only changes productivity in the manufacture of cheese. But if we are using the Fund concept, we have to say that the capital of the economy is reduced as a result of the invention. It still consists of the same physical goods, but it is reduced in Fund terms, because it can be replaced at a smaller sacrifice of consumption goods than before. The effect of such an invention cannot then be expressed in terms of simple reactions on the marginal products of the factors, for we have also to take into account the change in the 'quantity' of one of the factors which has occurred, *ipso facto*, as a result of the invention. The same difficulty arises with any change in technology, whenever there is a difference between the effects of the improvement on investment and consumption.[2]

[1] Concepts which in the order of their introduction Lerner calls *mpk*, the marginal productivity of capital, *meI*, the marginal efficiency of investing and *mpI*, the marginal productivity of investing. See A. P. Lerner, 'Capital', *International Encyclopaedia of Social Sciences*, 2 (New York: Crowell Collier and Macmillan, 1968), 276.

[2] Hicks, *Theory of Wages*, 348–9. My emphasis.

Alternatively, if one were comparing economies, output per unit of capital measured in terms of consumption goods in the consumption-good sector would vary unpredictably as the ratio of the wage rate to the net rate of return varied across the economies. For economies with identical fixed technologies, the movement of the price of the capital good in terms of the consumption good will depend on which sector is the more capital-intensive. For economies with identical variable technologies, positive, neutral or negative Wicksell *price* effects may be experienced and there is no reason to expect the capital intensities of production with capital measured in terms of consumption goods to be greater for economies with higher wage-rate/net-rate-of-return ratios. It is this kind of result which leads Hicks to say that '…it is only if one is using the Physical concept of capital that it is possible to have a Production Function which represents the state of technology in at all a straightforward manner.'[1]

Hicks makes only a footnote[2] reference to Mrs Robinson's concept of 'real capital' which, as is well known, entails the measurement of capital in terms of labour time.

Using 'real capital', I would write the production relationships as

$$Q = Q\left(L, \frac{K}{\overline{W}}\right)$$

or

$$C = C\left(L_C, \frac{(P_K/P_C)\,K_C}{\overline{W}}\right)$$

$$I = I\left(L_K, \frac{(P_K/P_C)\,K_K}{\overline{W}}\right)$$

A technical improvement in the capital-good sector would see a fall in the 'real-capital'/labour ratio. Alternatively, given the technology, a comparison of economies with different real-wage/net-rate-of-return ratios, would yield different ratios of 'real capital' to labour, and positive, neutral or negative *real* Wicksell effects. Accordingly, representation of technical relationships in 'real capital' terms leads to the same lack of straightforward results witnessed with the use of the forward-looking, or Fund, concept of capital.[3]

---

[1] *Ibid.*, 345.   [2] *Ibid.*

[3] Samuelson, 'Parable and realism', 203 and D. C. Champernowne, 'The production function and the theory of capital: a comment', *Review of Economic Studies*, XXI (2), 1953–4, 112–35.

Samuelson and Champernowne are both bothered by the peculiar behaviour of the ratio of 'real capital' to labour in relation to the ratio of the real-wage rate to the net rate of return, as contrasted with what was assumed to be the well-behaved relationship when capital was expressed in commodity-capital terms. As the 'switching' problem shows, however, the assumption of 'good' behaviour on the part of the traditional concepts was ill-founded. How do we choose now?

The standard concept of the production function is perfectly valid[1] when one is scanning across economies over time and space, where techniques are unchanged and exhibit constant returns to scale. In the one-commodity case, from

$$Q = Q(L, K)$$

one can meaningfully write

$$q = \alpha l + \beta k$$

where the proportionate rates of change may represent differences over time or across economies. If the economy has experienced accumulation with an unchanged labour force, q will equal βk (again, over time or across economies).[2] In the two-sector two-commodity case, from

$$C = C(L_C, K_C)$$

$$I = I(L_K, K_K)$$

one can meaningfully write

$$c = \alpha_C l_C + \beta_C k_C$$

$$i = \alpha_K l_K + \beta_K k_K$$

Again, there is no difficulty with this formulation over time or across economies.[3]

When there are more than two capital goods, the traditional aggregate concept breaks down. It will be recalled from Chapter 4 that measures of aggregate capital can be prepared. It is true in such cases that the aggregate concept will not help to prove anything – in particular, it cannot be used as a partial derivative of the net rate of return. The use of Physical Things, while valid, still leaves the determination of the rate of profit unsolved. In other words, completely exhaustive statements of the techniques available

---

[1] It should now be clear that by valid I mean only a representation of technical relationships where the outputs and inputs are physically specified. I do not mean any aggregation of whatever kind.

[2] If, for the same economy, with an unchanged constant-returns-to-scale technology, the instantaneous rate of growth one time 'period' later is $q^* = \beta^* k$, then the technology has an elasticity of substitution which is a function of the capital/labour ratio. If β fell while the capital/labour ratio rose, then $q \to q^*$ would be less than βk and greater than $\beta^* k$. In such discrete cases, an index-number problem exists. The same problem holds for the comparison across economies.

[3] In terms of prices, these relationships are for the one-commodity case,

$$1 = P(\overline{W}, R)$$

and

$$0 = \alpha \overline{W} + \beta r$$

and for the two-commodity case,

$$1 \equiv C(\overline{W}, RP_K/P_C)$$

$$P_K/P_C = I(\overline{W}, RP_K/P_C)$$

and

$$0 = \alpha_C \overline{w} + \beta_C(r + p_K - p_C)$$

$$p_K - p_C = \alpha_K \overline{w} + \beta_K(r + p_K - p_C).$$

167

to economies being compared, with a complete list of the commodity-capital goods involved, are all that can be made, no more.

In short, when no technical change is occurring and there are constant returns to scale, no problems are involved in comparing completely specified production relationships over time or across space. Such production relationships are well expressed in terms of Physical Things. In the one-sector case, application of the Fund concept leads, of course, to the same result as the Physical Things concept. Peculiarities in making such comparisons arise if the Fund concept is employed in the two-sector case. Application of Mrs Robinson's concept leads to peculiarities in both the one- and two-sector cases.

Hicks stresses that the peculiarities arise when we use the Fund concept to compare economies in which technical progress is occurring. Yet, in Hicks' line of thought, no difficulties emerge in the one-sector case when technical change is occurring – that is, we can, with impunity, continue to use either the Physical Things or the Fund concepts of capital. The peculiarities emerge in the two-sector case. 'It is only in the special case when the invention is neutral between investment and consumption that we get the same result whether we use the Physical concept or the Fund concept.'[1] Indeed, in the case where technical change occurs in the consumption-good sector alone, it would appear, as a converse to Hicks' case, that in the capital-good sector, at least, technical retrogression has occurred.

One might argue that Hicks' Fund concept must be rejected, since (*a*) it appears to generate peculiar results and (*b*) it appears to require the introduction of prices into what are essentially technical relationships. It would seem that, even in the face of technical change, we must continue to write our production relationships in terms of Physical Things. Yet there clearly is a sense in which Hicks is right to say that the current flow of capital goods (services) can, with technical change in the capital goods sector, be obtained at a smaller sacrifice in terms of consumption goods foregone. What is puzzling about Hicks' remarks is his reason for arguing, when discussing inventions, that the Fund and Physical Things concepts give the same result when 'the invention is neutral between investment and consumption'. How exactly would Hicks specify such a neutral invention?

In the chapter on the Production Function in his *Capital and Growth*, Hicks introduces technical progress in a discontinuous fashion, only for analytical clarity. He considers two stationary states, the sole difference between them being that techniques have improved. Comparison of the steady-stationary-state economies can, he argues, be undertaken in terms of Physical and Fund concepts. The production function, using the Fund

[1] Hicks, *Theory of Wages*, 349.

168

concept, $C = C(L_C, (P_K K/P_C))$ is called a 'sophisticated' production function.

We come now to what is to Hicks a central problem. If the 'sophisticated' concept of the production function is used, and if technical progress has been investment-biased (in Hicks' sense), then, from equilibrium to equilibrium, it would appear that the stock of 'capital' has not changed and the whole of the increase in the consumption-good output would be attributed to technical progress. To Hicks this is an unwarranted result. Capital formation should play some role in raising output. To capture this, Hicks argues that, at the discrete moment when the technical improvement occurs, the value of the stock of capital expressed in terms of consumption goods falls and is then built up to its stationary-state level by accumulation. Technical change and capital accumulation then both play a role in raising consumption per head. Hicks says

Such a reinterpretation involves a considerable shift in ideas; but it is the only interpretation which enables us to go on making sense of a production function during a process of transmutation [i.e. capital accumulation]. Every technical improvement implies a loss of capital: *capital being measured in terms of the consumption that has to be foregone in order that the productive power that is embodied in the physical instrument should be replaced.*[1]

And, he goes on immediately to say, in apparent contradiction to earlier statements, that

It is unnecessary (it should be noticed) to distinguish, for purposes of this definition, between improvements that affect the process of production of capital goods, and improvements that affect the efficiency of given capital goods in consumption-good production. Each works in the same way; in each case the improvement makes it possible to replace the productive power at a smaller sacrifice of consumption.[2]

The apparent contradiction is eliminated when the earlier discussion about improved capital goods and obsolescence is recalled in which it was shown that more capital goods, through technical change in the capital-goods sector, are identical in steady-state equilibrium to better capital goods associated with so-called 'embodied' technical change.

It is of the greatest importance to note that, in a world of technical change, Hicks argues that the Fund concept is the only one relevant.

So long as we measure saving in terms of consumption goods given up, the capital that is accumulated by it must be valued in the same terms. Thus (whatever may be the case when one is making a static comparison) *the only production function that can be used in a growth model is one which shows the product to be a function of capital that is measured (or valued) in this particular manner.* Such a production function can be constructed, but it is an artificial construction, quite different

---

[1] Hicks, *Capital and Growth*, 300. His emphasis.   [2] *Ibid.*

from the technological relation between product and physical capital which the economists who first used the notion had (often at least) in mind.[1]

The fourth piece of Hicks' to be reviewed is his recent 'The measurement of capital', given at the 1969 meetings of the International Statistical Institute. In this paper Hicks, I believe, has retrogressed. First, he attempts to make a distinction between Physical Things and 'effective' Physical Things.

He argues

...it is nearly inevitable that the only available price-index of capital goods will be biased in the direction of physical comparability. It is bound to have a tendency to measure capital in terms of physical content (sometimes even just 'so much steel'), instead of measuring it in terms of its productive efficiency, as for the theoretical measure would be required. Improvements in the manufacture of capital goods (as in 'steel' production) would be registered; improvements in the utilisation of capital goods would slip through.

I cannot myself perceive that there is any economic sense in such a physical measure. It is futile to erect great edifices of theory, and of econometrics, upon it. The estimation of production functions – involving a distinction between accumulation of capital (in some such sense as this) and technical progress (*residual* technical progress) – seems therefore to me to be a vain endeavour.[2]

I have already shown, in Chapter 6, that the distinction between capital in terms of Physical Things and in terms of its productive efficiency is wrong. Here Hicks seems to be re-introducing Solow's 'effective' capital, and, as I have shown, this is an empty concept. If price indexes were constructed according to Hicks' specifications, then he would presumably conclude that the estimation of production functions, involving the neoclassical separation of capital accumulation and Residual technical change, would be valid.

As Chapters 5 and 6 demonstrate, however, this view is incorrect. The important point is not whether capital goods improve over time (they surely do) nor how accurately we can measure such improvement (and I argue in Chapter 6 that we do much better than is commonly supposed), but that commodity-capital goods are reproducible. Even if we could arrive at a perfect price index for commodity capital, we should still be required to take account of the improved efficiency with which commodity capital can be produced. This is what the Harrod–Robinson measure does and what the neoclassical separation of technical change and commodity-capital accumulation fails to do. Neoclassical measures, as Chapter 5 showed, do take account of 'improvements in the manufacture of capital

---

[1] *Ibid.*, 303–4. The emphasis is mine.
[2] J. R. Hicks, 'The measurement of capital', *Bulletin of the International Statistical Institute: Proceedings of the 37th Session*, I, 261–2.

goods' but they fail to take such improvements into account in the assessment of capital as an input in the process of economic production. *This* is the reason why neoclassical estimation of production functions is a vain endeavour – not the reason Hicks suggests. Second, as a measure of the capital input, Hicks wants 'a measure of the *quantity* of non-human resources, inherited from the past, and available in the present to be worked on by labour to produce current output'.[1] This is merely a Who's Who, and the aggregate measure is of no use in its commodity-capital form, as the 'switching' problem shows. Third, he moves away from the Fund idea – that is, the expression of the aggregate stock of commodity capital in consumption-good prices. He argues

The efforts and sacrifices which were necessary, in the past, in order that some part of the equipment, which the present has inherited from the past, should be constructed, were no doubt of greatest importance *then*; but what is their present importance? What light do they throw upon the nature of our inheritance, as it is now? The *present* stock is the matter with which a useful measure (of the stock of capital) ought to be concerned. Once again, *bygones are bygones.*[2]

In the chapter of the Aggregate Production Function in *Capital and Growth*, the discussion about the Consumption Fund has no relevance whatever to past consumption. It is the efforts and sacrifices which would have to be made today to replace and augment today's collection of capital goods which are of importance. Here Hicks' slip seems to be connected with the fact that the stock of capital is sometimes thought of as an accumulation of past 'efforts and sacrifices'. In a world of technological progress, that concept is irrelevant – as Hicks says. That, however, is not the concept which is wanted.

8.3   A critique

In a roundabout and uncertain way, Hicks has thus come to a concept of capital drawn up in terms of consumption goods, after initially rejecting such a forward-looking capital concept. What has happened to the Physical Things concept – the standard 'neoclassical' production function subject to Hicksian technical change? It would appear that it has been abandoned. Does that mean that the Hicksian concepts of technical change have also been abandoned, or does it simply mean that they would have to be complicated with additional biases?[3] Apparently not. First, if the model

[1] Hicks, 'The measurement of capital', 259.
[2] *Ibid.*, 262.
[3] In the second edition of *Theory of Wages*, he says (349): 'I would not deny that it would be possible to work out a system of classification, on marginal-product lines, using the Fund concept; but it would have to be a four-way classification not merely into labour-saving and capital-saving, but also into investment-biased and consumption-biased.'

is for one commodity, then, again, there is no difference between the Fund and Physical Things concepts of capital and related production functions. Second, if the rate of technical improvements in the two sectors is the same (neither investment- nor consumption-biased), then again there is no difference between these concepts. Third, the artificiality of the 'sophisticated' production function, whereby prices play a role in relationships which traditionally have been regarded as technical conditions, identifiable independently of prices (remember: no aggregate stock of capital is being discussed), would appear to be unhelpful. Fourth, the loss in value of capital goods arising from technical change is more adequately handled, in my view, as 'depreciation by obsolescence' and again, I see no reason why alterations in consumption-goods prices should affect what are, essentially, technical relationships.

Yet clearly there is a sense in which Hicks is fundamentally right. Technical change in the capital-good sector does imply that the primary inputs indirectly[1] used to produce consumption goods have improved in their efficiency (in terms of a 'real cost' theory of production) while '*in terms of the consumption that has to be foregone in order that the productive power that is embodied in the physical instrument should be replaced*',[2] the capital input has fallen and there has been an improvement in efficiency (in terms of the theory of opportunity cost). As I have shown previously, this point is fundamental. It must be retained. This point is, of course, precisely what is captured by Harrod's concept of technical change.[3]

If it is true that capital is reproducible or augmentable, then any concept of technical progress must be expressed in terms of the inputs with which capital goods are produced.[4] Such an attempt encounters the well-known difficulty that an infinite regress into historical time is required.[5] If only static conditions over time or amongst countries are dealt with, then one need not bother with the 'reduction' of capital to its original inputs. The static production function, drawn up in terms of Physical Things, will see us through. If technical change occurs, however, infinite regress problems can be escaped, as was shown in Chapter 5, by solving simultaneously for the Harrod–Robinson concepts of technical change and backward-looking capital inputs.

[1] A. P. Lerner, 'On some recent developments in capital theory', *American Economic Review*, LV, May 1965, 284–95.
[2] Hicks, *Capital and Growth*, 300. Hicks' emphasis.
[3] In *Towards a Dynamic Economics* Harrod says, discussing neutral progress (23): 'The productivity of labour embodied in machines is raised in equal measure with that of those engaged on minding machines; it implies an equal rise of productivity on the part of all labour however far back or forward it may be between the inception and the final stage of production.'
[4] As Kuenne argued in *General Economic Equilibrium*, 229. See p. 97, n. 2.
[5] Lerner, 'Capital', 273.

In Chapter 5, it was argued that the Hicksian concept of technical change asks: what is the rate of improvement in the efficiency of primary (i.e. non-reproducible, non-augmentable) inputs and intermediate (reproducible augmentable) inputs required to produce output? From

$$Q = Q(L, K; t)$$

we have $\qquad\qquad q - (\alpha l + \beta k) = t$

In terms of prices, it would appear as

$$\alpha \overline{w} + \beta r = t$$

The Harrodian concept of technical progress *also* asks: what is the rate of improvement in the efficiency of primary and intermediate inputs required to produce intermediate inputs? In the dynamic context of technical progress, then, I can write

$$q - (\alpha l + \beta(k - t_R)) = t_R$$

or $\qquad\qquad q - (\alpha l + \beta k) = t_R(1 - \beta)$

or $\qquad\qquad q - l + (\beta/\alpha)(q - k) = t_R$

If Harrod-technical change, t_R, is neutral where $q = k$, then $q - l = t_R$. In terms of prices, it would be written

$$\alpha \overline{w} + \beta(r + t_R) = t_R$$

or $\qquad\qquad \overline{w} + (\beta/\alpha) r = t_R$

and, in the Harrod-neutral case where $r = 0$, then $\overline{w} = t_R$. A new backward-looking concept of capital as an input in the process of production is derived, not by introducing prices into technical relationships, but by capturing the 'interdependence' of the direct and indirect *technical* relationships associated in the production of output. In the dynamic context, the 'historical regress' problem is escaped. The concept of capital is $k - t_R$. What concept is this? The price equation tells us. In this simple one-commodity model, as I have shown, that concept, $k - t_R = (k - \overline{w})$, is the growth rate of Mrs Robinson's 'real capital', equal to the growth rate of the labour input. In this simple case, then, the backward-looking concept would appear to be equal to Mrs Robinson's concept. However, it clearly is not in more complex cases. Consider one possibility. From one kind of equilibrium to another, technical progress is neutral in that capital per unit of output remains unchanged. Changed rates of saving cause the net rate of return to fall. The rate of technological progress is unaffected and so the growth rate of 'capital' is $k - t_R$. Because the growth rate of real wages is greater than the rate of technical progress, the growth of 'real capital', $k - \overline{w}$, will be less. Mrs Robinson's 'real capital' concept would still appear to yield peculiar results. I am, of course, in this case, merely repeating the results shown before to hold in a static environment. I wish to emphasize this point. In the one-commodity case with Harrod-neutrality, the growth rate of Mrs Robinson's 'real capital' and the concept advanced here are the same. In steady equilibrium, with an unchanging rate of return, the labour-time spent on the construction of capital goods is being reduced at the rate indicated by the rate of Harrod technical change. If the rate of return is falling, such labour-time is compounded (over constant gestation periods – an important part of the assumption of a constant capital/output ratio) at lower rates of return and Mrs Robinson's 'real capital' will be growing less rapidly than the concept advanced here. The standard production-function analysis holds up in static comparisons of altering factor proportions, provided, of course, that no aggregation is pursued. The peculiar results described by Hicks when his Fund concept is employed, or those pointed out by Samuelson in his critique of Mrs Robinson's 'real capital', simply need not arise. However, while the standard production function is employable in static conditions, the concept of it being shifted by technical change must be abandoned.

The capital concept which must, in my view, be used for the analysis of growing capitalistic economies and technical progress is the backward-looking one advanced here. In the dynamic context, Harrodian technical change is derived by capturing the fundamental technical interdependence of the system, represented by the fact that commodity capital is repro-ducible. No prices need be introduced: only technology is employed. The Harrodian concept is therefore, *on this count only*, equal to the 'standard' Hicksian counterpart in that technology alone is being considered.

Economies with different techniques and rates of saving, in which real wage rates and output were rising at the same rates and in which the Physical Things/output ratios were constant but different, would be said to be experiencing the same rates of Harrod technical progress. The prices of labour and 'waiting' could be said to be rising at the same rate. In the various economies, save in the fluke case where production elasticities were the same, the neoclassical rates of technical change would all be different. In Chapter 5, I showed that such different rates would have no theoretical meaning whatever.

For one economy experiencing neutral Harrodian change, efforts have been made to separate such a result into the type of technology and the bias of Hicksian technical change. Thus, Harrod-neutrality tends to be associ-ated with an elasticity of substitution of unity ($<$ 1 or $>$ 1) with neutral (labour saving or capital saving) Hicksian technical change.[1] In any

[1] W. Fellner, 'Measures of technological progress in the light of recent growth theories', *American Economic Review*, LVII, December 1967, 1073–98.

economy, one would expect that the interaction of working and saving propensities and technical progress would lead over time to the result that output and prices, in terms of consumption goods per unit of labour and 'waiting', would rise proportionately. To test such a theory of induced technical change, the concept of capital as a factor of production to be used must be Harrodian.

All the analytical content is contained in the one-commodity framework. I have shown that in such a context Hicks' Consumption-Fund concepts of capital and related technical change are equal to his Physical Things concepts and, as such, are invalid. The backward-looking concept advanced here captures the essential reproducibility characteristic of Physical Things in a context of technical progress. This surely is what Hicks was trying to capture in the Fund approach. Why the difference? In a one-commodity context the opportunity cost of 'capital' goods, in terms of 'consumption' goods foregone (the marginal rate of transformation), remains equal to unity – technical progress or no – whereas the 'real cost of production' of a unit of output (input) of the one commodity falls with technical progress. Hicks' forward-looking Fund concept is drawn up in terms of 'opportunity costs', whereas the 'backward-looking' concept by which it must be replaced is drawn up in terms of 'real cost of production'.

The two-commodity context may be briefly used to illustrate the relationship between Hicksian concepts and those advocated here. It is important to note that in the two-commodity case both the Fund and Harrod concepts require the abandonment of the Physical Things idea, and with it, the abandonment of the standard concepts of technical change. In the standard format,

$$c - [\alpha_C l_C + \beta_C k_C] = t_C$$
$$i - [\alpha_K l_K + \beta_K k_K] = t_K$$

Whereas, in the format argued here

$$c - [\alpha_C l_C + \beta_C (k_C - t_{K_R})] = t_C{}^1$$
$$i - [\alpha_K l_K + \beta_K (k_K - t_K)] = t_{K_R}$$

For the capital-good sector, the foregoing argument for the one-commodity case may be repeated. If there is neutral technical progress in the production of capital goods, there is of course Harrodian technical change

---

[1] Again, in terms of prices, in the standard format
$$\alpha_0 \overline{w} + \beta_C (r + p_K - p_C) = t_C$$
$$\alpha_K \overline{w} + \beta_K (r + p_K - p_C) = t_K$$
And in the format advanced here
$$\alpha_0 \overline{w} + \beta_C (r + p_K - p_C + t_{K_R}) = t_{C_R}$$
$$\alpha_K \overline{w} + \beta_K (r + p_K - p_C + t_{K_R}) = t_{K_R}$$

in the consumption-good sector – even though in the standard sense there might not be any technical change at all. The technical interdependence captured by the backward-looking concept of capital is more clearly illustrated in the two-sector case. In the consumption-good sector, the Hicksian Fund concept and the backward-looking concept advanced here would appear to give similar results, but a glance at the capital-good sector reveals their fundamental difference. In the case where technical change occurs only in the consumption-good sector, the two concepts of Physical Things and 'waiting' are then the same – with the Fund concept leading to technical retrogression in the capital-good sector. If invention is neither investment- nor consumption-biased, one would expect an unchanged price of the capital good in terms of the consumption good or an equal rate of technical change in both sectors. A glance at the price equations shows once again that only when the Harrod concepts are employed will the movement of relative prices be predicted.[1] Again, as I demonstrated in the one-sector case, non-neutral change or a change in the equilibrium conditions will of course necessitate taking into account all elasticities of substitution, both technical and preferential. This holds, of course, for the more complicated two-sector models.

In Harrodian equilibrium situations, however, since the relative rates of technical change in the two sectors predict relative prices, there is a relationship between the capital concept advanced here and Hicks' Fund concept. Hicks' Fund concept would be

$$c - [\alpha_C l_C + \beta_C (k_C + p_K - p_C)] = t_C^{HF}$$

$$i - [\alpha_K l_K + \beta_K (k_K + p_K - p_C)] = t_K^{HF}$$

[1] In the standard case, if $t_C - t_K = 0$, then I would have

$$[\alpha_C \overline{w} + \beta_C (r + p_K - p_C)] - [\alpha_K \overline{w} + \beta_K (r + p_C - p_C)] = 0$$

or, assuming that $r = 0$, then

$$(\alpha_C - \alpha_K)\overline{w} + \beta_C - \beta_K (p_K - p_C) = 0$$

or

$$p_K - p_C = -\frac{(\alpha_C - \alpha_K)\overline{w}}{1 - \alpha_C - (1 - \alpha_K)} = w$$

Alternatively, if $p_K - p_C = 0$, then

$$\alpha_C \overline{w} = t_C$$

$$\alpha_K \overline{w} = t_K$$

and only where $\alpha_C = \alpha_K$ will $t_C = t_K$. In the Harrod case, if $t_{C_R} - t_{K_R} = 0$, I would have

$$[\alpha_C \overline{w} + \beta_C (p_K - p_C + t_{K_R})] - [\alpha_K \overline{w} + \beta_K (p_K - p_C + t_{K_R})] = 0$$

or

$$(\alpha_C - \alpha_K)\overline{w} + (\beta_C - \beta_K)(p_K - p_C) + (\beta_C - \beta_K)t_{K_R} = 0$$

$$p_K - p_C = -\frac{(\beta_C - \beta_K)t_{K_R}}{(\beta_C - \beta_K)} - \frac{(\alpha_C - \alpha_K)\overline{w}}{\beta_C - \beta_K}$$

$$= -t_{K_R} + \overline{w} = 0$$

Other cases of relative differences in Harrod-neutral progress are canvassed in Chapter 5.

which is, as I have shown, equal to

$$c-[\alpha_C l_C + \beta_C(k_C + t_{C_R} - t_{K_R})] = t_C^{HF}$$

$$i-[\alpha_K l_K + \beta_K(k_K + t_{C_R} - t_{K_R})] = t_K^{HF}$$

or

$$t_C = \beta_C(t_{C_R} - t_{K_R}) + t_C^{HF}$$

$$t_K = \beta_K(t_{C_R} - t_{K_R}) + t_K^{HF}.$$

Only in the case where $t_{C_R} - t_{K_R} < 0$ would Hicks' concepts of Fund capital and technical progress yield meaningful results (i.e., when $t_C^{HF} > t_C$ and $t_K^{HF} > t_K$). In the case where $t_{C_R} - t_{K_R} = 0$, the 'Fund' concepts collapse back to the 'Physical Things'. In the case where $t_{C_R} - t_{K_R} > 0$, even stranger results of technical retrogression apparently occur. This repeats the results found for the one-sector case.

In the case where $t_{C_R} - t_{K_R} < 0$, in Lerner's terms, the marginal product of investing is rising, and in equilibrium, the marginal product of capital must be falling, in order to keep the marginal efficiency of investing (Solow's social rate of return) unchanged. This is the critical link between Hicks' forward-looking Fund concept of capital and the backward-looking Harrod 'waiting' concept of capital.

Again, as I have shown, in a general model of n capital goods which, of course, includes intermediate inputs, such as coal used up, the standard Hicksian concepts would be

$$c - \left[\alpha_C l_C + \sum_{i=1}^{n} \beta_{C_i} k_{C_i}\right] = t_C$$

$$i_i - \left[\alpha_{K_i} l_{K_i} + \sum_{j=1}^{n} \beta_{K_{ij}} k_{K_{ij}}\right] = t_{K_i} \quad (i = 1, ..., n)$$

The Harrodian concepts are

$$c - \left[\alpha_C l_C + \sum_{i=1}^{n} \beta_{C_i}(k_{C_i} - t_{K_{iR}})\right] = t_{C_R}$$

$$i_i - \left[\alpha_K l_{K_i} + \sum_{j=1}^{n} \beta_{K_{ij}}(k_{K_{ij}} - t_{K_R})\right] = t_{K_{iR}} \quad (i = 1, ..., n)$$

In Harrod-neutral equilibrium, while Physical Things/output growth ratios ($k_{K_{ij}} - x_i \gtrless 0$) need not be zero, the 'capital/output' ratios in terms of the consumption good *will* be constant – exactly as the Harrodian rates of technical progress would predict.

8.4 Conclusion

In this chapter, I have shown that over nearly a decade of writing on capital and production theory, Hicks has come to the conclusion that, in a world of technical progress, only a 'sophisticated' production function drawn up in terms of consumption goods will do. I have argued in this chapter, however, that the Fund concept must be replaced by Harrod's backward-looking concept, if we are to make sense of technical progress and capital accumulation. I have dwelt upon the relationship between the two and have shown how Hicks' concept is contained within Harrod's. It must be emphasized, however, that the 'Physical Things' concept of capital and the traditional neoclassical distinction between technical progress and capital accumulation are to be abandoned.

9

A FINAL WORD

In this study I have demonstrated that the traditional neoclassical distinction between capital accumulation and technical change – the distinction between movements along, and shifts of, a production function – is invalid. I have shown that the correct analysis is contained in the growth and capital theories of Sir Roy Harrod and Joan Robinson.

In principle, this study deals with *ex post* concepts. No decision-maker need be concerned with the measurement of technical change: he wants to select or purchase or install the technology currently most profitable. Similarly, no decision-maker need be concerned with his stock of capital. At any time, his stock is given – a collection of physical things which, as Keynes taught, will be in the short run more or less intensely utilized. The decision-maker is concerned with additions to his stock, i.e. capital formation. In examining the outcome of all such decisions, however, the concepts of technical change and capital advanced here are the correct ones. The capital input concept is, of course, the fundamental one, as defined by all capital theorists. Ricardo distinguished between the value and the quantity of capital,[1] Senior spoke of abstinence,[2] Marx talked about the socially necessary congealed labour time embodied in his constant capital,[3] Rae,[4] Böhm-Bawerk,[5] and Wicksell[6] knew that 'original' factors and 'periods of production' were imperfect concepts which attempted to capture the fact that capital is essentially endogenous to the process of production, Kaldor dealt with capital's reproducibility and

[1] Ricardo, *Principles of Political Economy*, I, 95.
[2] N. N. Senior, *An Outline of the Science of Political Economy* (New York: A. M. Kelley, 1938), 79 ff.
[3] K. Marx, *A Contribution to the Critique of Political Economy*, trans. N. I. Stone (Chicago: Charles H. Kerr, 1918), 24.
[4] J. Rae, *Statement of Some New Principles on the Subject of Political Economy*, ed. R. W. James, *John Rae: Political Economist*, II (Toronto: University of Toronto Press, 1965), 91.
[5] E. von Böhm-Bawerk, *Positive Theory of Capital*, vol. II of *Capital and Interest*, trans. G. D. Huncke and H. F. Sennholz (South Holland, Illinois: Libertanian Press, 1959), 14.
[6] K. Wicksell, *Lectures on Political Economy*, vol. I, *General Theory*, trans. E. Classeen ed. L. Robbins (London: G. Routledge, 1934), 154.

augmentability,[1] Keynes was clearly sympathetic,[2] Harrod deals with an 'average basket of waiting',[3] and Robinson's critique of the neoclassical position is based fundamentally on her view that capital 'is a necessary condition for labour and natural resources to be productive. But it is not a factor of production independent of them'.[4]

I would argue that the intermediate and endogenous nature of the capital input is best understood in the dynamic context of technical change. Strangely enough, then, the fundamental attribute of the capital input becomes more amenable to theoretical consideration and empirical estimation outside the static environment, within which so many writers tried to understand and describe it. I believe that it is this intermediate and endogenous nature of the capital input, in a world where technical change is occurring, that lies behind part of the Cambridge controversy. Aggregation problems and non-smooth production surfaces are matters for secondary complaint. The oft-found suggestion[5] in the literature that consistent aggregation would blunt the attacks on the neoclassical structure clearly misses the main point. As this study demonstrates, the fundamental point of disagreement runs much deeper. To give Mrs Robinson the final word 'Looking at the matter in a philosophical light, the reason why there is no meaning to be attached to the marginal product of "capital" is that, from a long-run point of view, labour and natural resources are the factors of production in the economy as a whole, while capital goods and the time patterns of production are the means by which the factors are deployed.'[6]

If, then, in the long run, commodity capital is not a factor of production, what determines the equilibrium rate of return to capital? That is a question for another book which, I hope, will have more important theoretical content than this one.

[1] N. Kaldor, 'The controversy on the theory of capital', *Essays on Value and Distribution* (London: Duckworth, 1960), 155 ff.
[2] Keynes, *General Theory*, 213.
[3] R. F. Harrod, 'The "neutrality" of improvements', *Economic Journal*, LXXI, June 1961, 301.
[4] Robinson, *Accumulation of Capital*, 310–11.
[5] See, for example, Brown, *Theory and Measurement of Technological Change*.
[6] Robinson, *Accumulation of Capital*, 310.

BIBLIOGRAPHY

Books and Special Studies

Allen, R. G. D. *Macro-Economic Theory*, London: Macmillan, 1967.

Asimakopulos, A. *The Reliability of Selected Price Indexes For Measuring Price Trends*, Ottawa: Queen's Printer for Royal Commission on Banking and Finance, 1962.

Böhm-Bawerk, E. von. *History and Critique of Interest Theories*, vol. I of *Capital and Interest*, trans. G. D. Huncke and H. F. Sennholz, South Holland, Illinois: Libertanian Press, 1959.

Positive Theory of Capital, vol. II of *Capital and Interest* (see above).

Further Essays on Capital and Interest, vol. III of *Capital and Interest* (see above).

Brown, M. *On the Theory and Measurement of Technological Change*, Cambridge: Cambridge University Press, 1966.

Denison, E. F. *The Sources of Economic Growth*, New York: Committee for Economic Development, 1962.

Denison, E. F. with Poullier, J. P. *Why Growth Rates Differ*, Washington: Brookings Institution, 1967.

Dewey, D. *Modern Capital Theory*, New York: Columbia University Press, 1965.

Ferguson, C. E. *The Neoclassical Theory of Production and Distribution*, Cambridge: Cambridge University Press, 1969.

Green, H. A. J. *Aggregation in Economic Analysis: An Introductory Survey*, Princeton: Princeton University Press, 1964.

Harrod, R. F. *The Trade Cycle*, Oxford: The Clarendon Press, 1936.

Towards a Dynamic Economics, London: Macmillan, 1948.

Money, London: Macmillan, 1969.

Haavelmo, T. *A Study in the Theory of Investment*, Chicago: University of Chicago Press, 1960.

Hayek, F. A. *The Pure Theory of Capital*, London: Routledge, Kegan Paul, 1952.

Hickman, B. G. *Investment Demand and U.S. Economic Growth*, Washington: Brookings Institution, 1965.

Hicks, J. R. *The Theory of Wages*, 2nd ed., London: Macmillan, 1963.

Capital and Growth, Oxford: Clarendon Press, 1965.

Kendrick, J. W. *Productivity Trends in the United States*, Princeton: Princeton University Press for NBER, 1961.

Keynes, J. M. *The General Theory of Employment Interest and Money*, London: Macmillan, 1936.

Kirzner, I. M. *An Essay on Capital*, New York: A. M. Kelley, 1966.

Kuenne, R. E. *The Theory of General Economic Equilibrium*, Princeton: Princeton University Press, 1963.

Leijonhufvud, A. *On Keynesian Economics and the Economics of Keynes*, New York: Oxford University Press, 1968.

Lerner, A. P. *The Economics of Control*, New York: Macmillan, 1944.

Lithwick, N. H. *Economic Growth in Canada*, Toronto: University of Toronto Press, 1967.

Marx, K. *A Contribution to the Critique of Political Economy*, trans. N. I. Stone, Chicago: Charles H. Kerr, 1918.

Meade, J. E. *The Rate of Interest in a Progressive State*, London: Macmillan, 1933.

A Neo-Classical Theory of Economic Growth, 2nd ed., London: Allen and Unwin, 1968.

The Growing Economy, II, *Principles of Political Economy*, London: Allen and Unwin, 1968.

Patinkin, D. *Money, Interest and Prices*, 2nd ed. New York: Harper and Row, 1965.

Pigou, A. C. *The Economics of Stationary States*, London: Macmillan, 1935.

Rae, J. *Statement of Some New Principles on the Subject of Political Economy*, ed. R. Warren James, *John Rae: Political Economist*, II, Toronto: University of Toronto Press, 1965.

Ricardo, D. *On the Principles of Political Economy and Taxation*, eds. P. Sraffa and M. Dobb, *The Works and Correspondence of David Ricardo*, I, Cambridge: Cambridge University Press, 1951.

Robinson, J. *The Economics of Imperfect Competition*, London: Macmillan, 1933; 2nd ed. 1969.

The Accumulation of Capital, London: Macmillan, 1955; 3rd ed. 1969.

Essays in the Theory of Economic Growth, London: Macmillan, 1962.

Samuelson, P. A. *Foundations of Economic Analysis*, Cambridge: Harvard University Press, 1953.

Salter, W. E. G. *Productivity and Technical Change*, Cambridge: Cambridge University Press, 1960.

Senior, N. W. *An Outline of the Science of Political Economy*, New York: A. M. Kelley, 1938.

Shackle, G. L. S. *A Scheme of Economic Theory*, Cambridge: Cambridge University Press, 1965.

Solow, R. M. *Capital Theory and the Rate of Return*, Amsterdam: North Holland Publishing, 1963.

Sraffa, P. *Production of Commodities by Means of Commodities*, Cambridge: Cambridge University Press, 1960.

Stone, R. *et. al. Input-Output Relationships 1954–1966*, Paper no. 3 of A Programme for Growth, London: Chapman and Hall for Department of Applied Economics, University of Cambridge, 1963.

Uhr, C. G. *Economic Doctrines of Knut Wicksell*, Berkeley and Los Angeles: University of California Press, 1960.

United Nations, *A System of National Accounts*, New York: UNO, 1968.

Wicksell, K. *Lectures in Political Economy*, vol. I, *General Theory*, trans. E. Classeen, ed. L. Robbins, London: G. Routledge, 1934.

Interest and Prices, trans. R. F. Kahn, London: Macmillan, 1936.

Value, Capital and Rent, trans. S. H. Frowein, London: Allen and Unwin, 1954.

Selected Papers on Economic Theory, ed. E. Lindahl. London: Allen and Unwin, 1958.

Articles

Abramovitz, Moses. 'Economic Growth in the United States: a review article.' *American Economic Review*, LII, September, 1962, 762–82.

Asimakopulos, A. 'The definition of neutral inventions', *Economic Journal*, LXXIII, December 1963, 674–80.

Asimakopulos, A. and Weldon, J. C. 'The classification of technical progress in models of economic growth', *Economica*, XXX, November 1963, 372–86.

'Sir Roy Harrod's equation of supply', *Oxford Economic Papers*, XV, November 1963, 266–72.

'A synoptic view of some simple models of growth', *Canadian Journal of Economics and Political Science*, XXXI, February 1965, 52–79.

Barna, Tibor. 'Alternative methods of measuring capital', ed. R. Goldsmith and C. Saunders, *The Measurement of National Wealth*, London: Bowes and Bowes, 1959.

'The replacement cost of fixed assets in British manufacturing industry in 1955', *Journal of the Royal Statistical Society*, CXX (Series A), 1, 1955, 1–36.

Becker, G. 'A theory of the allocation of time', *Economic Journal*, LXXV, September 1965, 493–517.

Bliss, C. 'On putty clay', *Review of Economic Studies*, XXXV, April 1968, 105–32.

Bruno, M. *et al.* 'The nature and implications of the reswitching of techniques, Paradoxes in Capital Theory: A Symposium', *Quarterly Journal of Economics*, LXXX, November 1966, 526–53.

Christensen, L. R. and Jorgenson, D. W. 'US real product and real factor input, 1929–1967,' *Review of Income and Wealth*, XVI, 1, March 1970, 19–50.

Champernowne, D. C. 'The production function and the theory of capital: a comment', *Review of Economic Studies*, XXI (2), 1953–4, 112–35.

David, Paul A. 'The deflation of value added', *Review of Economics and Statistics*, XLIV, May 1962, 148–55.

'Measuring real net output: a proposed index', *Review of Economics and Statistics*, XLVIII, November 1966, 419–25.

Denison, Edward F. 'Theoretical aspects of quality change, capital consumption and net capital formation', *Problems of Capital Formation: Concepts, Measurement, and Controlling Factors*, Studies in Income and Wealth, Vol. 19, Princeton: Princeton University Press, 1957.

'Some major issues in productivity analysis: An examination of estimates by Jorgenson and Griliches'. *Survey of Current Business*, XLIX, May 1969, 1–30.

Diamond, P. A. 'Disembodied technical change in a two-sector model', *Review of Economic Studies*, XXXII, April 1965, 161–8.

'Technical change and the measurement of capital and output', *Review of Economic Studies*, XXXII, October 1965, 289–98.

Domar, E. D. 'On the measurement of technological change', *Economic Journal*, LXXI, December 1961, 709–29.

'On total productivity and all that', *Journal of Political Economy*, LXX, December 1962, 597–608.

'Total productivity and the quality of capital', *Journal of Political Economy*, LXXI, December 1963, 586–8.

Domar, E. D. *et al.* 'Economic growth and productivity in the U.S., Canada, U.K., Germany and Japan in the post-war period', *Review of Economics and Statistics*, XLVI, February 1964, 33–40.

Dorfman, R. 'A graphical exposition of Böhm-Bawerk's interest theory', *Review of Economic Studies*, XXVI, February 1959, 153–8.

'Waiting and the period of production', *Quarterly Journal of Economics*, LXXIII, August 1959, 351–72.

Emery, B. J. and Rymes, T. K. 'Price indexes in a social accounting framework', eds. J. Henripin and A. Asimakopulos, CPSA *Conferences in Statistics*, 1962 *and* 1963, *Papers*, Toronto: University of Toronto Press, 1964.

Fisher, F. M. 'The existence of aggregate production functions', *Econometrica*, XXXVII, 4, October 1969, 553–77.

Geary, R. C. 'The general price level and the external trading gain', International Association for Research in Income and Wealth, Ireland Conference, 20–6 August 1967 (mimeo).

Gigantes, T. and Pitts, P. R. 'An integrated input–output framework and some related analytical models', a paper presented to the 1965 CPSA Conference on Statistics (mimeo).

Gordon, R. J. 'Measurement bias in Price Indexes for Capital Goods', International Association for Research in Income and Wealth, Israel: mimeo, 1969.

Green, H. A. J. 'Embodied progress, investment and growth', *American Economic Review*, LVI, March 1966, 138–51.

'A note on the measurement of capital', *Canadian Journal of Economics and Political Science*, XXVIII, 1962, 281–2.

Griliches, Z. 'Hedonic price indices for automobiles: an econometric analysis of quality change', *Government Price Statistics*, I, Hearings before the Joint Economic Committee of the Congress of the United States, Washington: U.S. Government Printing Office, 1961.

'Capital stock in investment functions: some problems of concept and measurement', *Measurement in Economics: Studies in Mathematical Economics and Econometrics*, Stanford, California: Stanford University Press, 1963.

Griliches, Z. and Jorgenson, D. W. 'The explanation of productivity change', *Review of Economic Studies*, XXXIV, July 1967, 249–85, reprinted in *Survey of Current Business*, XLIX, May 1969, 31–64.

'Sources of measured productivity change: capital input', *American Economic Review, Papers and Proceedings*, LVI, May 1966, 50–61.

Hahn, F. H. 'On two-sector growth models', *Review of Economic Studies*, XXXII, October 1965, 339–45.

'On the stability of growth equilibrium', Memo from the Institute of Economics, University of Oslo, 19 April 1966.

'Equilibrium dynamics with heterogeneous capital goods', *Quarterly Journal of Economics*, LXXX, November 1966, 633–46.

Hahn, F. H. and Matthews, R. C. O. 'The theory of economic growth: a survey', *Economic Journal*, LXXIV, December 1964, 779–902.

Hall, R. E. 'Technical change and capital from the point of view of the dual', *Review of Economic Studies*, XXXV, January 1968, 35–46.

Harcourt, G. C. 'Some Cambridge controversies in the theory of capital', *Journal of Economic Literature*, VII, 2, June 1969, 369–405.

Harrod, R. F. 'An essay in dynamic theory', *Economic Journal*, XLIX, 1939, 14–33, reprinted in *Economic Essays*, London: Macmillan, 1952, 255–77.

'Supplement on dynamic theory', *Economic Essays*, London: Macmillan, 1952.

'Domar and dynamic economics', *Economic Journal*, LXIX, September 1959, 451–64.

BIBLIOGRAPHY

'Second essay in dynamic theory', *Economic Journal*, LXX, June 1960, 278–93.

'The "neutrality" of improvements', *Economic Journal*, LXXI, June 1961, 300–4.

'Themes in dynamic theory', *Economic Journal*, LXXIII, September 1963, 401–21.

'Are monetary and fiscal policies enough?', *Economic Journal*, LXXIV, December 1964, 903–15.

Hicks, J. R. 'The measurement of capital in relation to the measurement of other economic aggregates', ed. F. A. Lutz and D. C. Hague, *The Theory of Capital*, London: Macmillan, 1961.

'Thoughts on the theory of capital – the Corfu Conference', *Oxford Economic Papers*, XII, 2, June 1960, 123–32.

'The measurement of capital', *Bulletin of the International Statistical Institute: Proceedings of the 37th Session*, I, 253–63.

Jaszi, G. 'An improved way of measuring quality change', *Review of Economics and Statistics*, XLIV, August 1962, 332–5.

Johnson, H. G. 'Towards a general theory of capital accumulation', *The Canadian Quandary*, Toronto: McGraw-Hill, 1963.

Jorgenson, D. W. 'The theory of investment behavior', ed. R. Ferber, *Determinants of Investment Behavior*, New York: Columbia University Press for NBER, 1967.

'The embodiment hypothesis', *Journal of Political Economy*, LXXIV, February 1966, 1–17.

Jorgenson, D. W. and Griliches, Z. See Griliches, Z.

Jorgenson, D. W. and Christensen, L. R. See Christensen, L. R.

Kaldor, N. 'The controversy on the theory of capital', *Essays on Value and Distribution*, London: Duckworth, 1960.

'Alternative theories of distribution', *Essays on Value and Distribution*, London: Duckworth, 1960.

'A model of economic growth', *The Economic Journal*, LXVII, December 1957, 591–624.

'Capital accumulation and economic growth', ed. F. A. Lutz and D. C. Hague, *The Theory of Capital*, London: Macmillan, 1961.

'Increasing returns and technical progress – a comment on Professor Hicks' article', *Oxford Economic Papers*, XIII, February 1961, 1–5.

Kennedy, Charles. 'The valuation of net investment', *Oxford Economic Papers*, VII, 1, February 1955, pp. 36–46.

'Technical progress and investment', *Economic Journal*, LXXI, June 1961, 292–9.

'Harrod on "neutrality"', *Economic Journal*, LXXII, March 1962, 249–50.

'The character of improvements and of technical progress', *Economic Journal*, LXXII, December 1962, 899–911.

Keynes, J. M. 'The general theory of employment', *Quarterly Journal of Economics*, LI, February 1937, 209–23, reprinted as 'The general theory: fundamental concepts and ideas' in R. M. Clower, *Monetary Theory: Penguin Modern Economic Readings*, Harmondsworth: Penguin, 1970, 220–1.

Lancaster, K. 'A new approach to consumer theory', *Journal of Political Economy*, LXXIV, April 1966, 132–56.

Lerner, A. P. 'On some recent developments in capital theory', *American Economic Review*, LV, May 1965, 284–95.

'Capital', *International Encyclopedia of Social Sciences*, 2, 'New York: Crowell Collier and Macmillan, 1968, 270–8.

Lithwick, N. H., Post, G. and Rymes, T. K. 'Post-war production relationships in Canada', ed. M. Brown, *The Theory and Empirical Analysis of Production*, New York: Columbia University Press for NBER, 1967.

Lydall, H. 'On measuring technical progress', *Australian Economic Papers*, VIII, June 1969, 1–12.

Malinvaud, E. 'Capital accumulation and efficient allocation of resources', *Econometrica*, XXI, 1953, 233–68, revised in AEA, *Readings in Welfare Economics*, London, 1969.

'The analogy between atemporal and intertemporal theories of resource allocation', eds. J. E. Stiglitz and H. Uzawa, *Readings in the Modern Theory of Economic Growth*, Cambridge: M.I.T. Press, 1969.

Matthews, R. C. O. 'The new view of investment: Comment', *Quarterly Journal of Economics*, LXXVIII, February 1964, 164–76, reprinted in J. E. Stiglitz and H. Uzawa, *Readings in the Modern Theory of Economic Growth*, Cambridge: M.I.T. Press, 1969.

Meade, J. E. 'The rate of profit in a growing economy', *Economic Journal*, LXXIII, December 1963, 665–74.

Modigliani, F. and Samuelson, P. A. 'The Pasinetti paradox in neoclassical and more general models', *Review of Economic Studies*, XXXIII, October 1966, 269–301.

Naqvi, K. A. See Robinson, J. and Naqvi, K. A.

Nicholson, J. L. 'The measurement of quality changes', *Economic Journal*, LXXVII, September 1967, 512–30.

Pasinetti, L. L. 'On concepts and measures of changes in productivity', *Review of Economics and Statistics*, XLI, August 1959, 270–82.

'Changes in the rate of profit and switches in techniques', *Paradoxes in Capital Theory: A Symposium, Quarterly Journal of Economics*, LXXV, November 1966, 563–83.

'Switches of technique and the "rate of return" in capital theory', *Economic Journal*, LXXIX, September 1969, 508–31.

'Again on capital theory and Solow's "rate of return"', *Economic Journal*, LXXX, June 1970, 428–31.

Phelps, E. S. 'Substitution, fixed proportions, growth and distribution', *International Economic Review*, IV, September 1963, 265–88.

'Axioms for factor-augmenting technical progress', *Golden Rules of Economic Growth: Studies of Efficient and Optimal Investment*, New York: W. W. Norton, 1966.

Pitts, P. R. See Gigantes, T. and Pitts, P. R.

Post, G. See Lithwick, N. H., Post, G. and Rymes, T. K.

Read, L. M. 'The measure of total factor productivity appropriate to wage-price guidelines', *Canadian Journal of Economics*, I, May 1968, 349–58.

Redfern, Philip. 'Net investment in fixed assets in the United Kingdom, 1938–1953', *Journal of the Royal Statistical Society*, CXVIII, (Series A), 2, 1955, 141–92.

Robinson, Joan, 'The classification of inventions', *Review of Economic Studies*, V, 1937–8, 139–42, reprinted in AEA, *Readings in the Theory of Income Distribution*, New York: Blakiston, 1949.

'Economic growth and capital accumulation: a comment', *Economic Record*, XXXIII, April 1957, 103–8.

'The production function and the theory of capital', *Review of Economic*

Studies, xxi, 1953–4, 81–106, reprinted in *Collected Economic Papers*, vol. ii, Oxford: Blackwell, 1960.

'Accumulation and the production function', *Economic Journal*, lxix, 1959, 433–42, reprinted in *Collected Economic Papers*, vol. ii, Oxford: Blackwell, 1960.

'Some problems of definition and measurement of capital' in *Collected Economic Papers*, vol. ii, Oxford: Blackwell, 1960.

'Depreciation', *Collected Economic Papers*, vol. ii, Oxford: Blackwell, 1960.

'Harrod's knife-edge', *Collected Economic Papers*, vol. iii, Oxford: Blackwell, 1965.

'Equilibrium growth models', *American Economic Review*, li, June 1961, 360–69, reprinted in *Collected Economic Papers*, vol. iii, Oxford: Blackwell, 1965.

'Pre-Keynesian Theory after Keynes', *Collected Economic Papers*, vol. iii, Oxford: Blackwell, 1965.

'A reconsideration of the theory of value', *Collected Economic Papers*, vol. iii, Oxford: Blackwell, 1965.

'The General Theory after twenty-five years', *Collected Economic Papers*, vol. iii, Oxford: Blackwell, 1965.

'Comment on Samuelson and Modigliani', *Review of Economic Studies*, xxxiii, October 1966, 307–8.

Robinson, Joan and Naqvi, K. A. 'The badly behaved production function', *Quarterly Journal of Economics*, lxxxi, November 1967, 579–91.

Rymes, T. K. 'Professor Read and the measurement of total factor productivity', *Canadian Journal of Economics*, i, May 1968, 359–67. See also Emery, B. J. and Rymes, T. K.; Lithwick, N. H., Post, G. and Rymes, T. K.

Samuelson, P. A. 'Parable and realism in capital theory: the surrogate production function', *Review of Economic Studies*, xxix, June 1962, 193–206, reprinted in ed. J. E. Stiglitz, *The Collected Scientific Papers of Paul A. Samuelson*, vol. i, Cambridge: M.I.T. Press, 1966.

and Modigliani, F. See Modigliani, F.

'Indeterminacy of development in a heterogeneous-capital model with constant saving propensity', ed. K. Snell, *Essays on the Theory of Optimal Economic Growth*, Cambridge: M.I.T. Press, 1967.

'The monopolistic competition revolution', ed. R. E. Kuenne, *Monopolistic Competition Theory: Studies in Impact*, Essays in Honour of Edward H. Chamberlin, New York: Wiley, 1967.

Shell, K. and Stiglitz, J. E. 'The allocation of investment in a dynamic economy', *Quarterly Journal of Economics*, lxxxi, November 1967, 592–609.

Solow, R. M. 'The interest rate and transition between techniques', *Socialism, Capitalism and Economic Growth: Essays presented to Maurice Dobb*, ed. C. H. Feinstein, Cambridge: Cambridge University Press, 1967.

'Technical change and the aggregate production function', *The Review of Economics and Statistics*, xxxix, August 1957, 312–20.

'A contribution to the theory of economic growth', *Quarterly Journal of Economics*, lxx, February 1956, 65–94, reprinted in eds. J. E. Stiglitz and H. Uzawa, *Readings in the Modern Theory of Economic Growth*, Cambridge: M.I.T. Press, 1969.

'Technical progress, capital formation, and economic growth', *American Economic Review, Papers and Proceedings*, lii, May 1962, 76–86.

'Heterogeneous capital and smooth production functions: an experimental study', *Econometrica*, XXXI, October 1963, 623–45.

'Investment and technical progress', eds. K. J. Arrow *et al.*, *Mathematical Methods in the Social Sciences*, 1959, Stanford: Stanford University Press, 1960.

'On the rate of return: reply to Pasinetti', *Economic Journal*, LXXX, June 1970, 423–8.

Usher, D. 'Traditional Capital Theory', *Review of Economic Studies*, XXXII, April 1965, 169–85.

INDEX

CONTENTS

190